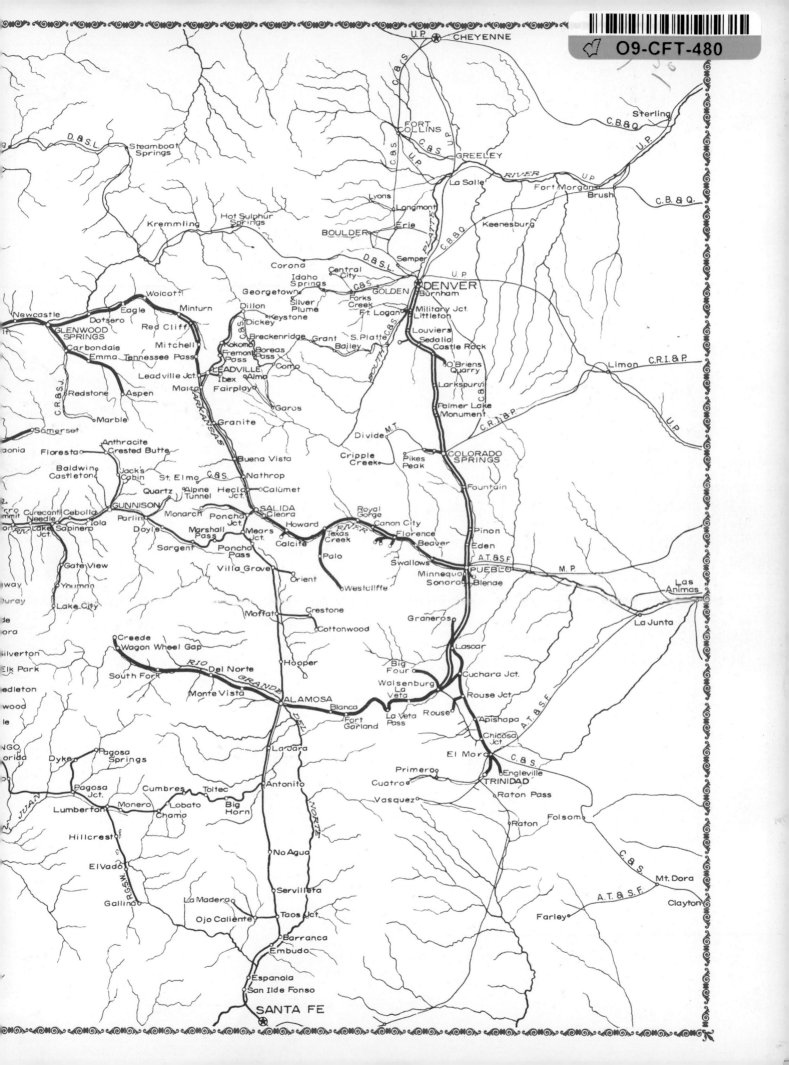

Rio Grande Railroad.

Rio Grande

The handsome period piece shown here by the *doyen* of railroad artists in his generation, Howard Fogg, of Boulder, depicts the original Rio Grande depot at Palmer Lake with an up train to Denver paused on a summer morning in the enviable nineties. It was from the platform of this primeval structure that a strong wind once toppled the diminutive engine *Montezuma* and its fragile coaches and here, according to Colorado legend, from its enclosed belfry the agent was in the habit of scanning the horizon with a telescope for smoke signals to announce an arriving train in an age as yet innocent of the magnetic telegraph.

Rio Grande
Mainline of the Rockies

BY LUCIUS BEEBE & CHARLES CLEGG

Berkeley HOWELL-NORTH California

1962

ACKNOWLEDGMENTS

Because of its geographic diversity and the protracted period of its coverage, the authors are indebted to an uncommonly long tally of sources whose collaboration of editorial and pictorial material have made this book possible. The degrees of this indebtedness cannot with any propriety be indicated without recourse to the refinements of typeset that characterizes the importance of players in a Broadway theatrical production and, with one exception, they are all given equal billing here. They include, Carlton Sills and Jackson Thode, archivists and repositories of the fact, legend and folklore of the Rio Grande Railroad; Mrs. Alys Freeze of the Western Collection, Denver Public Library; E. J. Haley, a cartographer of impressive dimensions who did the map; Glenn H. Johnson, Jr., of The State Historical Society of Colorado; Margaret Shepherd of the Utah State Historical Society; the Colorado College Library of Colorado Springs; The Pioneer Museum at Colorado Springs; Marshall Sprague, one of the foremost contemporary historians of the Rocky Mountain region; Howard Fogg of Boulder and Otto Kuhler of Pine who executed the color work; and the following photographers, collectors and custodians of railroad art and memorabilia: Jim Shaughnessy, Richard Steinheimer, John W. Maxwell, Everett De Golyer, Jim Ehernberger, Richard B. Jackson, Robert A. Le Massena, Otto C. Perry, Gerald M. Best, Arthur D. Dubin, Guy Dunscomb, Henry R. Griffiths, Jr., the Shipler Studios of Salt Lake, Johnny Krause, Gordon S. Crowell, Fred Jukes, Robert W. Edwards and Richard F. Lind. The exception to this democracy of our gratitude must be made in the case of Richard H. Kindig, *doyen* and ranking authority on Colorado railroading, a profound source of knowledgeable information, himself an expert photographer of the railroad scene and a surpassingly generous benefactor of his talents and resources. Mr. Kindig's unstinted assistance and enthusiasm for the project this book represents have been of a knightly dimension and in the grand manner of a Medici. In appropriate degrees, this book is as much the end-product of these several contributors as it is of the authors whose names appear on its title page.

RIO GRANDE, MAINLINE OF THE ROCKIES

Copyright © 1962 by Howell-North Books, a corporation, all rights reserved. No part of this book may be reproduced in any manner without permission in writing, except in the case of brief quotations embodied in critical articles and reviews.

Printed and bound in the United States of America.

Library of Congress Catalogue Card No. 62-13445

Published by Howell-North Books
1050 Parker Street, Berkeley 10, California

JIM EHERNBERGER

CONTENTS

The Silverton Mixed: A Narrow Gauge Portrait by Charles Clegg

A BABY RAILROAD IS BORN

HE STORY of the Denver & Rio Grande Western Railroad is in large measure the story of Colorado and the Rocky Mountain region from the reconstruction years following the Civil War to the immediate here and now. In the beginning it was first of all a mining railroad conceived on an inclusive scale but following with more or less fidelity the pattern of financing, construction and operations of other Western carriers whose destinies were involved in the recovery of precious metals. Only where most other railroads served a single region, the destinations reached by the primeval Rio Grande were multiple and widely dispersed.

It even followed in its first years the pattern of boom and bust, bonanza and borrasca that characterized mining everywhere in the Old West. One day the railroad rolled in metaphorical clover; the next its properties were being attached by creditors. It might have been the original inspiration of the song about off-again, on-again, gone-again-Finnigan. It followed an intricate pavane of suits, mergers and dissolutions, reorganizations, refinancing and incorporations that left even the most astute lawyers shaken at their contemplation.

It had the status, at various times, of a very poor relative and of a rich and enviable public uncle, but whatever its estate, be it a home owned industry or in the clutches of absentee empire builders, the story of the Rio Grande was never dull. It was always a railroad of bounce.

The Rocky Mountain region which was later to become the setting for the Denver & Rio Grande Railroad and its various and subsequent corporate entities existed long before the railroad both as a fact of geology and in the primeval economy of the Old West.

It had existed for the Spaniards working northward out of Old Mexico with one single-minded objective in view: gold in limitless abundance. The gold, for a variety of reasons, among them the native indolence of the Mexicans and the Spaniards' determination that slave labor should enrich them without effort, proved illusive and the tide of conquest receded to become firmly established in the overland trade to Santa Fe in which the Mexicans were to become brokers, tradesmen and satraps of an empire of commerce that was no longer one of conquest.

There followed the fur trade which, until the latter years of the thirties, populated the Shining Mountains with perhaps the hardiest race of pioneers the continent was to know, the *voyageurs, engagés, bourgeoisie* of the great fur companies, the American Fur Company and the competition, whose mountain men and long hunters became the stuff of legend as long as the gentlemen in London and Paris wore hats of beaver fur instead of felted cloth.

The tides of men and affairs that had lapped briefly against the mountains abated for the second time when the fur trade went into a decline. By the mid-thirties the last great spring rendezvous had been celebrated and again the silence of vastness pervaded and the hunting grounds returned to their original Indian tenants by default.

It wasn't as if, in the year 1870, the Rocky Mountain region of Colorado needed a railroad, could afford a railroad or held the slightest promise of supporting the existence of a railroad. The very idea of a railroad, to any responsible intelligence, must have seemed hilarious, a delusion of dimensions to match the mountains that would overshadow it.

There was no basic industry, no factories, manufactories, smelters or agriculture that demanded or justified as elaborate an agency of transport as what the British appropriately called "a permanent way."

—7

The entire population of the Territory of Colorado was fewer than 40,000 and its leading city, Denver, held 4,800 people, just ten more residents than had been on the scene in 1860. Colorado Springs was not yet a name on the map, while Colorado City and Pueblo, the principal scenes of activity and human habitation between Denver and Santa Fe, boasted a joint population of fewer than fifteen hundred. The stage between Denver and Pueblo carried an average of thirty paying patrons weekly and a muster of the residents at Trinidad on the southern boundary of the territory couldn't have come to over 500.

This was not the sort of teeming community that cried for the services of a railroad, a contriving which could only function on a recurrent daily basis and had its roots in a reasonably abundant traffic in humans and the goods they consumed, produced or traded. Desultory staging and freighting service across the Great Plains to Kansas supplied the every need of the Rocky Mountain region which, far from being an expanding economy, was in actual fact declining or barely static.

The reason Colorado had to have a railroad had nothing to do with any rational appraisal of its economy; it was an emotional compulsion and the depressing fact that somebody else had one. Railroad fever was a disease that was epidemic throughout the entire North American continent at the time. Its fever raged unabated in the industrial East and struck with equal devastation in regions where a day's travel failed to disclose a human habitation. Railroads not only brought communities into being; the absence of them could put communities out of business, and the moral bankruptcy suggested by being without a railroad was a ponderable affliction.

Denver and Colorado generally not only didn't have a railroad, but there was a working railroad of great prestige just a hundred miles to the north in the newly completed Union Pacific, whose rails for a few tentative and teasing miles around Julesburg actually crossed Colorado soil. The Union Pacific was in a fair way to eliminate Colorado from the map in an economic sense and, in the department of morale, it was driving Denver folk to drink if any of them needed special inspiration to this activity.

Not that the Union Pacific, now that the novelty had worn off, was seething with profitable business. It wasn't, but what it lacked in carloadings it supplied in optimism which by a slight switch in geography became the rankest pessimism by the time it reached Denver City on the banks of Cherry Creek. Denver, to hear tell in the saloons that were its principal industry, was doomed, and some of its business houses were in actual fact removing to locate along the U.P. at Cheyenne and Laramie.

Amidst the encircling gloom, hope gleamed feebly from two diverse points of the compass: the Denver Pacific Railway now, as of 1870, being built to connect the Queen City of the Plains with the U. P. mainline at Cheyenne, and the Kansas Pacific giving even more direct access to the Southwest Gateways of Kansas City and St. Louis.

On these two advancing railheads Denver's continued existence was predicated and nobody could look into the future to foresee the day when the Burlington, the Rock Island, the Missouri Pacific, the Santa Fe and the Union Pacific itself should all battle for traffic between Denver and the East over their own highly competitive main lines.

Some idea of Denver's remoteness may be gathered from the tariff on communications which priced a ten word telegram to New York or Boston at just under ten dollars and freight at $2.60 per hundred pounds from Kansas City. The cost of legally manufactured whisky including a government stamp was so exorbitant that the prevailing two-bit drink was an arrangement called Taos Lightning made down New Mexico way and freighted in on ox carts. The stuff was so powerful and often lethal that it was commonly remarked that nobody with a taste for it ever lived long enough to become addicted. The only comfort in the shortage lay in the fact that, farther to the west, the Salt Lake Mormons were reduced to drinking an even more formidable distillate called Valley Tan in comparison to which Taos Lightning was as veritable cognac of a comet year.

Amidst these desolations and uncertainties there was to arise a prophet of Colorado's destinies who was about as improbable a product of the Howling Wilderness that was the Old West as can be imagined. General William Jackson Palmer, whose military rank derived from the Union forces in the late war, had been one of the engineers of the Kansas Pacific. His background was Rittenhouse Square, Philadelphia, and the study of mining in England.

He was as out of place following in the footsteps of, say, Jim Bridger as a cowboy in full hair pants regalia of the time would have been at Blenheim Palace. His tastes ran to croquet and white flannels, circumstances that in no way reflected on his military record and, in the beginning anyway, the mountains and the engineering they implied, not to mention the manners of their inhabitants, aroused in him a profound distaste. It is notable in the record that the first projection of the Rio Grande Railroad had nothing at all to do with the Rocky Mountains.

It was the tangible fact, nevertheless, timeless, immutable and forbidding, of the Rocky Mountains that gave the Denver & Rio Grande Western Railroad its theme of wonder.

Without their presence as backdrop, challenge, refuge and perpetual sources of revenue and vitality, the Rio Grande might well have been nothing more than one more railroad from here to there and merchandise that characterized scores of other with the conventional traffickings in passengers carriers from Bangor to San Diego, useful all of them, beautifully maintained and operated some of them, but undistinguished for any great central and identifying fact of character. This the Shining Mountains gave the Rio Grande in limitless abundance. "Mountain railroading," men said with a swagger in their tone, "Mountain divisions, that's the Rio Grande!" Mountain railroading it was in the days of the narrow gauge teapot locomotives so fragile that a brisk breeze could, and in the record, did topple them from the tracks, and mountain railroading it remained when the heaviest motive power on the American continent shouted through the high passes where once the Mountain Men and the Long Hunters had gone before them.

The mountains gave the railroad its panache of grandeur, its essential validity over and above the mere occasions of commerce and economy. Men lifted up their eyes unto the hills and they beheld the smoke of the railroad's going, aye from Clear Creek to Tennessee, above the abyss of the Rio de las Animas Perdidas and at the Summit called

Soldier. Its writ ran from the Queen City of the Plains to the Kingdom of Deseret and it was mountains all the way. The more pity the word was not included in its corporate title.

It is doubtful if these metaphysical considerations bulked large, however, in the thinking of General William Jackson Palmer when he undertook to survey, locate, finance, build and eventually operate a railroad that should run from mid-Colorado to Old Mexico and, in so doing, keep Denver City on the map. He was perfectly aware of the mountains, and their presence conditioned his thinking in terms of routes, grades, motive power, meteorology and as sources of coal, iron, precious metals and even tourism that should justify the comprehensive scheme of things he envisioned. The mountains were full of wonderful things that would keep a fire burning under a crown sheet and grease the journals of revenue cars. It was only for this reason that General Palmer was eventually agreeable to accommodating himself to the facts of geology at all. His experience as an engineer in the construction of the Kansas Pacific had in no way conditioned him to grades up to nearly four per cent and it is probable that he shuddered inwardly in contemplation of the abyss of Animas where all those Spaniards had perished.

In the long light of hindsight, it is ironical that General Palmer's "baby railroad" conceived in terms of long tangents and gentle grades through the meadowlands that bordered on the Great Plains should become celebrated as the greatest mountain railroad of them all.

Any coherent and reasonably consecutive account of the Rio Grande's operations is conditioned by the fact in the record that its routes and destinations more closely resembled those of a logging railroad whose trackage shifts incessantly to accommodate its revenue loadings than it did more conventional carriers whose maps and profiles had a certain degree of permanency. New branches, new mainlines, abandonments, rerouting of traffic, shifts from narrow to double gauge and from double to standard, and in one amazing instance a reversal of this process to retrack the Farmington division from standard to narrow gauge, were of such diversity, frequence and microscopic detail as to stagger the imagination. Branches were projected, surveyed, located, built, operated and abandoned all in a space of months. The original purpose and destination of the overall pattern of operations was shifted to an entirely new quarter of the compass within a few years of the road's first incorporation and its mainline itself at various times occupied three different and widely separated routes. Standard gauge tracks were being laid while the vast majority of its mileage was still spiked to three feet and other narrow gauge was being built long after the overall policy of operations had shifted to standard.

The story of the operations of the Rio Grande is no more orderly a chronicle than its financial maneuvers, and these were very shifty indeed. Any map of the railroad must, purely and simply, seem the work of a demented cartographer.

General Palmer's original projection of a narrow gauge railroad running south out of Denver to connect with subsidiaries at the border and continue on into Old Mexico was a simple and plausible one. It was uncomplicated and available to casual financing which was about the only description that fitted the conduct of its moneyed affairs. That its narrow gauge should be the determining factor in its expansion in directions never foreseen by its sponsors is purely fortuitous. The three foot gauge which might very well have assured its failure had its traffic been in the direction it was first planned, in the end made its operation possible in remote mountain fastnesses that had never entered into General Palmer's primal thinking. It was a railroad of paradox.

The pattern of railroad financing and construction in the time and place that saw the beginnings of the Rio Grande was already well defined and a recognized *modus operandi* in the American West. Few rights of way were built outright by the companies incorporated to operate over them, but by contract firms operating as separate corporate entities no matter how closely they may have been allied to the railroad itself through interlocking directorates and community of interest. The prototypal Union Pacific had done its actual construction through the agency of Credit Mobilier, a contract company entirely owned by members of the Union Pacific Board of Directors, and the Rio Grande was similarly farmed out to the Union Contract Company. It was an arrangement that assured profit from the expenses of actual

construction even though none might be immediately foreseen from the traffic in passengers and merchandise.

The setup was an explicit one and required neither apology nor explanation from its participants. The President of Union Contract was Charles S. Hinchman, a neighbor in Philadelphia and Civil War companion-in-arms of General Palmer. Its secretary was W. S. Jackson, also an officer of the railroad, Robert F. Weitbrec was treasurer of the Rio Grande Railroad and also, by coincidence, treasurer of Union Contract. Colonel W. H. Greenwood, general manager of the railroad, was also general manager of the contracting firm of its builders.

The community of interest between railroad and railroad contractor was not merely parallel; it was absolute.

In the words of George L. Anderson, a Colorado scholar and student of the Rio Grande's early economy, "the relations between the two companies were so close that J. A. McMurtrie, senior engineer, declared they were one and the same thing. The surveys of possible railway routes were made under the direction of the railroad company, but they were paid for by the contract company. The railway company prepared specifications for the construction of the road, controlled the route, accepted or rejected surveys, and then the contract company built, equipped and operated the road until possession was demanded by the railway company. . . . The construction company obtained and paid for lands necessary for the right of way, but the deeds were made out to the railroad. It also used the right to condemn private property granted to the railroad company by Congress, but it had to pay all expenses of the proceedings and then deed the land thus obtained to the railway company."

Under the terms of a contract dated April 4, 1871, according to Mr. Anderson's carefully documented account, the Denver & Rio Grande Railway Company entered into agreement with the Union Contract Company for the construction and equipment of the entire mileage of the then projected route from Denver to El Paso. The first division, running between Denver and Colorado City, a distance of seventy-six miles was to be available to the operation of trains by January 1, 1872. Obligations of the contractor included the installing of all rails, spikes, ties, sidings, bridges, trestles, passing tracks, depots, sheds, engine houses, shops, water tanks and incidental structures and the provision of all locomotives, freight and passenger cars, machinery, tools, shopping facilities and a complete telegraphic system of communications.

In return for its services, the Union Contract Company was to receive $14,000,000 first mortgage, seven per cent gold bonds of the railway company, another $14,000,000 in capital stock, all the municipal, state or county bonds which might be available to the railroad as subsidies, all lands acquired by the railroad aside from those actually included in its right of way and all and any other forms of subsidy that might come to the railroad in the construction of its line. The finished railroad was to be turned over by the builders in sections of twenty miles at a time, the details of its surrender to be subject to arbitration as occasion arose. Since the community of interest between both contracting parties was absolute and identical, the prospect of any difference of opinion was remote.

The actual construction and initial operations of the Rio Grande seem to have been largely devoid of the commotions and tumults which accompanied the progress westward of Union Pacific and were part of the established pattern of progress in Texas, North Dakota and elsewhere as enlightenment and commerce rode westward on the cars. General Jack Casment's Irish paddies picking them up and setting them down across Nebraska, Wyoming and finally Utah had been so dedicated to incidental hooray that the ribald communities that moved with the end of track were called Hell on Wheels. Continual holiday reigned as the only recently discharged veterans of Shiloh and The Wilderness, fought, whored, gambled and drank in a prolonged saturnalia of continental dimensions. As trackside graves multiplied and work stoppages after payday became an actual impediment to the work in hand, the directors of Union Pacific at length commissioned special officers and company deputies who hanged the worst offenders and at least restored a semblance of order in the saloons and bagnios that rumbled across the Great Plains and over Sherman Hill, although nobody who investigated them at first hand ever emerged with the sentiment that Green River, Co-

rinne or Promontory Point were an extension of such abodes of culture as Cambridge, Massachusetts, or Chatauqua, New York.

There is no record of epic convulsions as the light iron of the Rio Grande inched at an average mile and a quarter a day down from Denver toward the future site of Colorado Springs. Although the division was supposed to have been completed by July of 1871, it was actually late in October that representative members of the community and the Denver press were invited on the first excursion over what was coming to be known as "the baby railroad" and partake of company hospitality at Manitou. Among the guests who lined the General's buffet were N. C. Meeker of Greeley, a stanchly prohibitionist community, who could have been relied on to confine his attention to the lobster aspic, William N. Byers, the valorous and combative founder of the fortunes of *The Rocky Mountain News* and Dr. William A. Bell, a regional magnifico and ardent advocate of the projects of his friend General William Jackson Palmer.

As the rails moved south out of Colorado Springs and Manitou in the direction of the Arkansas River the facade of tranquil and ordered progress so dear to the heart of General Palmer began rudely to be shattered by an atmosphere in which low recriminations, distrust of the company's motives and the threats of the competition were to culminate in outright warfare between the Rio Grande, the oncoming Atchison, Topeka & Santa Fe Railroad and a number of Colorado communities which deemed it prudent to ally themselves to one or the other of the contestant carriers. For a considerable time there was doubt as to whether the baby railroad would pass through Pueblo at all or would diverge from its direct north and south axis at the Cotton Place, twenty-five miles south of The Springs, and thence south and west directly to Canyon City which was its immediate objective at the time. There were coal fields in the neighborhood of Canyon City and coal that had to be freighted in from Golden, far to the north, was proving more unsatisfactory every day. On one occasion the coal in the tender of the little *Montezuma* proved completely immune to combustion and, twenty miles north of The Springs, it was necessary for crew and passengers alike to get down and gather buffalo chips to get up enough steam to bring the train to its terminal. The coal fields of Labran and Canyon City were urgently indicated.

Perhaps the railroad was not above cultivating a climate of uneasiness at Pueblo, for uncertainty about the future was in the time and place a prime incentive to subsidies to railroad builders. In any event, Pueblo voted railroad bonds until it was on the verge of bankruptcy, the railroad inclined an appreciative ear and in November 1871 it was definitely announced that the rails were going to Pueblo. Had they not, it is difficult to foresee what would have been the fate of the great complex of railroad subsidiaries headed by the Colorado Fuel & Iron Company which was soon to claim Pueblo as its epicenter.

The next exchange of insults between the railroad and a community with a fancied grievance was with the important mining town of Trinidad in Southern Colorado and the entrepot to the all-important Raton Pass through which access would eventually be had to New Mexico and the entire Southwest. The management of the Rio Grande outraged public sentiment in Trinidad by letting it be known that it was considering a diversion over Veta Pass in the direction of Fort Garland before quitting itself of a long standing promise to proceed directly to Trinidad. Perhaps the misunderstanding was deliberately cultivated in the hope of more subsidies from neglected Trinidad, but if this was the case it was a miscalculation that was shortly to have fatal results to the Rio Grande's hope of achieving the river of its corporate title at El Paso.

Trinidad and its surrounding hamlets was extremely railroad minded and if the Rio Grande wouldn't play ball, it would, in this pass and perforce, find a railroad that would. This, as it happened, was the Atchison, Topeka & Santa Fe.

The Santa Fe, at this stage in its affairs, was not the resolute and determined force of nature it was shortly to become. It stood on the threshold of an enormous empire of freight and passenger business which it could achieve via the Raton Pass if it could obtain access to it, but the resolution was lacking, for the time being in any event, to seize and hold this formidable geographic advantage. The Santa Fe was momentarily so undetermined as to the immediate future that a report

was in wide circulation that its plan was to turn northward to Colorado Springs and thence westward and to Leadville over Ute Pass, eventually the right of way of the Colorado Midland. Rumors, passions and ambitions were fused in a farrago of bad feeling with the Rio Grande, perhaps innocently, perhaps culpably, on the receiving end.

Both carriers, on the very verge of an incalculable bonanza beyond the Pass of The Rat paused at Trinidad, eyeing each other like cats on a fence. From El Moro, where its rails now terminated, the Rio Grande was closer to the actual pass itself than the graders of the Santa Fe and the circumstance may have contributed to the complacency in the Rio Grande camp which eventually lost the day for it. Its engineers completely failed to file any plat and profile of their proposed route up the Raton so that when the day dawned that found the Santa Fe in factual possession it had no legal alternative but to withdraw. It was a tactical error of the first magnitude, but one which contributed notably to the Rio Grande's education in times to come.

The deciding action which eliminated the Rio Grande forever from the high plains of New Mexico and gave its rival a green light to California was of brief but dramatic duration and transpired, as such cloak and dagger engagements should, in midnight hours and dark of the moon.

In February 1878 the atmosphere at Trinidad was tense with only thinly veiled expectancy. Undercover agents for each of the contestants were as thick along the margins of Purgatory Water as international spies were reputed to be in the corridors of the *Istanbul Express* in the Carpathians. Shrouded figures haunted the ravines by dark and coded telegrams to Boston and Denver were thick as autumn leaves on Valombrossa.

Key figure in this game for high stakes was the venerable relic of another day in Colorado history named Uncle Dick Wootton, a veteran of pioneer times who had been a legendary killer of Indians, one of the original Long Hunters and practically a mythical hero in the bars of the old frontier. Uncle Dick was now old and the marks of Indian warfare on his person a veritable palimpsest of history in the Shining Mountains before the railroad was dreamed of. He had bought the toll road to the Raton and erected a spacious hacienda and toll house to control it where the old gentleman was his own bar's best customer. He admired to sit up nights with the mule skinners and wagon train drivers who put up at his shebang, drinking Taos Lightning by the keg and telling lies that compared favorably with the fabled mendacities of Baron Munschausen.

Another companionable soul who patronized Uncle Dick's mahogany and listened politely to his tales of great days gone was Ray Morley, land-seer and advance man for the Santa Fe Railroad. Morley, too, liked a good night's fandango with the Spanish girls who came down from the Pass. He strummed a romantic guitar and held his own with the Patron when the bottle was passed. He made himself as attractive to Uncle Dick and his riff-raff of followers and partisans as the Rio Grande had made itself unattractive to Trinidad generally.

When, therefore, one dark and gusty night, Morley knocked at Uncle Dick's door and told the hangers-on at the bar that he had a silver dollar for each man who would come out and throw a few shovels of dirt for a railroad grade, the response was gratifying. The customers, reinforced with deep draughts of Taos, took over the road-mender's store of picks and shovels and went into the night to strike a blow for Uncle Dick and for Cyrus K. Holliday, a silk hatted gentleman in far-off Boston who wouldn't have cared for their company in Commonwealth Avenue.

There have been many picturesque interludes in the history of railroad building in the Old West, but none more fragrant than those brief hours before dawn half way up river from Trinidad to the Raton as the dirt flew in the light of flickering lanterns, possibly to the music of a guitar in the hands of the versatile Ray Morley of the Atchison, Topeka & Santa Fe Railroad.

When rival graders for the Rio Grande, a temperance organization that didn't recruit its ranks from the local saloons, arrived at a conventional hour next morning, it found the Santa Fe in possession. True, the location stakes lurched drunkenly up the ravine and the graded gravel itself was a barely discernible elevation along the riverbank, but they were sufficient. Where the *Super Chief* today snores its way up to the portal of a tunnel at the apex of the Raton, once in the chill hours before dawn, the Rio Grande lost an empire. Uncle Dick's toll house is still there and it is pleasant to think that his cheery genius presides over the Pass of the Rat as it did that epic night of destiny.

"The preliminary surveys of the Rio Grande Railroad compelled a mammoth corps of engineers, explorers and surveyors," wrote Arthur Ridgway of the carrier's early days. "It is estimated that at one time the engineering corps consisted of upward of 500 men. Their work lay . . . in virgin forests, through untraversed canyons, over untraveled passes, along precipitous slopes and rocky cliffs. There was no mode of travel save pedestrian or equestrian; mountain storms were a source of terror. To be snowbound often meant starvation." The drawings on the page opposite from *Harper's Weekly* depict the Rio Grande's locating engineers in the Rockies and, while they do not suggest starvation, indicate nevertheless the rugged character of the Colorado winters.

No other railroad construction in the Old West, not even the Northern Pacific in the mountains of the Northwest, presented the hazards and difficulties of the terrain first penetrated in the seventies by the Rio Grande. All supplies and construction material had to be freighted in for the route over Veta Pass by mule team or trains of oxen. Ties were transported lashed to the backs of burros while rails were tied to saddles and allowed to trail on the ground. The clement climate and easy gradients that allowed the Union Pacific engineers to lay ten miles of track a day and to expedite construction with steam power were unknown. Men and mules alone accounted for the mountain grades that brought the three foot iron at last to Alamosa and Silverton and over Marshall Pass into the Gunnison country. In terrain where geography permitted, supplies came in by patient ox-teams guided by bullwhackers whose legendary profanity and dexterity in overcoming obstacles made them a race of men apart, even among the pioneers.

The first depot restaurant on the infant Rio Grande was this classic frontier edifice, The Log Cabin which had been built in 1870 at The Springs by Governor Alexander Cameron Hunt, who became Palmer's agent in many of his big real estate and promotional deals. When the three foot iron of the baby railroad was laid right past its front door in 1871, Hunt thoughtfully converted it to serve hungry and thirsty travelers who were set down from the cars at his very threshold. At a somewhat later date it became a Fred Harvey eating house and part of the system that brought civilization to the Old West. Governor Hunt, appropriately attired in top hat, appears at the left in this rare photograph from the Pioneer Museum at Colorado Springs. Others are members of the family of Major John H. McDowell, Hunt's son-in-law, who ran the establishment. The organization man in General Palmer's scheme of things almost invariably had a military title. *(Pioneer Museum, Colorado Springs.)*

That the Rio Grande was aware of tourism even in narrow gauge times is evidenced by this builder's photograph of a narrow gauge Pullman tourist sleeper dated 1889 from the collection of Arthur D. Dubin. That artists for the pictorial press never tired of Colorado snowscapes is suggested in the strip from Leslie's in 1878 captioned "A Snow Blockade in The Rocky Mountains of Colorado: Four Engines Stalled With Two Cars."

By the year 1890 it was apparent that the major trackage of the Rio Grande was headed for standard gauging and that his first little official car *Nomad* was rapidly being outmoded, so General Jackson ordered from Pullman the fine conventional size car *Ballyclare*. Not only was this gleaming private varnish car more in keeping with the dignity of the railroad's president, it was available to interchange with connecting and friendly carriers which, of course, *Nomad* wasn't. *Ballyclare* soon was turning up on the Florida East Coast bound for Palm Beach which was then emerging as the most splendid dream of another strong willed railroad president, Henry M. Flagler. General Palmer and Flagler saw eye to eye in many things, none more so than the grand manner in travel and the advantages of Palm Beach under a January sun. *(Two Photos: Pullman Standard.)*

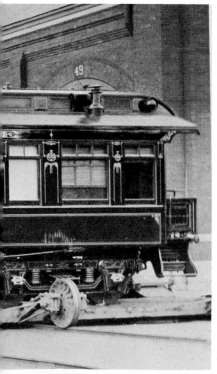

General William Jackson Palmer, at about the time *Ballyclare* was built to his personal specifications, was one of the handsomest men in Colorado and a stickler for form in speech, manners and attire. An aristocrat to his fingertips, he resented Jay Gould and Gould's intrusion into the affairs of his railroad, but by 1892 Gould was dead and the general had many more years of usefulness ahead of him. *(Colorado State Historical Society.)*

The baby railroad's first resort of health and fashion at Manitou Springs, shown above in 1877, offered scant opposition to the winds that whistled down from around Pike's Peak in the background, but its first rolling stock, also of baby dimensions and including four wheel baggage, smoking and freight cars, was more available to winter gusts. The same year the sketch above appeared in *Leslie's* a Rio Grande passenger train was blown from the rails near Palmer Lake, a contretemps which, although nobody was seriously injured, embarrassed the management and became a stock source of local humor. *(Pioneer Museum, Colorado Springs.)*

In 1896 the Rio Grande ordered two new and more powerful type ten wheelers from Baldwin guaranteed to haul eight cars between Pueblo and Denver in three and a half hours. Here the prototypal engine of this class No. 701 is shown in Denver after a trial run with special housing for instruments on its pilot beam and a sort of early day dynamometer car behind the engine as well as the eight cars stipulated in the contract. *(Western Collection, Denver Public Library.)*

Four years later the 700 class was hauling most first class trains and No. 709 posed in 1900 with its crew and some friends in Denver on the head end of *The Trans-Continental, San Francisco, Butte & Portland Express. (R. H. Kindig Collection.)*

The line over La Veta Pass of the Fort Garland Extension was located by the veteran team of Rio Grande engineers, J. A. McMurtrie and J. R. DeReemer and grading contracts awarded the firm of Carlile, Orman & Mersereau of Pueblo. In one tracklaying gang there were two unfrocked clergymen, a former professor of mathematics at Indiana University, two Yale men and forty Irishmen who were paid $2.50 to $3.00 a day, good pay for the times but board was $6 a week. Mike Green, a celebrated foreman, devised a coat of arms for the division: a shamrock on a sun rayed disk, the latter as tribute to the many Mexicans on the payroll.

This was Sumsion's Camp in the construction of the Scofield section of the Pleasant Valley Railroad, predecessor of the Rio Grande Western. *(Robert Edwards Collection.)*

Here is the veritable look of railroad building in the Old West: the hand hewn ties of untreated timber, the loose fill and light narrow gauge iron, the Ames shovels and picks, the spike mauls of the layers and the uncouth agents of destiny who spiked the rails. The scene is on the barren Utah uplands at Colton, east of Soldier Summit in the construction of the original line of the Pleasant Valley Railroad, soon to become an element in the ever-growing Rio Grande Western. *(Robert Edwards Collection.)*

— 23

Often reproduced because it is one of the earliest top quality photographs of the Rio Grande in operation, William H. Jackson's fine still of a narrow gauge double header with the engine *Kokomo* as helper shows a five car train on the Fort Garland run soon after the inauguration of service on the extension. In the background, Dump Mountain shows in almost the identical projection as on the page opposite, an angle of this geologic outcropping as conventional in the Colorado iconography of the seventies as Fuji from The West in classic Japanese art. *(Western Collection, Denver Public Library.)*

The wild and lonely scenery through which the narrow gauge ran in its ascent of Dump Mountain to Veta Pass fascinated pictorial reporters of the Old West just as its grade of 217 feet per mile bemused railroaders. Both these drawings are from *Harper's* in the eighties, the one above by Thomas Moran, the lower by H. Worrall.

This drawing by *Harper's* staff artist Charles Graham occupied a page in the issue of February 4, 1888 with the caption: "The Great Loop on The Denver & Rio Grande Railway."

TO THE SAN JUAN MINES
THE BEST AND SHORTEST ROUTE!

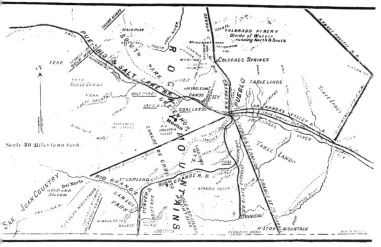

Scale 30 Miles to an Inch

Via Pueblo, Colorado,
The Southern Terminus of the Denver and Rio Grande Railway.

Daily Line of Coaches between Pueblo and Del Norte
DISTANCE ONLY ONE HUNDRED AND TEN MILES.

PUEBLO, THE METROPOLIS AND BUSINESS CENTER OF SOUTHERN COLORADO
Is Ninety Miles the nearest Railroad Terminus to the San Juan Mines.

HOW TO GET TO THE SAN JUAN MINES.

Passengers arriving at Denver, Colorado, on their way to Del Norte and the San Juan Mines, will find their shortest, cheapest and quickest route, to be by way of the Denver and Rio Grande Railway, (Narrow Guage,) to Pueblo, distance 118 miles, thence by coach to Del Norte, 110 miles.

Passengers arriving at Las Animas, Colorado, the terminus of the Kansas Pacific and Arkansas Valley Railway, on their way to Del Norte and the San Juan Mines, will find their shortest, cheapest and quickest route, to be by coach to Pueblo, distance 90 miles, thence by coach to Del Norte, 110 miles.

Persons arriving at Grenada, Colorado, the terminus of the Atchison, Topeka and Sante Fe Railroad, on their way to Del Norte and the San Juan Mines, will find their shortest, cheapest and quickest route, to be by coach to Pueblo, distance 140 miles, thence by coach to Del Norte, 110 miles.

PUEBLO THE OUTFITTING DEPOT FOR THE SAN JUAN MINES.

It should be borne in mind that outfits of every description for traveling, camping and mining can be obtained in Pueblo, as good quality and at prices as low as in any other part of Colorado. Large stocks of everything necessary, are always on hand, and travelers will find no difficulty in obtaining all that they require. Families or parties of young men from the States arriving in Pueblo by rail, can purchase their outfit of wagons, horses, harness and provisions, together with everything they desire, much cheaper than they could bring the same with them.

Published by Direction of the Board of Trade, of Pueblo, Colorado.

LAMBERT & Co., PRINTERS, DAILY COLORADO CHIEFTAIN, PUEBLO, COLORADO.

In 1879, when the Pueblo Board of Trade had the *Colorado Chieftain Press* run up the poster at the left, the Rio Grande's narrow gauge tracks ran as far as Pueblo and no further and the town of Pueblo itself was in business as the entrepot to the newly opened mining districts of Del Norte and the San Juan while Creede was still a full decade in the future. Adventurers, homesteaders and "parties of young men from The States" were exhorted to pause in Pueblo to outfit their parties before taking stage to Del Norte 110 miles to the west. The map also, and optimistically, showed a highly visionary "Pueblo & Salt Lake Railroad" up the Canyon of the Arkansas where eventually the Rio Grande was to run but which was not yet so much as a gleam in General Palmer's eye. Above, after the building of the Fort Garland Extension and the elimination of the staging route to Del Norte, passenger trains paused at Veta Summit so that travelers might enjoy the view. The line was still narrow gauge when this photograph was taken. *(Two Photos: Western Collection, Denver Public Library.)*

As far back as the nineties the snowsheds at Marshall Pass had attracted the attention of sketch artists, as witness the above drawing from *Harper's Weekly* of the time. They were still there, dark, dank and cavernous when Otto Perry took the below photograph in 1943.

By 1943 when Otto Perry took the above shot, the Marshall snowsheds were showing signs of wear, but back in 1935 when Richard B. Jackson made this atmospheric photograph of the westbound local at Cimarron, they had been in good operating order.

Now few traces remain at the summit of Marshall Pass to show the snowsheds and turntable where once the engines turned drowsily in the winter night to go down the grade, but once there was life and activity sheltered under their sloping roof and protective covering of snow. Below: the venerable Durango switcher No. 271 makes up the *San Juan* for its morning run to Alamosa in the days when passenger service was one of the endearing aspects of life in the southwestern regions of the Columbine State. *(Above: Otto Perry; Below: Edgar T. Meade Collection.)*

Where once, in the not so distant past, the Rio Grande's brakemen had to be sure footed as mountain goats to tie them down on the winter car tops going down Cumbres Pass *(left)* summer finds a pastoral setting for the Rio Grande's narrow gauge No. 485 on the head end with No. 487 helping from behind going up the same grade. It was scenes such as this that established continuity with the heroic past of Rocky Mountain railroading and endeared the slim gauge to sentimentalists long after the railroad's management had come to view the three foot gauge as obsolescent. *(Otto Perry.)*

The original photographs from which these drawings were made by staff artists for *Frank Leslie's Weekly* were taken by the celebrated Salt Lake City photographer Colonel Charles R. Savage and depict winter scenes on the Rio Grande Western near Soldier Summit, Utah. Snow blockades supplied Eastern editors with picture material in abundance and with seasonal regularity. Colonel Savage is more celebrated in the iconography of the Old West as one of the two photographers present at Promontory Point, Utah, at the Golden Spike ceremonies in 1869 and as the author of the immortal photograph of the "engines touching head to head" that is the most important single photograph in the annals of continental conquest. There was another photographer present in the person of A. J. Russell, a New York specialist in stereoptican views for illustrated lectures and confusion exists to this day as to just whose photos at Promontory are which, but Colonel Savage's seem to have arrived in the East before Russell's and as a result were the basis of most of the drawn pictorial art which apprised the world of the big day on the Utah uplands.

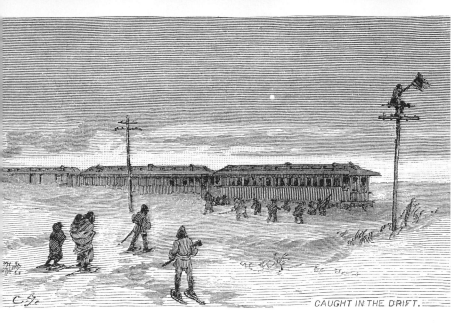

CAUGHT IN THE DRIFT.

Sometimes failure to make the shelter of the snowsheds atop Marshall Pass caused the narrow gauge cars to stall in the drifts after a midwinter blizzard, and relief parties had to be organized. Eastern artists (in this case for *Leslie's*) found the transcontinental snowbound and serenaded by wolves under a full moon irresistible as subject for their talents.

THE SERENADING PARTY.

The look of the narrow gauge and its Marshall Pass operations in 1885 is explicit in the three views all dating from that year on these two pages. Below is a very rare action shot from the omniscient camera of William H. Jackson showing a narrow gauge Rio Grande passenger train heading up the grade on the west side of Marshall Pass. Above and opposite is Salida depot of the period with a tank type switcher at the right sporting an outsize headlight for night yarding operations and, in the center, the ghost of somebody's dog who, ignorant of shutter speeds and light readings, achieved ectoplasmic immortality before his time. Below is the interior of a narrow gauge Pullman open section sleeper, its diminutive berths demonstrating their capacity for but a single occupant that is reported to have recommended them to General Palmer. All photographs are from the Western Collection, Denver Public Library.

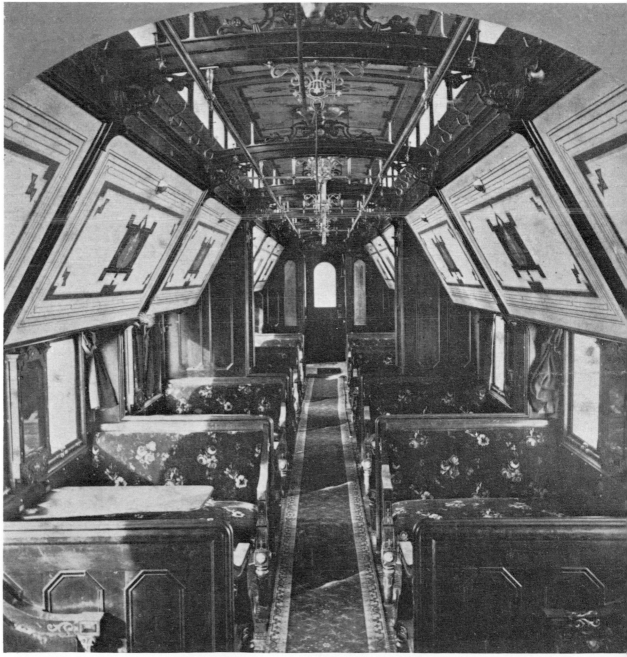

The Currecanti Needle, a rocky pinnacle pointing skyward a few miles east of Cimmaron in the Black Canyon of the Gunnison, was for many years the trade mark and symbol of the Rio Grande and part of the insigne of the road. On this page it is shown in a photograph by William H. Jackson; opposite in a line drawing for *Harper's* in 1890 by Charles Graham who incorporated it in a drawing called "Behind Time." Although he took liberties with the factual terrain followed by the railroad in the Currecanti shadow, the artist was aware of its symbolism in Rio Grande thinking, pointing *ad astra* as the destinies of the carrier itself mounted not only toward the stars, but ever westward.

Denver's second Union Station, built in 1880, was destroyed by fire in 1894 and was followed by the third structure at the same site which stands today. It was on the corner of Seventeenth Street and Wyncoop, shown in the lower photograph at the right that Soapy Smith, King of the Thimbleriggers and one of the Rio Grande Railroad's most sincere admirers, was accustomed to pitch his kyster while Doc Baggs and Judge Van Horn worked the crowd for suckers. (*Two Photos: Western Collection, Denver Public Library.*)

Denver's first Union Station serving the Denver Pacific and infant Denver & Rio Grande was built in 1871 and lasted nine years until the second structure of the same name was built at the foot of Seventeenth Street. The first interlocking was placed in operation in the Rio Grande yards south of the depot in 1881 as shown below in a contemporary sketch. *(Two Pictures: Western Collection, Denver Public Library.)*

In an age when railroading in its every aspect was a national preoccupation, the readers of *The Illustrated Police News*, published in Boston as direct competition to *The Official Police Gazette*, were in April 1888 thrilled by this hairbreadth 'scape recorded in the Queen City of the Plains. "A Blushing Maid in Peril," read the caption to the drawing which occupied the entire front page of the issue. "A Lady, Whose Foot Was Caught at a Railroad Crossing in South Denver City, Colorado, Rescued by a Gallant Hackman. His Brave Act Cheered." No knightly gesture escaped the *Police News'* attention, especially if it invited viewing a lady's ankle.

In the glorious noontide of the ten wheeler the several times a day run with commuters between Denver and Fort Logan and Littleton was known for the first engine assigned to it as the *Uncle Sam Train* and was usually powered by one of the road's 500 series. The stub track in Denver depot used today for private cars and the spotting of special equipment next to the depot commemorates the little shuttle run in the name "Uncle Sam Track." (*Two Photos: R. H. Kindig Collection.*)

The prototypal engine named *Uncle Sam (above)* had an uncommonly tall stack and its name painted on the cab. No. 502 *(below)* a few years later boasted such refinements as mudguards and a cord to the cab for control of the patent shutter dimming its stately headlamp when meeting another train at night.

In an age innocent of the boons of jet speeds, taking in the mail on the fly and sorting it aboard the cars was thrilling evidence of progress and the last word in enterprise. A sketch artist for *Harper's* depicted for its readers the railway post office on the Denver-Pueblo run in the mid-eighties.

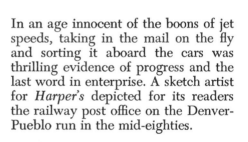

Symbolic of the great tradition of the Railway Post Office that rode both the narrow and standard gauge in the age of steam, this elevation of a Rio Grande mail car presents for posterity the unassailable likeness of a service that was impervious to the elements, mischance and devisings of evil men. *(Rio Grande Railroad.)*

Merry Xmas.

OYSTERS.

CELERY.   LETTUCE.   QUEEN OLIVES.

FRESH LOBSTER.

CONSOMME ROYAL.

FRESH COD FISH, MADEIRA SAUCE.

BAKED WESTPHALIA HAM, CHAMPAGNE SAUCE.   ROAST TENDERLOIN BEEF.

WILD TURKEY, STUFFED WITH CHESTNUTS.
TAME DUCK, HUNTERS' STYLE.
SADDLE OF ANTELOPE, A LA SALIDA.

ROAST YOUNG PIG, STUFFED WITH TRUFFLES.

OYSTER PATTIES, A LA FRASCATTI.   QUAIL, ON TOAST.

CHARLOTTE OF PEACHES.   DEVILED CRABS.

HOT RUM PUNCH.

MASHED POTATOES.   BOILED SWEET POTATOES.   ASPARAGUS

SUCCOTASH   FRENCH PEAS.

ENGLISH PLUM PUDDING COGNAC AND HARD SAUCES.

PUMPKIN PIE.   MINCE PIE.   LEMON MERINGUE PIE

FRUIT CAKE.   COCOANUT CAKE.

ANGEL FOOD.   SILVER CAKE.   MACAROONS.

NEAPOLITAN ICE CREAM.

SNOW APPLES.   MALAGA GRAPES.   ORANGES.

ASSORTED NUTS.   LAYER RAISINS.   EDAM CHEESE.

BLACK COFFEE.

MONTE CHRISTO,
SALIDA, COLORADO.
DECEMBER 25, 1888.

In the eighties, before the *Colorado & New Mexico Express* set out a sleeper at Salida and the rails were narrow gauge *(below)* travelers found the fare at the Monte Christo Hotel something to write home about, especially on Christmas Day.

In 1935 the Rio Grande Trains No. 15 and 16, the *Colorado & New Mexico Express* furnished overnight communication between Denver and Alamosa, Salida and Grand Junction through the agency of Pullman standard sleepers to be set out at each of the three terminals. There were coaches to Grand Junction via Leadville and head-end revenue but no diner. It was strictly a sleeper hop. Here the *Colorado & New Mexico Express*, a train that had been running since it carried a Creede sleeper in the nineties, rolls into Denver of a winter's morning with snow on the ground and a bleak sky overhead in contrast to the warm berths of three Pullmans on the drawbar of No. 800, a light Pacific. *(Otto C. Perry.)*

Obviously inspired by one of the Rio Grande's sleepers after the passing of the narrow gauge so dear to the proprieties of General Palmer was this drawing in the *Police Gazette* which kept an eye on the West as well as the Bowery. The caption read: "She Thought It Best To Be On the Safe Side: A Bride on a Sleeping Car of the Rio Grande Line in Denver Pins Her Marriage Certificate to the Curtain of Her Berth." It was not the sort of publicity to amuse the General.

By 1892 the original narrow gauge sleepers with their single occupancy berths had been retired to secondary runs such as the Durango-Silverton service and such beautiful standard gauge equipment as the Pullman *Taro* were in service between Denver and Salt Lake-Ogden. The coming of standard equipment made possible such lapses from the standards of decorum as that depicted above. *(Pullman Standard.)*

By the time *Taro* was in service, Rio Grande sleeping car patrons were becoming accustomed to all the amenities and luxuries of Pullman travel including some of the most ornate interior decors in the world with rare woods and intricate paneling in abundance, Turkey carpets, bevel-edge French mirrors, thickets of potted palms and elaborate crystal lighting fixtures. In 1935 the Rio Grande's *Colorado-New Mexico Express,* shown below, carried Pullman Standard sleepers for Alamosa and Grand Junction via Pueblo, diner, coaches and head-end revenue. *(Left: Pullman Standard; Below: Otto Perry.)*

Clubbing down the hand brakes on narrow gauge high cars, a universal technique in the nineteenth century, is almost a forgotten technique today. Here a brakeman demonstrates the classic stance and leverage with a hickory club which halted the cars on signal from the engineer in the eighties. *(Rio Grande Railroad.)*

Decorating the car tops on Tennessee Pass on a winter's night could be a dangerous occupation although the low narrow gauge cars and four or five mile speeds were not apt to be fatal in the event of missing a grabiron. The legend and folklore of the narrow gauge in early time abounds with hair raising tales of brakemen thrown from the cartops at night and having to make their way through blizzards and other calamities of the elements to wayside depots and maintenance stations, but few of them are identifiable with details of names, dates and places. Train crews did ride their cars down mountainsides, as witness the celebrated wreck of the *San Juan* on the Alamosa-Durango run in the fifties, but the record of injuries is sparse and of fatalities almost none.

— 49

Two views of the much pictured *San Juan* on the Lobato Trestle, both by Otto Perry show varying angles of the highest bridge on the Alamosa-Durango run while the different stages of growth in the foreground indicate the passage of time between the two exposures.

Lobato Trestle may well have been the setting for the stirring scene depicted above which appeared in the *Police Gazette* in 1905 with the caption: "Trainmen To the Rescue; A Pretty Girl's Pluck When Surprised by the Limited on a Colorado High Bridge." Such occurrences were not infrequent and the distinguished historian Bruce Catton recalls just such an experience at first hand on the Gunnison line many years back. Below, in a rare action shot from the collection of Robert A. LeMassena, a diamond stacker noses out on Lobato with a stock extra on its drawbar not long after the turn of the century.

Any resemblance between the groups of characters assembled around the yard goats No. 824 and No. 813 on the page opposite in Denver yards in the year 1900 to a troupe of early Mack Sennett comedians is purely incidental, but the suggestion is nonetheless implicit. Yarding was casual at the turn of the century and corncob pipes, walrus mustaches and shirts outside one's trousers raised no eyebrows in a Denver that was still a cow town and very much part of the Old West. On this page the Burnham Shop's switcher with a saddle tank and clerestory on its cab was something of a pet around South Denver and *(below)* only at Alamosa in recent years was it possible to see standard gauge switchers of the 1100 series yarding narrow gauge equipment such as the caboose on the drawbar of No. 1161. *(Page Opposite: R. H. Kindig Collection; Above, Same; Below: Jim Ehernberger.)*

Seemingly endless tangents of track against a backdrop of the Sangre de Cristo Mountains made the Salida-Alamosa run one of the most picturesque of the entire narrow gauge. Above, shown double headed, is the same train which in the lower frame leaves the San Luis Valley via the grade up Poncha Pass just north of Round Hill, Colorado. (Two Photos: Otto C. Perry.)

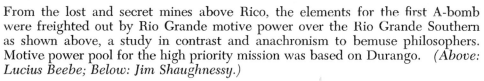

From the lost and secret mines above Rico, the elements for the first A-bomb were freighted out by Rio Grande motive power over the Rio Grande Southern as shown above, a study in contrast and anachronism to bemuse philosophers. Motive power pool for the high priority mission was based on Durango. (*Above: Lucius Beebe; Below: Jim Shaughnessy.*)

Although competition for passengers from automobiles, buses and airplanes had yet to materialize, the opening decades of the twentieth century saw rising operational costs and the immense vogue for interurban railways casting a long shadow over the steam passenger train. Between 1906 and 1940 a luxuriant variety of railbuses and other adaptations of automotive units flowered everywhere that steam had formerly been undisputed king, most especially on branch lines and short hauls where traffic was thin. Most celebrated and successful of these ventures were the portholed rail cars devised and built by the Union Pacific's Superintendent of Motive Power and Machinery in the Harriman regime, William R. McKeen, whose cars at one time or another ran over many main lines between Maine and California, and short lines as well. Fascinated by the success of McKeen's gasoline driven, heavy traction all-steel vehicles, many carriers improvised railcars of their own with varying degrees of success. This Mack truck was rebuilt by the Rio Grande at its Burnham Shops in 1926 and is shown here on its trial trip out of Denver. It has air brakes, a Baker heater, toilet compartment and an engine bell just to establish continuity with more conventional operations of its time. *(Rio Grande Railroad.)*

Few pieces of railroad equipment had as long and varied a career in two centuries as the Denver & Rio Grande Western's Motor Car No. 592. Originally built by Pullman at Pullman, Illinois, in May, 1898 as a fifty-two foot wooden daycoach and numbered RGW 216, it was renumbered as 784 in 1909 and in 1920 rebuilt as a combined coach-baggage car and renumbered 592. In 1927 it was overhauled again and appeared with two Continental six-cylinder 100 horsepower motors and ran for ten years upon its owners' various occasions with mail, express and passengers, making its last mileage as a self-propelled unit in 1930. In 1938 its motors were removed and it reappeared as a combine on the daily mixed train between Glenwood Springs and Aspen. In 1951 it was retired and its body sold, for purposes undisclosed, to T. M. Steel of Denver. This, it is believed by Jackson Thode, archivist for the railroad, to be the most versatile car ever to have appeared on the carrier's roster of equipment. *(Rio Grande Railroad.)*

Locomotives of the class later renumbered 700 such as No. 759 shown below were Vauclain compounds built in 1902 and remaining in service until the middle twenties. A rare view of two of them double heading the *Scenic Limited* in the Royal Gorge *(above)* dates from about 1920 and shows the versatility of this graceful but lightweight motive power in passenger service for approximately two full decades. *(Above: Robert A. Le Massena Collection; Below: Rio Grande.)*

No. 701 was one of the original group of 4-6-0 passenger engines received by the Rio Grande in 1896 from the Baldwin Locomotive Works in Philadelphia and, seven years later when the above photograph was made in Denver depot waiting for a highball for Pueblo, it was still in mint condition and a haughty example of the locomotive erector's workmanship. If the appearance of the head-end crew is not too reassuring and their friend in the Homburg seems a reasonable facsimile of a Balkan spy, it must be remembered it was an age of beards and that head-end crews were as yet innocent of the antiseptic cabs of Diesels. A commentary on how very wild the railroading West was, even after the turn of the century, are the link-and-pin coupling and wooden pilot still acceptable in Colorado at a time when mainline carriers in the East had long since outlawed such primitive practices. The sleeve atop the stack of No. 701 appears in many photographs of Rio Grande motive power of the period and was an improvement apparently added by the railroad. (*R. H. Kindig Collection.*)

Focus and epicenter of the industrial empire that was to support the railroad was the complex of mills and furnaces of the Colorado Fuel & Iron Company at Pueblo, shown at the left. From them rails radiated to the four points of the compass as is suggested by a sturdy 2-10-2 *(left above)* photographed by R. H. Kindig and *(right)* an ex-Norfolk & Western 2-8-8-2 purchased during the 1941 war. *(Everett De Golyer Collection.)* Genius of this all-embracing scheme was General W. J. Palmer *(below)* a looming figure of the Age of the Moguls.

—61

Recruited in the seaports of entry of the East, numbers of emigrants from Central
Europe were imported by the Rio Grande in zulu cars *(above)* to operate the vast
Bessemer furnaces and other heavy industries of the Colorado Fuel & Iron Com-
pany at Pueblo.   *(Two Pictures: Rio Grande Railroad.)*

The huge industrial complex of Pueblo, originally intended as the private feudal domain of the Rio Grande Railroad, eventually came also to be served by a network of carriers that included the Santa Fe, Colorado & Southern, Missouri Pacific and Colorado & Wyoming. *(Two Photos: Colorado State Historical Society.)*

Although the lettering on the depot nameboards differs and summer has given place to winter, the two photos of Tennessee Pass about 1930 give the feel of this remote and desolate outpost of the Rio Grande's mountain operations and main line before the Moffat Tunnel. The train in the winter scene is the *Scenic Limited,* abbrevi- ated to suit the season. Now the station at Tennessee is only a memory and trains whistle for the tunnel under the roof of the world without stopping where once the orders were handed up, front and rear, by the eyeshaded operator. *(Rio Grande Railroad.)*

The massive Rio Grande depot at Pueblo shared with the Missouri Pacific, Santa Fe and Colorado & Southern as it appeared in 1910 is evidence of the volume of passenger traffic in that now remote and perhaps romantic era. The coaches in the foreground bear on their nameboards the lettering of the St. Louis, Iron Mountain & Southern Railroad, evidence of the interchange point between the Rio Grande and another influential Gould carrier, the Missouri Pacific of which the Iron Mountain was by now a part. *(Rio Grande Railroad.)*

After the flood waters subsided Rio Grande Business Car No. B-5 was found a victim on the private car track in Pueblo depot *(above)* while below is a general view of the devastation looking over the yards to Nuckoll's Packing Plant. *(Rio Grande Railroad.)*

The sudden violence of mischance to moving trains is not the only form of catastrophe to which railroads are available, as witness the flooding of the Arkansas River on June 3, 1921 that left in its wake seven deaths and destruction to railroad plant and rolling stock running into millions. The fatalities took place aboard the Rio Grande's Train No. 3, the *Salt Lake-San Francisco Express* which passed through Pueblo in mid-evening and was caught by the full fury of the flash flood on the edge of town. Below is a scene on the tracks in Pueblo station the next morning; at the left a vignette of violence among the tracks and trestles of the outer yards. (*Two Photos: Rio Grande Railroad.*)

Early in the game, cattle ranching and the beef industry became important factors in the Rio Grande's scheme of things as great spreads appeared on the ranges of the lower Arkansas Valley and shorthorns, Herefords and other superior stock replaced the Texas longhorns. Stock trains for Denver and the East loaded at Antonito, Lamar, Julesburg, Sterling and other points both on the Rio Grande and its competing railroads. Here steers of the great "J.J." Ranch of the Prairie Cattle Company in the Arkansas Valley are loaded from the Rio Grande's pens for shipment to Denver.

Popular imagination doesn't closely associate cowboy cutups with Colorado, but until 1880 they were the most numerous single occupational group in the state and the *Police Gazette* in 1883 captioned this stirring scene: "Cow Boys on a Racket; They Took Over the Ranche at Lamar, Colo." Below, in 1945 a double headed stock extra heads east out of Alamosa. *(Charles Clegg.)*

In the years of steam two short lines of pronounced personality fed the Rio Grande in the San Luis Valley, the San Luis Central *(above)* running fifteen miles from Center to Monte Vista on the Rio Grande's Creede Branch, and the San Luis Valley Southern *(below)* running mixed trains over thirty-one miles of improbable iron from Jaroso to Blanca. Agricultural products supported both little roads and the S.L.V.S. carried passengers in a hand-me-down Rio Grande combine. *(Above: Gordon S. Crowell; Below: Charles Clegg.)*

The San Luis Valley Southern's yards and loading pens at Blanca *(above)* for all their forlorn appearance, fed hundreds of carloadings annually to the Rio Grande to be carried eastward behind such mighty mainline motive power as the carrier's articulated No. 3617 highballing smokily out of Blanca in 1949. *(Above: Charles Clegg; Below: Rocky Mountain Railroad Photos.)*

In the photograph at the top of the page opposite one of the Rio Grande's nobly proportioned three cylinder Mountain type freight hogs with its third cylinder showing plainly under the smokebox poses for its likeness by R. H. Kindig at Grand Junction in 1948.

In late 1920 when summer brought the tourist trade to the Rockies, Train No. 3, *The Westerner*, eastbound with through Pullmans for interchange with the Missouri Pacific at Pueblo, sometimes ran double headed with sixteen cars as shown in this heady action photographed by Otto Perry. The R.P.O. interior is from an earlier time when mail by rail was a wondrous convenience and the only connection with the outer world for many lonely ranchers between the Rockies and the Wasatch.

In 1883 when the through line from Denver to Salt Lake was only recently in operation, a herd of antelope running ahead of the engine of his train at Green River so delighted the famous sketch artist Charles Graham of *Harper's Weekly* that he drew this picture of the scene. Seventy years later at nearby Castle Gate, Richard Steinheimer shot this winter scene as two helpers start a coal drag toward Soldier Summit, rattling windows with their going. A 2-10-2 and a 2-8-8-2 show in the photograph and another 2-8-8-2 is up at the head end.

The three vignettes of the *San Juan* shown above and variously entering Antonito, near Coxo, Colorado, and at dusk and in the twilight of the narrow gauge off the Cumbres in 1949, are all from the incomparable camera of Otto Perry.

One of the enchantments of riding the legendary narrow gauge *San Juan* from Alamosa to Durango through Toltec Gorge and over Cumbres Pass as long as the little train lasted was the chance to see the fabled Colorado mountain vistas from its diminutive observation-parlor-cafe cars, in this case *Durango*. Ample resources of food and drink were available from a venerable steward and here the *San Juan* is shown passing the margin of an upland a mere four miles from Cumbres Summit in an ambrosial scene by Henry R. Griffiths, Jr., taken in the summer of 1947.

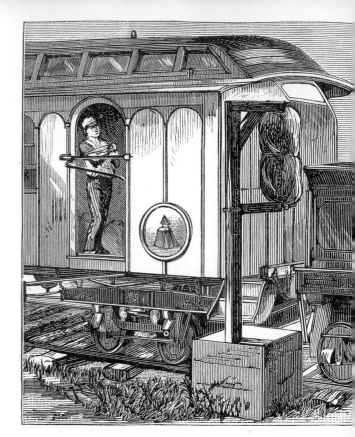

In 1941 the successor to the Uncle Sam run of the nineties between Denver and suburban Fort Logan and Littleton was Train No. 9 shown here with four cars behind a fleet footed Pacific No. 803, the very paradigm of stylish maintenance of motive power and rolling stock in the glory years of steam. At various times the run included a Railway Post Office for sorting the suburban mail but in this atmospheric action shot by R. H. Kindig only a mail storage and express car contributes to the head-end revenue.

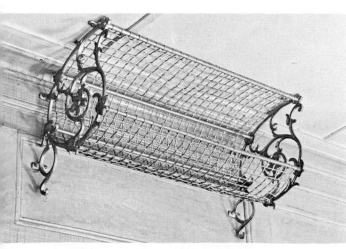

The Pullman coaches built for the Rio Grande by the ranking carbuilder of the age maintained Pullman standards of excellence in everything from flowered seat upholstery to handsome Pintsch lamp figures and the frivolous but ornate baggage racks everywhere in vogue at the time. (*Above: Pullman Standard; Left: Homer G. Comstock.*)

— 79

The first rails for the Fort Garland Extension that eventually became the Alamosa-Durango run were brought into the wintry mountains by well loaded burros with two lengths of rail on each.

For a time, in 1939 the *San Juan* from Durango and the mixed daily out of Santa Fe met at Antonito and continued into Alamosa as a single operation as depicted in July of that year with No. 473 on the smoky end in a rare action shot by Richard B. Jackson. On the opposite page Robert Hale's vignette of winter railroading suggests the narrow gauge approach to the elements, while Johnny Krause records for posterity No. 345 switching the Durango yard after the arrival of the *San Juan* in the lower frame.

From earliest times the narrow gauge railroads of the Rockies engaged the attention of artists and photographers to an even greater and more devoted degree than did their neighboring standard gauge operations of greater moment and consequence. The endearing diminutive of the three-foot trains appealed to early day photographers such as William Henry Jackson and Colonel Charles Savage of Salt Lake and exercised a still discernible charm for such celebrated sketch artists of the nineteenth century as Henry Farney, A. W. Waud, Henry R. Poore, Charles Graham, T. de Thulstrup and the famous team of Paul Frenzeny and Jules Tavernier of *Leslie's Weekly*. A new generation of photographers discovered the narrow gauge just in time to perpetuate its final years and included Otto Perry, Robert Hale, Richard Kindig, Richard B. Jackson, Jim Shaughnessy, and Gerald Best, all of whom are represented in this book. The portrait of No. 227 taken shortly after the turn of the century at Durango by Fred Jukes, an almost legendary old timer in Western railroad photography, shows its cab embellished with lace curtains on the engineer's window, a touch of whimsy only infrequently encouraged in later years. Above a view of the shops at Alamosa by Neal Miller for Rocky Mountain Railroad Photos.

Most dedicated of a later generation of narrow gauge photographers was Otto C. Perry, a one-time Denver letter carrier, who took No. 480, as shown below curving on a wooden trestle for a portrait of the slim gauge in its final years.

The rare photographs on this page show Durango yards and depot after the completion of the Farmington branch in standard gauge and before its conversion to three foot tracks, with three rails running everywhere to accommodate both freight and passenger traffic. Below, in 1923, Durango depot presents a busy picture as Train No. 116 arrives from Silverton behind the engine *Elk Creek*, a Grant product of 1881 that was only retired in 1926. Two gauges are much in evidence. *(Above: John W. Maxwell Collection; Below: Rio Grande Railroad.)*

For some reason now lost to history, the *San Juan's* observation-parlor car *Alamosa* at the rear end of the train is carried backward as it rounds Windy Point, half a mile west of Cumbres Summit, in 1910. Passengers on the *San Juan* (below) always enjoyed the narrow gauge adventure of riding an authentic train to happy yesterdays. (*Above: Robert A. Le Massena Collection; Below: Rio Grande Railroad.*)

In January 1881, less than two years after the completion to Alta of the Wasatch & Jordan Valley Railroad to that point, a series of avalanches wiped out the railroad grade and occasioned substantial loss of life amongst the mining communities that paralleled it. Snowsheds, tracks and cabins were all carried to irretrievable ruin on a scale so spectacular that on February 5, *Leslie's Weekly* devoted its entire front page to the catastrophe. The line was rebuilt when spring came with snowsheds of more substantial design that proved impervious to future attack.

Incorporated in 1874, the San Pete Valley Railroad between Morrison and Nephi was presently absorbed by the ever expanding network of the Rio Grande Western. Here a San Pete mixed train poses for its portrait in pastoral mood. *(Robert Edwards Collection.)*

A companion road to the Bingham line, the Wasatch & Jordan Valley Railroad, was incorporated in 1872 to build a narrow gauge line from Sandy to Alta in Little Cottonwood Canyon, the southernmost canyon in the Salt Lake Valley area. It was completed in 1879, but between Wasatch and Alta the grade was better than 600 feet per mile and motive power of the time was unequal to it so that empty cars were drawn up by horses and allowed to coast back, at some peril to life and limb, with ore from the mines. Above Granite the rails were continuously covered with snowsheds and a ride down was reported by contemporaries to have been "quite a thrilling experience." The Rio Grande acquired the Wasatch & Jordan Valley in 1881 when the below photograph *(Denver Public Library Western Collection)* was made of a party of English visitors, prospective investors in mining properties, being brought up by covered horse cars. The line drawing at the left is purely imaginary, no such roller coaster ride ever having been recorded. *(Utah State Historical Society.)*

In 1889 *Harper's Weekly* devoted a full page to this drawing by the well known sketch artist Henry Farny with the caption: "Down the Grade From the Divide in Colorado—Section Hands Going to Camp For Provisions." Although not specified the background is strongly suggestive of Tennessee Pass with Pando in the valley below.

88 —

Although the festive whisky jug so conspicuously in evidence on the page opposite doesn't figure in these portraits of Rio Grande Western section gangs posed at American Forks, Utah, about 1905, the down to earth types that tamped the ties and wielded spike mauls is much the same as that headed for Saturday night on the town a decade and a half earlier. The handcars alone show evidences of progressive mechanization. *(Two Photos: Robert Edwards Collection.)*

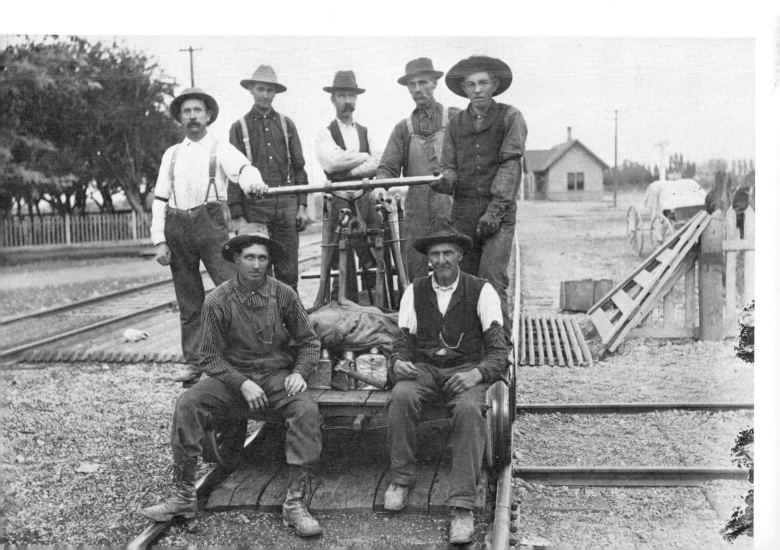

Against an unfinished water tower for background and with bunting awash, Rio Grande Western's No. 2 brings the first train into Richfield, Utah, the lettering on its headlight glass showing the date to be 6-2-1896. Fifteen years later the depot platform, derby hatted agent and platform loafers at Springville appeared as shown at the right. *(Four Photos: Robert Edwards Collection.)*

In 1900 the Junction House at Thistle, Utah, was the gathering place for train crews between runs, its lunch counter handy to the Rio Grande Western's main line, standard gauged this past decade and showing in the foreground. Below is a general view of the railroad's yards at Thistle in the same year with eight stall roundhouse, coal tipple, water tower, all the properties of railroading in far places of the Old West when the century was new.

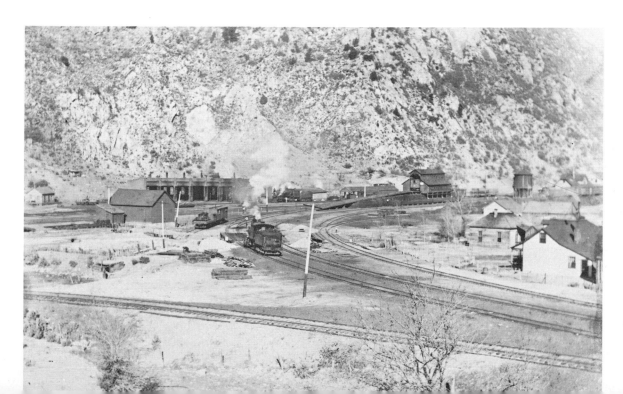

When a staff artist for *Frank Leslie's Illustrated Newspaper* in its issue of December 15, 1877 drew this sketch of the western terminal of the Union Pacific, he captioned his picture "Ogden Junction" which it indeed was as the meeting point of the U.P., the Central Pacific and the Rio Grande Western. No attempt was made to identify the trackage depicted, but it may safely be presumed that the artist was looking south and that the facade of the Beardsley House faced west toward the lake. The first departure of the *Scenic Limited* with Rio Grande Western No. 33 on the head end from today's depot at Ogden is shown below in a rare photograph from the collection of Robert A. LeMassena.

In the above scene the Rio Grande Western's No. 59 pauses for water at the tank at Lehi Junction in 1911, while *(below)* is a wide angle view of the same carrier's original depot at Salt Lake with three foot rails, stub switches and pastoral simplicities of operation. *(Above: Robert Edwards Collection; Below: Utah State Historical Society.)*

Railroading without frills and almost unchanged since the first transcontinental was completed twenty-one years earlier is suggested by the Denver & Rio Grande Western's No. 174 on the narrow gauge track at Scofield, Utah, in 1890. The dimension of standard gauge had been achieved more than a decade ago on most of the Rio Grande's Utah operations when the caboose-hop shown below paused in its work train activities near Springville in 1900. *(Two Photos: Robert Edwards Collection.)*

Originally known as Pleasant Valley Junction, Colton, Utah, in 1905 was the junction point of the main line of the Rio Grande Western and the Pleasant Valley Railroad and these two views, taken in that year, show the look of a raw and windswept railroad yards of the time in the Utah uplands. The water tower shown at the left above is the same one that appears from another angle in the lower photograph. *(Two Photos: Robert Edwards Collection.)*

A *rara avis* in the operations of any railroad, a triple headed freight with all three engines working steam on the head end, thunders through Castle Gate, Utah, about 1920 for a classic silhouette of railroading in the grand manner in a geological frame that has long been a hallmark of the Rio Grande. On the page opposite, an Eastern magazine artist's version of "a snow block-ade on the Castle Gate line in Utah" shows more spirit than familiarity with the Wasatch scene. Below is the Rio Grande Western's business car *Wasatch* on an inspection tour of the Western Lines in December 1912, a period when ranking executives still wore wing collars and morning coats on line. *(Below: Rio Grande Railroad; Opposite: Harry Shipler, Salt Lake.)*

In 1908, with the consolidation of the Denver & Rio Grande and the Rio Grande Western into a single corporate entity, on-line improvements were in order including the replacement of this wooden trestle with a steel span at West Thistle. In the lower frame is the departure of the *Scenic Limited* on its first run from the new Rio Grande depot at Salt Lake City. *(Above: Robert Edwards Collection; Below: Robert A. LeMassena Collection.)*

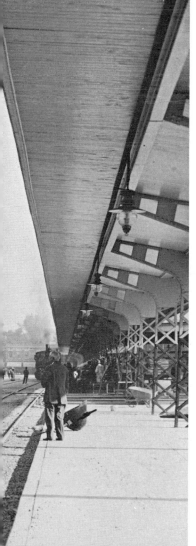

About 1895 the Rio Grande Western's No. 106 was hauling a construction train through an unidentified town with the Wasatch in the background for an atmospheric souvenir in the collection of Robert Edwards. Below is a contemporary drawing of the road's first depot at Lehi.

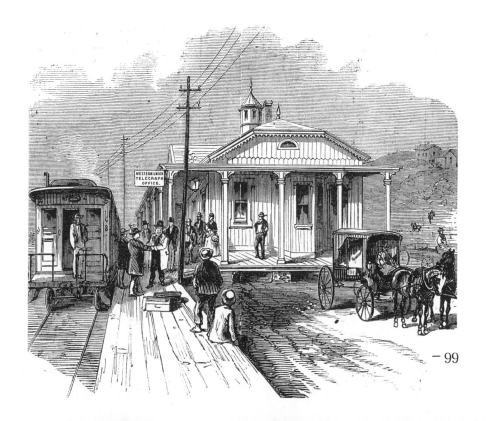

The Rio Grande Western's gleaming ten wheeler No. 54 poses with a consist of head end cars, open platform coaches and Denver Pullmans in the company depot at Salt Lake after the gauge had been standardized. Photographer was Colonel Charles R. Savage of Salt Lake whose photographs of the Gold Spike ceremony at Promontory in 1869 are classics in the iconography of the Old West. *(Rio Grande Railroad.)*

Here the same engine, No. 54 that is shown opposite is depicted again, this time with a two car local train in Salt Lake depot. Its profile differs for a straight stack stands where previously there had been a capped chimney. Below is an artist's version of a Salt Lake street scene in the seventies, a country town of the familiar wide streets of today, but unpaved and populous with the horses and vehicles of an age innocent of internal combustion. *(Above: Robert Edwards Collection; Below: Denver Public Library, Western Collection.)*

The depot at Soldier Summit on the Rio Grande Western in the nineties can have represented few comforts to the operator stationed there at his lonely telegraph key, and the recently unloaded stove on the platform at the right and the snow fence in the background suggest the winter significance of the elevation of 7,465 feet noted on the station signboard. In the below photo with R.G.W. No. 114 emerging from the Soldier Summit snowshed, the well polished rails have been standard gauged for a full decade when it was taken in 1900, but the switches leading to the passing track are still stub type as they had been when narrow gauge ruled everywhere between Denver and Salt Lake. *(Bob Edwards Collection.)*

That even the best managed corporation can sometimes make blunders of an impressive dimension is the moral implicit in this photograph taken at Soldier Summit in 1919 where now a single shack for the telegraph operator stands on a windy and barren Utah upland. Acting on advice that Helper terminal, 71.3 miles west of Green River was badly located and that vast advantages would derive from its relocation at Soldier Summit almost equidistant between Green River and Salt Lake, an entire operative community was established there. To this end sums in excess of $1,581,000 were spent to build a helper engine station on Soldier Summit. An engine house, shown in this photograph, car shops and several hundred employees' cottages were constructed, a vast network of tracks laid out to accommodate fuel for road and helper engines coaling at this point. Ten years later the entire project had been abandoned, the helper station restored to Helper and the whole costly experiment charged off to education. Understandably, almost no mention of the undertaking appears in the company's annual reports for the period. *(Rio Grande Railroad.)*

In 1911 the Rio Grande management had this celebrated and spectacular photograph of its crack *Panoramic Limited* taken on the ruling grade at Soldier Summit, Utah, where one road engine and four helpers were required to get eleven steel coaches and Pullmans over the hump. The picture was posed for the camera of Harry Shipler, a Salt Lake photog-

— 104

When, two years after the photograph on the page opposite, in June 1913, the assignment of Rio Grande Mallets to the helper run over Soldier Summit reduced the number of helper engines and crews to two, the second of what turned out to be a series of progressive photographs of the *Panoramic* was made by Shipler in the identical spot and is shown above. A third was taken in September of 1913 when the Mallets had been replaced by a single road engine, one of the 700 series Vauclain compounds, with an unidentified helper on the rear end. *(The Photos: Shipler, Salt Lake.)*

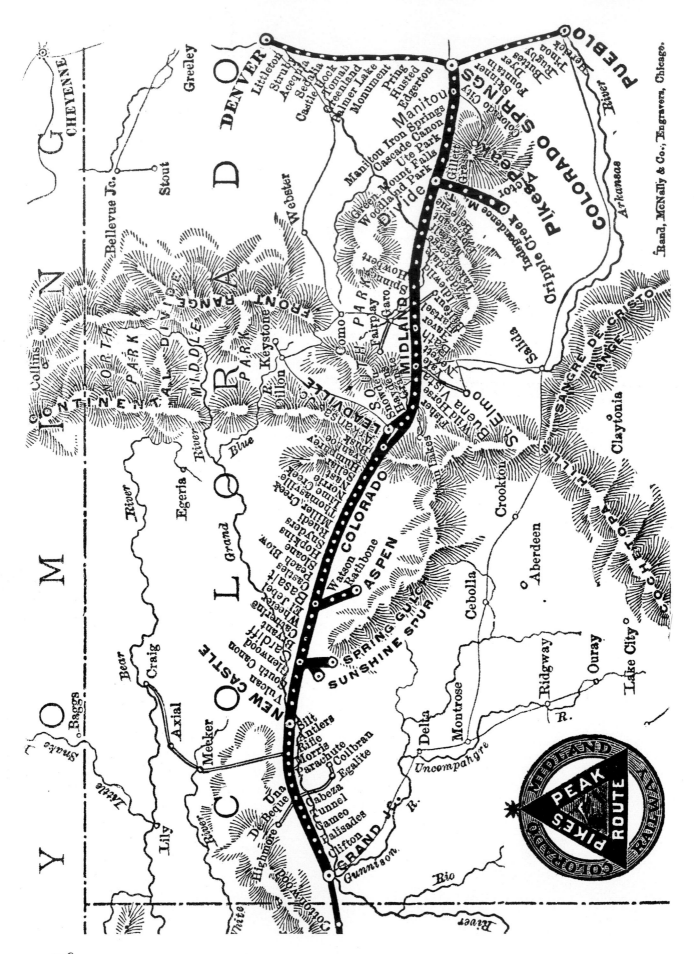

THE COLORADO MIDLAND

HE SHINING MOUNTAINS are populous with the ghosts of departed railroads, once operable, beloved, even prosperous but now in the roundhouses of eternity: the South Park, the Rio Grande Southern, the Florence & Cripple Creek, the Gilpin Tram, the Argentine Central and the once numerous narrow gauge branches of the Rio Grande itself, to name but a handful.

Best remembered of mainline operations, and one whose ghost assumes the outline of a well defined white elephant was the Colorado Midland, a standard gauge operation of continental ambitions and radiant auspices whose rights of way are now returning to the elemental earth and whose souvenirs are only to be found in the accredited repositories of yesterday. Its story is one to bemuse philosophers and economists alike.

That the Midland was doomed from the beginning is obvious in the easy wisdom of hindsight. It had three strikes against it at birth: gravity, the elements and the Denver & Rio Grande; they were formidable adversaries. Add to these the element of idiot bureaucracy and the tensions of a major war which finally sank the Midland almost without trace and you have a combination against which only great good fortune could prevail, and the Midland was not lucky.

The competition against which the Midland found itself pitted throughout its brief but dramatic lifetime was murderous. Wherever its surveys ran, to Leadville, Cripple Creek, even to remote and distant Aspen, other railroads were there ahead of it or directly on its heels. For miles its sixty pound rails paralleled both gauges of the Rio Grande, the three foot dimensions of the Denver, South Park & Pacific or the complex of competing lines converging upon the Cripple Creek District.

It changed owners and managements with the rapidity of Greek restaurants and its finances were a compound of chaos and catastrophe to frighten even the easy going bankers of the Colorado nineties. Its operations were often of the baling wire sort and it was hoodooed with wrecks, derailments and cornfield meets to freeze the marrow of division superintendents. At times not a wheel turned on its system for days on end while trains stalled in snowdrifts and rescue operations followed them into immobility.

And yet for all the frustrations, bankruptcies and grief that dogged its wayward progress, the Colorado Midland's memory is green with sentimental souvenirs and its ghost, for all its white elephant dimensions, is a friendly one. Perhaps it was the excursions that accomplished this. The wildflower picnics that it ran in an age of simple pleasures crown its recollection with garlands of childhood innocence. There was a fey cheeriness about the Colorado Midland that has long outlived all its other attributes.

In 1883 the Denver and Rio Grande was still Colorado's "baby road," its endearing diminutive belying a tough and determined management that was learning its way around in the school of experience. The Centennial State itself was only seven years removed from territorial status. Among numismatists, 1883 is remembered as the year the United States Mint forgot to incorporate the word "cents" on its half-dime coins. Just the Roman V appeared on its reverse and they were made from dies identical with those employed to strike five dollar gold pieces. To certain irresponsible people this suggested the practice of thinly gilding a five cent coin with gold and fobbing it off for five dollars. Moral philosophers have been able to discern a symbol of the times in this chicane.

The Colorado Midland Railroad, had it operated in a vacuum, would be a rewarding study. As direct competition to the Rio Grande it was a well defined victim type and quite properly the subject for brief consideration in this context.

The Midland came into emergent being at a time when railroading was the national American preoccupation, and the financing of new carriers was the easiest enterprise to float of all those available to the ever crescent wealth of the country. Only seldom did realism intrude itself when a new route was proposed, and the immense fortunes being acquired by the Vanderbilt family, Jay Gould and other Eastern capitalists served to emphasize a profit potential in terms of millions. That the Vanderbilts were legitimate operators and Gould a man of unmitigated disaster, made no difference. Both were railroaders, both were rich, enviable and to be imitated. Rails between nowhere and nowhere found their stock issues oversubscribed as soon as the books were opened. Inconsiderable communities, wishing to become considerable and finding themselves left off the surveys of main trunk lines, built their own short lines, connecting lines and bridge railroads in the sure knowledge that the coming of the cars would resolve all problems other than death and taxes.

There was another aspect of railroading, at this remove so trivial as often to be overlooked by historians and economists surveying the American scene. Railroading was a socially impeccable occupation and the railroad operator in any community was accorded the respect and admiration hitherto reserved for bankers and some bishops. The railroad president in the silk hat and frock coat of ultimate respectability was top man on the financial totem pole in any community and, by the same token, his wife was elevated to the estate then boldly capitalized in the newspapers as "Society." The Vanderbilts were again invoked as examples not only of astute financial operations but of the most exalted social dimensions. Their newly financed hauteur was relegating to the discard in New York, London and Paris older families of bankers, merchants and landholders, and ambitious nabobs in Kansas City, Chicago and San Francisco were exhorted by their wives to do likewise. Many substantial fortunes achieved in smelting, pork packing and coal mining were translated into railroading channels. The urge to acquire respectability and recognition on the part of bored

and inconsequential Texas oil millionaires is still a national phenomenon, as witness the fatal acquisition of the New York Central by a petroleum syndicate.

In the case of the Colorado Midland this facet of railroading is not to be ignored. In Colorado itself General Palmer, an unimpeachable aristocrat, had shown the way, and even in the modest terms of the Rio Grande in 1883, railroading was already synonymous with country estates, English connections and the *bon ton* generally. It is significant that none of the originators of the Midland had had previous railroad experience. Also that the scene of its incorporation was Colorado Springs, an enclave of manners and privilege so well established as even then to be known throughout the Rockies as "Little Lunnon."

The ancestral names that were to gleam in The Spring's later social hierarchy, Penrose, Tutt, Stratten, Jackling and Carlton had not yet emerged upon the general awareness when a lumberman named Homer D. Fisher with pineries at Woodland Park up Ute Canyon came up with the idea of a railroad to connect his mills at Colorado Springs with the timber growth eight miles up the mountain. Intuition told Fisher that his best bet would be a standard gauge line; all the carriers with which he wanted to interchange for the East were standard and he foresaw, with almost clairvoyant clarity, that he wouldn't be doing much business with the narrow gauge Rio Grande.

It may be assumed that he mentioned his plan to various semi-retired businessmen around the Springs, one of whom was Jerome Wheeler, a former executive of the even then important dry good merchants of New York, R. H. Macy & Company, who was one of the heaviest investors in the then booming mining camp of Aspen on the far side of also booming Leadville.

In the absence of evidence to the contrary, it may be assumed that either Fisher or Wheeler dropped the idea conversationally in the lap of James J. Hagerman, a Milwaukee ironmaster who had made a bundle in the iron ranges of Northern Michigan and in so doing had so impaired his health that he was now a permanent resident on a valetudinarian basis at The Springs. Hagerman wasn't so far gone that he hadn't, like Wheeler, picked up some properties at Aspen which included in their portfolio the superlatively satisfactory Mollie Gibson, a silver mine. Hagerman and Wheeler had interests in common to begin with; both were businessmen of proven astuteness with venture capital available and a lively interest in putting it to work. Neither had much on his mind except his private opinions of the most recently arrived British milord at the Antlers Hotel, and probably jumped at the chance of something to relieve the boredom of suburbia and at the same time turn a penny.

Hagerman, whose name is still remembered in the annals of Colorado, did not enjoy a reputation that was altogether stainless, and various of his deals, particularly in Cripple Creek and Aspen mining shares, were looked upon as suspect by such highly ethical operators as Penrose and Carlton. The Count James Pourtales, an enterprising German who was for a time proprietor of the Broadmoor Casino where the Broadmoor Hotel now stands, spoke of him in his memoirs variously as "sickly, elderly and loud-mouthed" and broadly suggested that he was a tin horn playing the part of a consequential wheeler. To a marked degree he possessed a faculty for unloading properties in which he was involved without apprising his partners and associates of his intentions and he was finally ruinously overextended in a promotion scheme in Texas' Pecos Valley.

His memory, for better or worse, is part of the fabric of the Midland legend.

Others who became, at first conversationally, and later actively interested in the overall project were Irving Howbert, a well established Colorado Springs pioneer banker, and Orlando Metcalf, a steel manufacturer of the pre-Carnegie era at Pittsburgh who was to supply the greatest amount of ready cash when the time came.

Here in microcosm was the entire pattern of financing that characterized the golden era of railroad expansion in the United States; the acquisition of private fortunes in mills, mining, merchandising and other profitable forms of endeavor and their channeling into rights of way, motive power and operating timetables.

Radiant paradigms of this fluidity were, of course, the translation of Commodore Cornelius Vanderbilt's ferryboat earnings into what was to become the New York Central, the Sacramento

hardware profits of Crocker and Huntington into Central Pacific, the ancestral rents of English landholders into Chicago & North Western, Standard Oil, through the agency of Henry M. Flagler, into Florida East Coast, and the department store millions of Levi Leiter and Marshall Field into the splendidly remunerative enterprise of clever George Mortimer Pullman. The Pittsburgh steel money of Orlando Metcalf even had its almost precise parallel, although in a far more spacious dimension, in the multiple millions taken out of the great split-up of the Carnegie property at Pittsburgh by the Moore brothers and promptly reinvested in the Chicago, Rock Island & Pacific Railroad. The Moore money came in hodsful where Metcalf's was, comparatively, in demitasses, but the parallel is there.

But while all these interested and lively participants in the first act of the Colorado Midland's drama thought in terms of railroading, and standard gauge railroading at that in a region hitherto dominated exclusively by narrow gauge thinking, they didn't at first see eye to eye in the matter of how it should be built. Metcalf and Hagerman, the advocates of the Aspen-Leadville axis, felt that construction should begin at that end of the route with the idea of financing it by hauling ore from Aspen to the smelters at Leadville and fuel and mining equipment back to Aspen while tapping the rich resources of coal and coke near Glenwood Springs to fire the Leadville smelters. The scheme in outline strongly resembled the New England triangle trade in slaves, cane and rum which laid the foundation of so many Beacon Street fortunes in Boston. That this wealth in turn was invested in immense sums in the railroads of the west including the Santa Fe, the Rio Grande's arch rival, is just part of the long cycle of capitalist economy.

The other faction of railroad entrepreneurs in the corridors of the Antlers and possibly at the Count James Pourtales Broadmoor Casino wasn't so much interested in the Aspen deal as it was in lumber from Woodland Park and interchange with trunk lines leading East at Colorado Springs. In spite of this divergence of opinion, the Colorado Midland was organized and incorporated at Colorado Springs on April 2, 1883, thereby missing by a day the possibility of a founding date that could have been prophetic. The Colorado Midland was at least notable for adopting a style and title that said what it had in mind and no more in an age which witnessed few such projects without including the word Pacific.

The Colorado Midland's empire builders soon learned the facts of life regarding the proposal to build the Aspen-Leadville connection first. Unless the builders were to resort to teaming all construction material up from the Springs via Ute Pass, across South Park and two ranges of mountains, everything they needed would have to be routed via Leadville over two railroads the Colorado Midland was seeking to put out of business. The overland freighting notion was discarded at once as ruinously impractical, and neither the Rio Grande nor the Denver, South Park & Pacific, already happily sabotaging each other for the Leadville trade, had any least intention of further dividing it on a three-way basis. A community of interest that might a few years later, after the passage of the Sherman Anti-Trust Law have attracted the attention of the Justice Department, suggested that both the Rio Grande and the South Park quote a tariff of $1.00 per hundred pounds of rails, Denver to Leadville. Curiously enough, the Santa Fe quoted the identical rate on rails between Chicago and Denver. Nobody rolled any rails at Pueblo at the time, and if they had, it could only have been the furnaces of the Colorado Fuel & Iron Company and their charges, too, might be expected to be uncommonly high.

The Colorado Midland didn't have the sort of money to buck this setup and gloom was at a discount in The Springs.

But Hagerman hadn't become one of the three wealthiest men in the Milwaukee seventies without having good connections in the banks of Chicago and railroads of the same region. If the Union Pacific, as the then owner of the South Park, and the Rio Grande, for once seeing eye to eye with the Santa Fe, wanted to play it that way, Hagerman could be rough too. He went east and laid his case before Charles Elliott Perkins, Boston Brahmin-bred head of the Boston-financed and controlled Chicago, Burlington & Quincy. No love was lost between the Burlington and the Santa Fe, whose directors walked to Trinity Church on opposite sides of Copley Square and avoided each other at lunch at the Union Club.

Perkins stroked his ample white moustaches and allowed that his railroad would lose no money hauling rails between Chicago and Denver for sixty cents, whence they could go to Colorado Springs by any way its owners wanted. He couldn't for the life of him see how he could get them up to Leadville, and the Colorado Midland at once saw the wisdom of starting nearer home and achieving their Leadville-Aspen-Glenwood axis through the back door.

At almost the moment this triumph was achieved, fortune was again favorable to the Midland in bringing as a social visitor to Little Lunnon, L. R. Busk, whose brother-in-law was an august figure in Threadneedle Street, London, where he was Governor of the Bank of England. Busk tipped off William Lidderdale that there might be something worth picking up in the way of Colorado properties and, anyway, there were a lot of other Englishmen at Colorado Springs and the climate was dandy, so why not come on out and case the joint? Lidderdale did come out, was enchanted with what he saw of the American West, much of it in Colorado and Wyoming populated by the younger sons of British earls, and bought into the Midland to the extent of $6,000,000.00 of its bonds purchased through the Bank of England's New York representative.

It all added up to one more tie with what, so far as The Springs was concerned, was the Mother Country, and marked one more place on the map of the world where the sun of empire never set.

By the mid-eighties the Midland was off with a whoop and a holler and blood in its corporate eye over the obstructionism practiced by the Rio Grande and the South Park. A survey of the entire line was made by Chief Engineer Thomas Wigglesworth and a ponderable portion of the Bank of England's six million was being paid out to Streator & McMurtrie who had contracted for the section between Leadville and The Springs, and to Orman & Crook, who, according to the Midland's recognized historian, Morris Cafky, had 1,000 Irish, Mexicans and other hard cases picking them up and putting them down when the graders had finished out of Leadville on the way to Aspen. The entire distance between Colorado Springs and Leadville, a total of 135 miles, was completed and the first train run on September 1, 1887. The fifty-six pound rails went into Aspen on February 4 of the following year, and the Colorado Midland was in business.

But by this time, the Rio Grande had come of age. It had survived two all-out railroad wars, one of which was an ignominious defeat and both of which had been highly educational. Just because its initial successes had been those of a "baby railroad" was no reason why it should remain in short pants while playing games with big boys in long trousers, and the Midland's standard gauge was all that was needed to get the news to General Palmer's men that their road was ready for the big time.

The Rio Grande met the Midland challenge where it meant the most first. It promptly prepared to lay a third rail so as to maintain both gauges between Pueblo and Leadville, and made preparations to relocate the line from Leadville over Tennessee Pass in standard gauge.

"West of Pueblo, the third rail was extended from Florence to Canyon City in 1888," wrote Ridgeway succinctly, "and large sums expended preparatory to carrying it westward therefrom. A third rail was also laid from Eilers to Leadville, a distance of three miles on account of interchange of standard gauge cars with the Colorado Midland to and from the Leadville smelters."

The amount of money sunk in the Midland by the time it had achieved its maximum trackage, according to Cafky, was $20,000,000.00 representing the initial buy of $6,000,000.00 in bonds by Lidderdale, $8,000,000.00 from the original incorporators, and another $6,000,000.00 from miscellaneous sources in Denver and The Springs. In addition to its own trackage, rolling stock and other equities, the C. M. owned half the capital stock in the so-called Rio Grande Junction Railway, which it had formed in conjunction with the Rio Grande itself to build the jointly owned right of way into Grand Junction. This investment, seemingly innocuous at the time it was underwritten, proved to be in fact a time bomb since it was one of the incentives to the Palmer road to complete its own broad gauging all the way to Salt Lake. Under the Continental Divide and to eliminate the fantastic loops and grade over the 11,000 foot crest of Hagerman Pass, it had contracted to rent a tunnel known as the Busk-Ivanhoe be-

tween those two points that had been constructed through independent financing and planned to amortize its debt by charging the Midland a quarter for every passenger who went through its 9,394 expensive feet of excavation and the same for every ton of freight.

Adequate passengers and freight equipment had been built by Pullman and other carbuilders and business promised a fine future. Livestock raising was booming in South Park, a growing tourist business was a really ponderable factor in gross revenues, coke from Glenwood Springs and ore from Leadville and Aspen all added up to a modest net for what Cafky characterizes as "the West's newest and steepest standard gauge railroad."

But James J. Hagerman was not happy, and this was very bad indeed, for Hagerman, in addition to being the largest single holder of Midland securities, felt strongly that the other backers whom he had induced to come along were entitled to a better return on their investment than was now showing or could be assured in any foreseeable future.

In 1890, just as most people felt that the Colorado Midland was getting into its stride, it was unloaded on the Atchison, Topeka & Santa Fe, at one time the Rio Grande's particular bête noire and arch enemy. The Santa Fe's President Allen Manvel paid the Midland's investors $20.00 cash and $30.00 in Santa Fe securities (soon to prove no such bargain as they then appeared) for each share of Midland stock which added up to a substantial $6,350,000.00 but still came to less than a third of what had been sunk into it.

The Colorado Midland continued operations as a wholly owned subsidiary of the Santa Fe with its own corporate name and officials, and in the Santa Fe interregnum it still seemed as though the C. M. was a railroad with a future. General Manager was Harry Collbran and, at his instigation, another subsidiary, the Midland Terminal Railway was built to connect the Midland mainline at Colorado City with the wildly booming diggings at Cripple Creek. The Midland Terminal was destined to outlive its ill fated parent and lasted until 1949, the last of all the carriers that once served the Cripple Creek District.

In 1893 the seemingly unthinkable happened when, a victim of the nationwide depression of that year, the parent Santa Fe defaulted interest payments and went into bankruptcy. The Midland, of course, followed suit and went into receivership. Four years later, the receivership also failed to make even its operating expenses and Federal courts sold the entire property, this time for an ignominious $295,000.00 to the mortgage trustee, and as of October 1897 it emerged as a new Colorado Midland Railway Company, controlled by an Eastern syndicate.

By now, however, it was becoming apparent that the Colorado Midland had not been born under benevolent stars and that its lifetime, such as it might be, was going to be spent in a series of orphanages. In 1899 a syndicate composed of the Rio Grande Western, by now the independently maintained road over which the Denver & Rio Grande achieved its western terminals at Salt Lake and Ogden, and the Colorado & Southern took a fancy to the Bartered Bride of the high passes. A little more than $8,400,000.00 in cash and securities went to the incredulous directors of the much sold C. M. and once again the road was under new management. But the fates had been saving their Sunday punch which was delivered in 1901 when the Rio Grande Western was acquired in toto by the now high-rolling Denver & Rio Grande and the Midland found itself a property in the portfolio of the railroad it had planned to put out of business back in the optimistic eighties. The two Rio Grandes were thereafter operated as a single railroad system although it was not until seven years later that complete corporate union was achieved.

In actual fact its deliverance into the hands of the enemy was the beginning of the Colorado Midland's happiest and most effulgent years. Its passenger trains routed out of Denver as far as The Springs over Colorado & Southern tracks and west of Grand Junction over the Rio Grande were accorded the status of members of the family instead of, as hitherto, mere paying guests. To spare its then unimproved main line and avoid wear and tear on slender resources of equipment, the Rio Grande routed much profitable tonnage east from Grand Junction over the Midland cutoff which clipped many miles off the Pueblo division. Leadville was out of borrasca and again operating in bonanza, this time in lead and zinc as well as the

rich outcroppings of gold and silver that had brought it fame.

And it was in this interlude that the Midland evolved the institutions for which it is perhaps best remembered in the Colorado community and which still bring enchanted memories to the mention of its name, the wildflower picnic trains. These immediately popular and well patronized extras headed out of The Springs and up Ute Pass every Thursday in the vacation months to destinations in South Park. Passengers took box lunches which were eaten in the verdant meadows at Spinney, Howbert and elsewhere that convenient sidings offered, and gathered arm loads and hampers of columbine, gentians, asters, Mariposa lilies and Indian paint brush. Tubs of water in the baggage car ahead assured their fresh transport back to town at the end of a day under the matchless skies of the Rocky Mountain summer. To a generation of blasé sophistication, gathering blossoms may not seem an occupation of ecstacy, but in 1905 Colorado's more than 700 varieties of mountain wild flowers were very much of an asset and figured in the state's tourist promotion on a par with its mountain scenery and salubrious airs.

In addition to the Midland's four per cent grades, multitudinous tunnels, shuddering abysses and dizzying altitudes, all of them achieved on the fifty and sixty pound rail of the period and largely without benefit of ballasted track or tie plates, it possessed one hazard which then, and now that it is only a memory, still congeals the marrow of engineers. This was the system of whorls and loops by which it crossed the Continental Divide, the High Line over the 11,500 foot pass at Ivanhoe which the Busk-Ivanhoe Tunnel had been designed to obviate.

Three huge loops which included in their survey ten long wooden snow sheds and ten bridges of ponderable dimensions were part of the attack on the formidable altitudes of the Sawatch Range. Double heading was indicated on anything at all, and the trains rumbling across the great curved trestle of timber 1,084 feet long crawled, swaying over an abyss at which strong stomachs were known to churn in apprehension. In 1897 during the Midland's first great reorganization, the management felt that the toll charges of the Busk-Ivanhoe management were excessive and terminated their agreement with the proprietors of the bore. Trains were rerouted over the old High Line and the smoke of their going was visible to observers half a hundred miles distant, plumed knights of railroad chivalry riding for a disastrous fall.

Nearly $70,000.00 had been spent to put the High Line in shape after years of complete disuse, but all went well until the winter of 1899 which proved to be a farrago of meteorological misfortunes. Then on January 24 the grandfather of all blizzards moved in ahead of a cold front that swept down from the plains of Manitoba, drifting in the cuts and passes and stalling traffic in less exposed altitudes than those achieved by the Midland west of Leadville.

A snowslide of Alpine dimensions roared down the slope above the right of way at Hagerman Station, stalling a stock extra filled with bawling cattle for Denver market. The crew killed their engines and hit out down the track, hopeful to reach Leadville alive, and the cattle froze into masses of congealed damage claims. Conventional rotaries and a borrowed Santa Fe Jull plow, a Rube Goldberg confection of sensational ineffectiveness, bogged down behind the big cattle dieup. All traffic was diverted to the Rio Grande mainline over Tennessee Pass and passengers reached Denver a day late and in mood grumpy.

For a month no wheel turned over. Hagerman and the stock extra disappeared completely in the drifting snow, a necropolis of rib steaks and Porterhouse. The first week in February another blizzard surged in from up Montana way, trapping another borrowed rotary powered by six straining engines and breaking a 500 pound casting necessary to its operation. It took seven days and a team of eight trained Alpinists on skis to get the new part out of Leadville.

Failure piled atop frustration for the rest of the winter and it was a paralyzing seventy-eight days before a Chinook abated the drifts enough to drag out the by now well aged steer meat. Seventy-eight days is a long and costly time for a railroad's main line to be blockaded, and the Midland promptly bought up the Busk Tunnel and dismantled the High Line and its expensive memories.

After the abandonment of the Midland in 1917 and the failure of the Carlton regime to interest buyers in reopening it at the close of the war, the much disputed tunnel became part of the Colorado system of state highways and was known in the automobile age that had helped kill the railroad as the Carlton Tunnel for its last owner. Irony was another of the non-revenue commodities that rode the Midland rails.

Passenger operations on the Midland in its noontide of prosperity between 1905 and the entry of the United States into the 1914 war were representative of the *belle epoque* that still evokes wistful admiration from amateurs of the days of railroading greatness. The Midland was not a great transcontinental trunkline like its opposite numbers, the U. P. to the north and the Santa Fe to the south with name trains, limited consists and extra fares on its timetable. It couldn't rival the splendor of library cars and barber shops on the *California Limited* or the drawing room-observation cars that Pullman built for the *Overland*, but its coaches, for their time and place, were eye-poppers and its Pullman sleepers on trains No. 4 and 5, the *Pacific Express* which were taken on west of Grand Junction by the Rio Grande were in the great tradition of leaded Gothic windows, Honduran mahogany berth fronts and green baize partition curtains behind which the strange jungle night life of the Pullmans pursued its stealthy occasions.

At one time Pullman passengers rode aboard some of the finest and most expensive varnish equipment ever to be outshopped by Pullman in its Palace Car days, the sleeper-observation cars *Sybaris* and the less ornate but equally reposeful and atmospheric *Starlight* whose likeness is reproduced at an appropriate place in this book.

Sybaris had been built at Pullman at a cost of $19,500.00, boasted a library in addition to its sleeping accommodations and an observation platform from which a Venetian doge might not have been ashamed to acknowledge the cheers of his constituents.

In 1890, if the files of *Harper's Weekly*, "The Journal of Civilization," are to be credited, the Midland was running, probably over the eastern portions of its trackage between The Springs and Florrisant, a sort of all-glass-enclosed observation car from which primeval camera fans snapped eagerly at the landscape and recoiled in terror as the tunnels of Ute Pass suddenly engorged the train.

"Badgered and beset on all sides," to use the words of Morris Cafky, the railroad passed again into receivership in 1912. Receiver George Vallery was a highly competent operator and under his administration a number of new sources of freight revenue were explored which resulted in greatly increased shipments of base metal ores out of Leadville and a sharp rise in the carriage of perishables out of the Arkansas Valley. But all to no avail and, after five years of legal maneuvering, the United States District Court at Denver ordered a foreclosure sale under the first mortgage of 1897.

The last years of the Midland's operations in 1917 and 1918 were to see it once more returned to close integration with the Colorado Springs community that had seen its birth and to witness its demise under the most exalted social auspices. If ever a railroad had a fine funeral it was that provided by its final owner Albert E. Carlton, Cripple Creek mining millionaire, teaming magnate and such an adroit practitioner of mining legalities through the agency of the so-called "apex statutes" that Coloradoans maintained that his initials stood for "Apex Everybody."

The sale of the railroad had been set at the Colorado City roundhouse and on the appointed day the premises swarmed with vultures in the persons of junk dealers who anticipated a quick job of converting the Midland into scrap which was then selling at wartime prices. Just as the bidding commenced a taxi rolled up, and, to the surprise of everyone, out stepped Apex Everybody Carlton, flanked by a corps of lawyers and advisers who struck a chill into the hearts of the assembled junkies. They well knew that Carlton's millions which flowed in a ceaseless torrent from Cripple Creek's deep diggings, from Cripple Creek Central's complex of trolley and industrial lines and from the vast Holly Sugar Corporation could easily outbid them if their owner was so minded, as he soon proved. Every bid for junk was topped with an even $25,000.00 additional from Carlton's banker and in the end, Special Master W. L. Dayton knocked the property down to Carlton for $1,425,000.00.

On May 31, 1917 the carrier was reorganized as the Colorado Midland Railroad Company with Bert Carlton as its president and such associates in its ownership and management as Spencer Penrose, C. M. McNeill, Charles L. Tutt, Charles Boettcher, Irving Howbert and Gerald Hughes. Seldom has so socially exalted a board of directors graced a railroad's stationery as that of the Midland in the last few months of its far from dull lifetime.

Forgotten were the tinhorn ways and suspect devices of Hagerman's time; everything was first class from here in.

Carlton, headman and guiding spirit, was a peculiar manifestation of his times, a fashionable playboy and mining speculator on such a scale as to remain a Colorado legend thirty odd years after his death. Born in Illinois in 1866, he had emigrated, like so many early residents of The Springs, to Colorado for his health in 1889 and first found employment driving a streetcar and clerking in Ed Giddings' dry good store. Later, with a grubstake provided by his father, of $10,000.00 he started a teaming business hauling ore from then wildly booming Cripple Creek to the railhead of the oncoming Midland Terminal Railroad. Bert's wagons brought so much business to the stub line that General Manager Harry Collbran gave him a monopoly on incoming freight as well. The Colorado Trading & Transfer Company that resulted was the foundation of one of the greatest of Western fortunes of the era. Carlton's association with the Colorado Midland through its subsidiary Midland Terminal began long before he was to become the railroad's last and most spectacular president.

Spencer Penrose, associated with Carlton and his lifelong friend, was a Philadelphian of Rittenhouse Square standing and a Harvard graduate whose brother was the august Senator Boise Penrose of Pennsylvania. Colorado Springs took an instant shine to tall, incredibly handsome Penrose who stayed on to become in his final years, Colorado's first citizen, builder of the Broadmoor Hotel, patron of the entire countryside and a towering figure of legend in the Rocky Mountain chronicle.

Charlie Boettcher was the state's leading moneybags at the time, owner of the Brown Palace Hotel in Denver and co-owner of almost everything in sight, while Irving Howbert, who had in 1869 become Clerk of Court for El Paso County which fortunately embraced the entire Cripple

Creek District, was a pioneer who had gotten in on the ground floor of so many useful and profitable deals that he was now The Springs' leading banker.

Although the Colorado Midland Railroad has been dead for more than four decades, the name of any one of its new directors and owners is one perfumed with remembrance wherever Coloradoans meet to salute the great days that are gone.

With its acquisition by Bert Carlton and his socially exalted associates, the Midland became more than ever a property of Colorado Springs and invested with the elegant attributes of Little Lunnon. Carlton, Penrose, Tutt & Company were as famous in their generation of wealth for their entertainments and generally hospitable *ton* as had been General Palmer in the spacious days of Glen Eyrie. Notables from the East and from the Old World made The Springs a Mecca for titles, wealth and the polite muses, so that *Collier's* editor, Mark Sullivan sent a staff reporter in the person of the much admired Julian Street to introduce his readers, vicariously, to the heady delights of the Broadmoor aristocracy. *Collier's* was then an influential periodical on a par with *Harper's* and *Munsey's* and Street was given the red carpet treatment to such a degree that he was captivated. What he had planned as a visit became a visitation of The-Man-Who-Came-to-Dinner proportions. What was to have been a brief survey became an epic, and back in New York, Sullivan was forced to use editorial scissors on a panegyric of Miltonic dimensions.

Along with the rest of the Midland, Carlton had acquired a fine business car or, as nobody in those days hesitated to call it, a private car, No. 100 built by Pullman for a predecessor in office. It was promptly renamed *Cascade* and became the scene of many well appointed junketings on which, according to the Count Pourtales, guests assembled for dinner attired *de rigueur* in tailcoats and boiled shirts "or the new smoking called a tuxedo."

"It was a beautiful car and we loved it dearly," Mrs. Carlton, by now the grande dame and unquestioned arbiter of Springs society, told the authors near the end of a long and useful life. "But mostly it was designed to ride our own trains where speeds were not excessive. Once, while we were in the East on business, Mr. Carlton had to leave me and I rode home alone, except for the servants, on the Santa Fe's *Fast Mail*. You have no idea how rough it was. All the table service was broken and I myself smelled of arnica for days after we got home."

One of the notables to arrive at The Springs aboard *Cascade* was Spencer Penrose's brother, the formidable Senator Boise Penrose of Pennsylvania, a very pattern of senatorial splendor and a magnifico in his own right in a time when the toga implied more distinction than it was later to do. The senator was an epicure whose table at home was celebrated for its profusion of good things and he had lately been experimenting with a private invention that was an infusion of bourbon whisky and fresh peaches which he stored in great earthen jars and allowed to blend potency and aroma for a secret period of time. The drink made a profound impression on Colorado, laying Broadmoor's most accomplished tosspots in windrows, even pole-axing Antelope Jim Hamlin, a local character of legendary capacity. A later generation was to know the senator's invention in its commercial redaction as Southern Comfort.

During its operating years the Midland had its share and perhaps more of mishaps due, in large measure, to the mountain terrain it covered, its hasty construction and a deficit economy which prevented replacement of worn or obsolete equipment. It had wrecks of varying degrees of fatality, savage cornfield meets, derailments and runaways, boiler explosions and the like, none more frequently than those involving its locomotive No. 22, a Schenectady ten wheeler whose roster number, according to popular superstition, coincided precisely with the number of people it had killed in a gruesome variety of accidents.

"One of these occurred on a Saturday in 1891 at Basalt," wrote Linwood Moody years afterward in *Railroad Magazine*, "where the Aspen Branch swung off the main line. It was the Midland's custom to run Saturday afternoon trains from Aspen to Glenwood, where it owned the hotel, so the Aspenites could enjoy the invigorating effects of the hot springs there, and, incidentally, swell the revenues of both the railroad and the hotel. Railroad men referred to these trains contemptuously as the laundry trains.

"At Basalt, on the way back to Aspen, the train had to back up the main line to take water, and then back down past the branch line switch again. One night, as Uncle Billy Switzer was backing the laundry train down, an extra crew was letting No. 22 out of the roundhouse track onto the main. Before either the extra crew or the passenger brakeman saw what was coming, they were too close to stop.

"The impact tore off the boiler check on the engine, and live steam from the boiler poured through an open coach window, killing two of the 13 passengers outright. Eight others died later. Thus No. 22 figured in the first Midland wreck in which a passenger lost his life.

"Later on, No. 22 went through what was perhaps the Midland's worst wreck. Engineer Ostrander was at her throttle, coming up from Grand Junction with a freight train, when he met a D&RG passenger train. Before either Ostrander or Fireman Hynds could jump, they came together, the freight traveling about thirty and the passenger around forty mph.

"The wreckage caught fire, and only one sleeper could be saved. It was cut off, pushed back to clear by crew and passengers. The engine crews of both trains and nine other persons went to their death. Since the charred remains of Ostrander's body were not found until late the next day, the story was circulated that he had jumped and taken to the woods to avoid responsibility for the collision.

"So far as we can discover, all the Midland's engines were used more or less regularly until the line folded up. That is, all except No. 35. Her story is brief. When she was only eight years old — on August 15, 1896 — she met with sudden death at Basalt, where she was being used in switcher service. At 10:00 a.m. Engineer Danielson and his fireman parked her on the 'whisky' track opposite the coal chute while they scoffed on company time. The fireman was in the switch shanty, and Danielson was down at the station, when No. 35 got disgusted (or maybe too dry?) and blew up with a bang that carried for miles.

"After the junk stopped falling, they found a ton or two of the boiler in a man's dooryard three blocks or so away, the firebox on the roundhouse tracks hard by the other side of the coal chutes, and the front end not far from the wheels. A man and a little girl in different parts of the town were hit but not badly injured by flying pieces. The official verdict was that defective staybolts had caused the explosion — which was an unusual decision, since there was a responsible engine crew to pin the blame to."

Apparently, although many informed people were aware that the United States was drifting irrevocably into the European conflict, the new owners of the Midland were confident that their railroad had a bright future before it and, indeed there was no valid reason to anticipate anything but good times for carriers everywhere, war or no war.

Carlton and his backers in 1917 alone expended more than a million dollars in on-line improvements. Ninety pound rail began appearing where sixty pound iron had been before. More than 100,000 fine oak ties replaced worn and splintered underpinnings. Wooden trestles were replaced with steel spans and 120 new freight cars in various categories were acquired from the now defunct Denver, Laramie & Northwestern. Carlton eyed the Denver & Salt Lake's newly acquired Mallet haulers with professional interest and studied the performance records of compound engines already in service on the Rio Grande's mainline.

But over and above mere improvements to plant, Apex Everybody Carlton fixed his sights on getting the Midland through on its own right of way all the way to Salt Lake and Ogden without the necessity of tipping its hat to the Rio Grande. Elements in this ambitious project were to include access to Denver through the purchase from the Colorado & Southern of its narrow gauge division east of Bath, the acquisition of an existing interurban line between Grand Junction and Fruita and the construction of an eight mile connecting line from Fruita to Mack. From there it was planned to take over the fearsome grades and operative hazards of the celebrated Uintah Railroad and broad gauge it to gain access to Utah by way of Daniels Pass over the lofty Wasatch Mountains. Testimony to the narrow margin by which this plan failed was the renewal of miles of Uintah narrow gauge ties with standard gauge in the anticipation of an early broad gauging of the entire mountain railroad.

The conduct of the affairs of American railroads during the First World War was something less than a glittering advertisement for government control of anything that had previously been a privately administered industry. Early in the war, and be it said while the carriers were still under private control, priorities had been established with an eye to expediting essential materials of war while curtailing unnecessary freight shipments and eliminating the duplication of much passenger service. A fantastic snarl of traffic was induced almost overnight when various government agencies armed with priorities sought to favor the projects with which they were entrusted ahead of other military and defense measures.

In December 1917 the Federal government, acting under the authority provided by the Possession & Control Act, seized the carriers and placed them all under the administrative head of William G. McAdoo as Director General of Railroads for the duration of the war and twenty-one months after the expected termination of actual hostilities.

Knowing that great things were expected of him because of the enormous authority he had received, McAdoo, in a veritable frenzy of activity, set about regulating, restraining and reorganizing so that chaos and confusion from being regional and sporadic, in brief order became endemic to the entire carrier network of the nation. Passenger schedules were slashed, passenger runs merged, freight facilities pooled and, most drastic of all, stringent controls of the flow of freight over the mainline carriers were introduced on a sweeping scale. Out of all this fever of activity nothing very great resulted and from the almost total dislocation of a vast and important industry, the statistics when they were compiled showed that McAdoo's hysterical administration had resulted in a microscopic increase of two percent in freight traffic between 1917 under private management and 1918 under government control.

A major casualty of Federal ineptitude was the Colorado Midland.

Although during the early months of 1918 freight moved over its mainline in greater quantities than during any previous period in its varied lifetime, its very profusion spelled disaster, for congestion began to manifest itself to a degree that would soon achieve total immobility. Sidings and passing tracks were jammed with merchandise,

some of it perishable, awaiting man power and motive power to move it. Movement over the entire railroad threatened to grind to a halt simply because there were not enough engines and train crews to expedite it.

The Railroad Administration, confronted with a situation which might well have been available to remedy, acted with the whole-hog hysteria which was characteristic of its every activity. All freight of every sort was ordered routed elsewhere, much of it over the Rio Grande while the overflow went to the Union Pacific and Santa Fe. Suddenly, from being swamped, the Midland was without any source of revenue whatsoever save strictly local and on-line loadings which were insufficient to warrant its wartime existence.

In July of 1918 the Colorado Midland was ordered into receivership and closely following this decree, there came an order to suspend operations as a measure of wartime conservation.

The last train between Grand Junction and Colorado Springs received its orders on August 4 and as the shadows lengthened across the tangents and vacant passing tracks for the last time, the much loved railroad passed into history. It was the largest mainline abandonment to date in the history of the industry.

With the end of hostilities in Europe there was talk of its revival. Various interested competitors including the Santa Fe surveyed the wreckage with an eye to possible reactivation, but the case was hopeless. No most optimistic estimate could conjure up a vision of sufficient revenue to justify the outlay of money and material that would be needed, and so the Colorado Midland passed into legend.

With the passage of time it became enshrined in the folklore of the vast and still remote regions it had been designed to serve, one with the Red River carts of Sir St. George Gore, the sweeping gestures of Horace A. W. Tabor and Baby Doe, the peer of the Unsinkable Mrs. Brown and the girls and guns and gold of Leadville. It will come not again, for the dead return not, but there are those that say the Colorado Midland never really went away.

Who can say them nay?

Seeking a competing route through mountains whose most advantageous passes had already been pre-empted, the Colorado Midland penetrated a wilderness of untamed ferocity as is suggested on these two pages. Financial economy suggested the rustic ore loading platform at Nast siding *(right)* and the do-it-yourself tank *(below)* on the west side of Hagerman near Hell Gate. On the page opposite, forest primeval forms a construction frame for the camera of C. L. McClure. *(Three Photos: Western Collection, Denver Public Library.)*

The polite amenities of tourist travel are suggested by the drawing above captioned "Aboard The Cars—Pike's Peak Route" from the Midland publicity pamphlet "Heart of The Rockies" in 1890, while in its capacity of fun railroad, it served a number of lighthearted resorts along its track, none more agreeably than the Green Mountains Falls Hotel where, at the right, a double header paused of a summer's day in the halcyon nineties. Above, opposite, is a scene when the Midland set its passengers down on the station platform at the end of its run at Ogden, Utah, in 1899. *(Above: Western Collection, Denver Public Library; Right: Pioneer Museum, Colorado Springs; Top, Opposite: Colorado College Library.)*

Here, at its "eating station" the Colorado Midland set down its passengers at Cascade in the year 1899 as a spacious century came to a close. The massive wooden storm lantern, proof against winter gales in the Rockies, the tailcoated conductor and the resolute lady passenger in mannish shirtwaist and sensible alpaca traveling skirt of modest length, all bespeak a way of life and travel free of urgency in the annals of an ill-fated but well remembered carrier. *(Colorado College Library.)*

A familiar figure, shown here seated on a pile of untreated ties, was the old Swedish knife maker who sold cutlery to Colorado Midland passengers as the cars paused at Cascade. Below, a second section, double headed follows the first into Cascade with a minimum of clearance in 1899. *(Two Photos: Colorado College Library.)*

Although The Antlers Hotel at Colorado Springs was closely associated in owner-ship with the Rio Grande Railroad, its omnibus cheerfully met trains of the Colo-rado Midland as well. The runner at the left is holding a bunch of old time brass baggage checks with which travelers identified their Gladstones, Saratoga trunks and tophat boxes. Below: a Colorado Midland diner interior after the advent of electricity.   (*Two Photos: Western Collection, Denver Public Library.*)

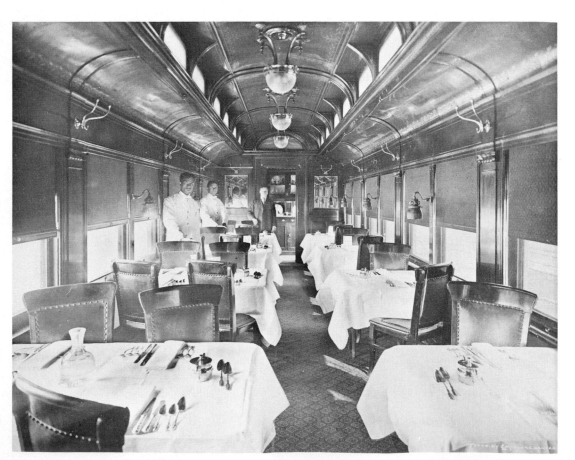

A chapter in the history of the receding frontier is implicit in the above photograph where, as the railheads advanced toward their various terminals and objectives, the staging routes that had once been the only means of communication became shorter and shorter. This one briefly connected the end of track of the Midland Terminal at Grassy with Cripple Creek and shortly, when the rails arrived at Cripple, was no more. Below Colorado Midland No. 25 is shown in a classic pose at Glenwood Springs with train crew, loungers and faithful Towser all anxious to be in the picture. (*Two Photos: Western Collection, Denver Public Library.*)

The stuff of romance still gathers about the legend of the Matchless Mine *(above)* from which Horace Tabor took millions in Leadville's golden noontide of fortune. "Never sell the Matchless," had been his dying words and his wife Baby Doe never did, dying there in the ghostly hoisting works in 1935 having outlived everything but the fame of her romance. Below are teamsters loading ore on the Colorado Midland platform at the turn of the century, perhaps from the Matchless. *(Above: Charles Clegg; Below: Colorado State Historical Society.)*

The atmosphere of holiday which associated itself with the annals of the Colorado Midland is suggested by a Presidential Special, assigned for one of Theodore Roosevelt's Colorado visits and shown above, and the group of wildflower picnickers posed in the lower photograph on some happy occasion far away and long ago. *(Top: Western Collection, Denver Public Library; Below: Colorado State Historical Society.)*

The Colorado Midland approached the summit of the Sawatch Range via ten vast, heavily timbered snowsheds, the longest of which was 2,110 feet in extent and the contemplation of these vast subterranean warrens never failed to arouse the enthusiasm of the sketch artists of the eighties and nineties.

Throughout its brief but eventful lifetime, the Colorado Midland was a railroad devoid of the traffic control and signal devices such as semaphores and position lights already in almost universal acceptance on roads of greater traffic density. It operated on telegraphic train orders handed up to crews at control points, and flags to protect unscheduled stops and track torpedoes were essential to even a semblance of safety. Mishaps were not unknown, but in view of the mountain terrain involved with impaired vision, sharp curves and heavy grades, the wonder is they were so few. Here, if only to satisfy the artist's requirement of drama, a train crew places torpedoes on a night track with the following section already painfully close.

The tourist Pullmans, an interior of which is shown opposite were a ponderable factor in the C.M.'s passenger traffic in the days before the 1914 war. Their rattan seats were a staple of humor, but aboard them many a happy vacationist rode who could never have afforded the Palace Cars. *(Colorado State Historical Society.)*

Operations on the Midland Terminal, all that remained in 1945 of the once pulsing Colorado Midland, were a daily freight shown here rolling into the curve at Manitou Park Station in smoky glory. *(Charles Clegg.)*

In the noontide of its somewhat errant fortunes, this two car Colorado Midland local was photographed by McClure against a background of Pike's Peak in the distance on the curve at Manitou Park Station. The U. S. Weather Bureau Station atop Pike's Peak *(below)* was one of the first in the Rockies, but it failed to warn the Midland of a blizzard of misfortunes that were in store. *(Below and Right: Western Collection, Denver Public Library.)*

Forty years after the McClure photograph reproduced below, the great curve at Manitou Park Station looked much the same as it had in 1905 when the rails had been those of the Colorado Midland itself. *(Charles Clegg.)*

The Colorado Midland's wildflower excursions such as the one
aboard two double header specials below, never went as far
afield from The Springs as the
great trestle at the Hagerman
Tunnel *(right)*. Mostly they
stopped in the meadows of Spinney or Howbert. *(Above: Western Collection, Denver Public
Library; Below: Colorado State
Historical Society.)*

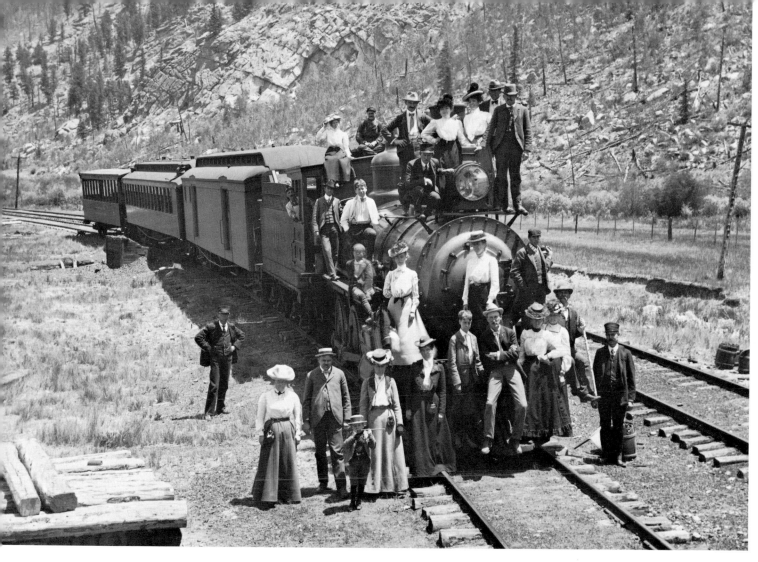

That the Colorado Midland took a leaf from the Rio Grande's book and provided a variety of observation cars for its excursion trains is suggested by the closed and open models, above and below, respectively. Although the name rock hound had not yet been coined, the lower picture depicts a safari after rare mineral specimens, a type of excursion second in popularity only to the railroad's celebrated wildflower trains. *(Two Photos: Western Collection, Denver Public Library.)*

— 133

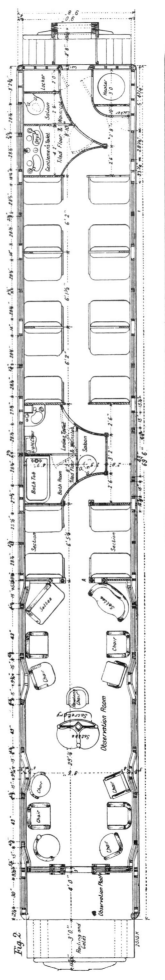

Fig. 2

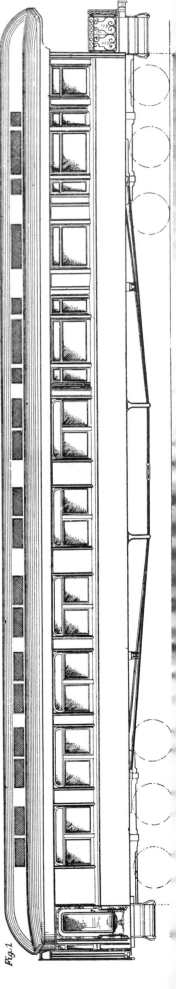

Fig. 1

The beautifully ornate library-buffet-smoking car *Tryphena* was one of the earliest observation cars outshopped by the Pullman Palace Car-Building Company and, while its earlier assignment is clouded, it definitely appeared on a Colorado Midland timetable for 1904 in service on the Denver-Salt Lake run. The legend read: "The only observation car running through the Rocky Mountains of Colorado without change and running through the Rockies by daylight. *Tryphena* and its twin *Tryphosa* each cost $17,034 and contained sleeping sections as well as lounge appointments. Few more beautiful cars ever saw service. On this page a happy group of excursionists *circa* 1907 pose in Denver station on the observation platform of an unidentified varnish car, obviously not *Tryphena*, but perhaps an off-line car of another carrier as was the happy custom in a day when charter cars for well heeled vacationists were available from Pullman and a wide variety of regional carriers. Private varnish occupied by railroad nabobs or charter parties with insignes of the Pennsylvania, or New Haven on their nameboards raised no eyebrows in the Rockies. (*Opposite: Pullman Standard; Above: Colorado State Historical Society.*)

— 135

This scene aboard the smoking car of a transcontinental limited was drawn in 1893 for *Harper's Weekly* by an uncommonly urbane artist, T. de Thulstrup, whose specialty was scenes of travel by land and sea and worldly sophistication such as horse shows and opera. His overland travelers reproduced here may well have been sketched by the artist in the noontide of the Midland Terminal's fortunes amidst the ample glories of *Tryphena* headed toward Leadville. On the page opposite an equally engrossing and engrossed group of pilgrims watch the uplands of Colorado roll past the observation platform of *Tryphena* in a pose recalling the glory times of American railroading when the hallmark of elegance on a name train was the brass railed observation verandah headed for Ultima Thule or Grand Junction, as the case might be. (*Two Drawings: Bancroft Library, University of California.*)

The Colorado Midland's presidential car No. 100 was built to the carrier's order by Pullman in 1898 and was identified by its number until the Carlton regime when it was named *Cascade*. It is shown above on the transfer table as it came from the Pullman shops. Below is a montage of Bert Carlton's guests aboard it as *Cascade* toward the end of the railroad's untranquil life. (*Above: Pullman Standard; Below: Western Collection, Denver Public Library.*)

Less luxurious than the private car of A. E. Carlton, the Midland's last president and a mine operator so versed in apex law that it was said his initials stood for "Apex Everybody," were the carrier's coaches shown here in examples from the collection of Arthur D. Dubin.

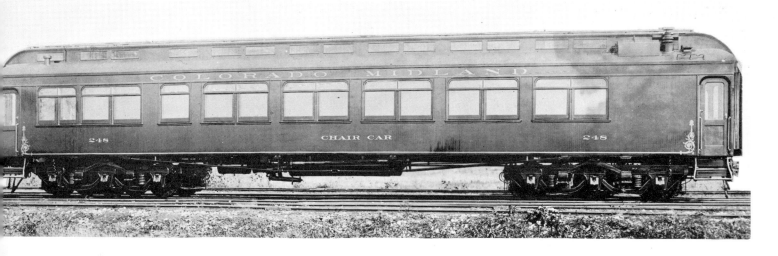

The spirit of the gayest nineties is implicit in this group about to board the Colorado Midland's observation car *Starlight* for a trip to romance the year Dewey took Manila. *(Colorado State Historical Society.)*

A carrier of faltering destinies and great charm, the Colorado Midland achieved in death the status of a legend it only imperfectly occupied in its active lifetime. Here a double header in the grand manner with 4-6-0s No. 18 and 20 on the head end, pauses for its portrait. It was a classic consist of head-end revenue cars, coaches and Pullman observation on the rear at Green Mountain Falls in 1913. *(Collection of R. H. Kindig.)* At the left is Allen Manvel, President of the Santa Fe when that road purchased the Colorado Midland and briefly was arbiter of its destinies.

— 141

A Colorado Midland construction train in Granite Canyon is neatly framed in a photograph by the road's official cameraman, C. L. McClure, while below a view of the combined C. M. and Rio Grande yards at Grand Junction in 1911 suggests a great deal of business with no fewer than six switch engines visible under a reading glass. *(Two Photos: Western Collection, Denver Public Library.)*

The wild flower picnic shown here must have required most of the Midland's excursion equipment since it embraced eight daycoaches and four open air observation cars running in three sections. In the photograph below a variation on the wild flower theme is depicted in the form of a mineral specimen outing patronized by what a later generation would call rock hounds. (Above: Pioneer Museum, Colorado Springs; Below: Colorado State Historical Society.)

— 143

Although Leadville's fortunes were in decline by the year Dewey took Manila, three actively competing railroads, the Rio Grande, Colorado Midland and the narrow gauge South Park were all operating into the Carbonate Capital in 1899 and the C.M. roundhouse and its crew in that year are shown on the page opposite. The engine shown there is No. 5, a Mogul of the same series of freight locomotives as No. 2 and 9 depicted on this page. No. 2 poses at the top of the page *in propria persona;* No. 9 vicariously in a beautiful scale model reposing in the Western Collection of the Denver Public Library. It was fashioned of burnished brass and copper in its graceful dimensions by Claude E. Harris, a onetime fireman and later engineer on the Colorado Midland. *(Three Photos: Western Collection, Denver Public Library.)*

By the end of the 1941 war, the last remaining vestiges of the Colorado Midland were the operations of its subsidiary Midland Terminal still hauling ore from Victor and Cripple Creek down to the Springs for processing. Gone and almost forgotten were the great wains of Bert Carlton's Colorado Trading & Transfer Company *(page opposite)* that hauled the rich ores of Cripple as far as the on-coming railhead. Gone indeed was Bert himself, although his capable widow, Ethel Carlton ruled in his stead for many years as The Broadmoor's most durable dowager. In the below photograph taken on a zero day above Divide, the M.T.'s No. 60 still surged up the grade with a string of empties on its drawbar, but the end was near. A few years later a giant cyaniding plant at Victor obviated the need to freight out the ores and the Midland Terminal went the way of its parent into the roundhouse of eternity. *(Lucius Beebe.)*

Durango was still a roaring town in 1950 when this picture was taken on the narrow gauge at Cumbres Summit by Jim Shaughnessy. Precious metals and the old frontier no longer made it roar, but oil across the New Mexican border. Most of the narrow gauge traffic out of Alamosa to Farmington via Durango was in pipes and drilling material for the New Mexican oil fields and this is an empty train of pipe cars going back to Alamosa for more.

THE ROARING TOWNS

ROBABLY no railroad in the record served such a multiplicity of roaring communities that roared so long and loud or were, in their essential economy, railroad towns and the extension of the railroad's personality as did the Denver & Rio Grande Western. The Virginia & Truckee, to be sure, and the Comstock Lode it represented, maintained a continuity of tumult until well after the turn of the century, but the V & T was, by all standards, a short line and Virginia City and the small complex of its suburbs but a single community. Bodie, on the California-Nevada border and the shootingest mining diggings of all time, had a brief lived narrow gauge, the Bodie & Benton, but it didn't connect with the outside world at any point and it again was the shortest sort of short line serving a single massed disorder masquerading as an outpost of civilization.

The Central and Southern Pacific between them probably came closest to the Rio Grande in leaving the impress of its character on an entire countryside, since at the height of its domination in the eighties and nineties the entire state of California owed allegiance to Collis Huntington and his hard headed associates, but the Southern Pacific's empire was agricultural and industrial and, if one excepts Promontory, Corinne and a water stop or two in Nevada, its on line dependencies never knew the gaudy infamies of Leadville, Creede and Silverton, the effulgent wickedness of Durango, Gunnison, Lake City, Alamosa and Telluride, the last of which it achieved by slight indirection through the agency of the Rio Grande Southern.

In greater or less degree these suburbs of Hell were railroad towns evolved, maintained and controlled in the image of the railroad. Their bravura eras began when the railroad arrived and their great days rode in aboard the baggage cars, coaches and sleepers of the Rio Grande, largely in its narrow gauge dimension. Some of them, like Alamosa, were essentially agricultural in their original character and remained so down to the immediate here and now, but mostly their economies were founded on precious metals, and where gold and silver were produced, the Old West found its apotheosis in gunsmoke, smashing glass and the cheerful tumults of Maiden Lane after dark.

Cripple Creek alone represented oversight on the part of the Rio Grande propensity for getting in on a good thing and on the ground floor. It had railroads in abundance but the Baby Railroad was not among them. It is almost the sole instance of a major mining excitement in Colorado that did not count the Rio Grande among those present.

That the railroad was explicitly and factually the agency which put the Rocky Mountain mining towns on the Howling Wilderness map is amply attested by the chronology of crimes of violence, the density of saloons and the illumination provided by lights of discernibly crimson hue. It was not until after the arrival of the railroad at Leadville in 1880 that the town's night life mounted to a crescendo of screaming that attracted national attention to the deadfalls and love stores of the carbonate capital as the quintessence of chaos. Creede's finest flowering was achieved and its most notable assassinations after the rails extended a through connection from the outer world by way of Wagon Wheel Gap. Durango celebrated through train service to Denver with its first legal hanging and it was at Silverton that the chance phrase of the wife of a Rio Grande sleeping car porter was the inspiration that fired its author to write "There'll Be a Hot Time in the Old Town Tonight."

Sanctimonious chroniclers have ever been avid to hail the railroad as an agency of civilized achievement and cultural progress whose freight was law and order, religion, education and the amenities of gentility generally. That its traffic could in equal and perhaps even more abundant measure be in roulette wheels, bar fixtures, burlesque queens, bogus stock salesmen, high pressure promoters and inmates of love stores was demonstrated by the Rio Grande with fine impartiality. The highest moral tone might prevail in Colorado Springs, which General Palmer was pleased to view as the Rio Grande's finest advertisement and show piece, but when railroad connections broke down to Telluride during a particularly severe winter, civil panic prevailed in the ensuing shortage of drinking whisky until volunteers might be recruited to break the blockade with the aid of mule teams. Never was a community's dependence on the railroad more dramatically demonstrated.

Doctors and clergymen might achieve the hitherto impervious frontier aboard the steamcars. Soapy Smith and Ed Kelley, who killed Bob Ford at Creede, and other less diligent servants of the Lord found the train connections equally convenient. Denver in the days of the Elephant Corral and wagon trains wasn't half the town for night life it was to become once the Colorado & Southern, Union Pacific, Santa Fe, Rock Island and, of course, the Rio Grande converged on the Queen City of the Plains.

The Rio Grande's rails reached Leadville on July 20, 1880, antedating the advent of the competition in the form of the Denver, South Park & Pacific narrow gauge by a satisfactory two years, and an immediate and considerable rise in the communal blood pressure of the city was the result. Like the other glittering diggings of the Shining Mountains, its beginnings had been relatively tame. Leadville was the child of the Oro City postmaster, Horace A. W. Tabor, who was to become the perhaps ranking figure in Colorado mythology and legend if not precisely its most attractive personality. Tabor's rise from rags to transcendent riches was an epic to stir the pulse of gamblers everywhere and congeal the marrow of reasonable, prudent and industrious people on an equal scale. Tabor, a storekeeper, as well as postmaster at Oro City, had grubstaked a couple of not too prepossessing prospectors named George Hook and August Rische to the necessities of an expedi-

tion into the hills in search of precious metals. Among the necessities they requisitioned was a gallon of proof whisky, and a mile or so out of town they decided that the sun had crossed the yardarm and sat down to sample the stuff. Inspired, they commenced to dig in a tentative fashion right at the scene of their picnic. Had they sunk their exploratory shaft twenty feet to the north or forty feet over yonder, they would have encountered country rock, but right smack dab under their feet and amidst the debris of sandwiches and hard boiled eggs, there crowned the incredible Little Pittsburgh Mine.

Tabor lost no time in becoming a millionaire. His grubstaker's one-third of the Little Pittsburgh he parlayed into stock and cash which he spent wildly and rashly in all directions. Fantastically inept investments turned into bonanzas. Kind friends, knowing the postmaster for a sucker, sold him a salted mine, but when he dug a few inches below the planted ore he came up with the Crysolite, which promptly began paying him dividends of $100,000 a month. Other kind friends unloaded a mine called the Matchless on him for $117,000 and the Matchless ran true to Tabor form and became the source of seemingly inexhaustible riches. Tabor became banker to Leadville and founded life and fire insurance companies, street railway systems, real estate and illuminating gas businesses and at length purchased himself the lieutenant governor's office of Colorado.

Leadville boomed with a great booming and it was inevitable that the Rio Grande should mark it for another company town. When the rails arrived, Leadville was reeling in sarabands of wildest wealth and profligacy; after service began over them Leadville became Saturnalia. The first train into town brought as the guest of Haw Tabor, Ulysses S. Grant and his arrival may well have been prophetic. Grant was never a man to say no to anyone's hospitality and Tabor himself was usually falling down drunk by late afternoon. In a few months Leadville qualified as the drinking capital of the known universe. Murder on the public streets became a commonplace. A syndicate of criminals engaged in the promotion of real estate laid claim to half the town's most desirable house lots and a form of civil war ensued in which homes were resold to their rightful owners at pistol point while others were illegally sold to equally illegal purchasers over the heads of their occupants.

An aspect of breezy Leadville that attracted attention was the circumstance that nobody paid any taxes. One brothel keeper claimed she was being unfairly taxed and the chain reaction that resulted found well heeled mine owners, real estate operators and householders also defying collection. Chaos and Old Night ruled. The police force disintegrated, sanitation was non-extant, the town swarmed with vultures who rode in on the cars and made hurried exits before they should be overtaken by vigilance committees or one of the epidemics that ravaged the populace at frequent intervals. As a company town, Leadville was no credit to the Rio Grande, but it was a source of substantial revenue, and two years after its entry the rival South Park commenced services and still there was enough profit for everybody. By the time the Colorado Midland arrived on the scene, however, the cream of Leadville's traffic had been skimmed and the circumstance, in the long run, contributed appreciably to the bankruptcy of that ill-starred carrier.

Another company town held in fee by the Rio Grande was Durango which, unlike Leadville and later Creede, was not assimilated after it was a going concern but located, platted and developed as a Rio Grande outpost from the very beginning. So strategically located was Durango that it eventually justified the foresight of the railroad management by becoming the focus of four narrow gauge railroad operations and the recognized capital of the narrow gauge world.

The Rio Grande tracks arrived from Alamosa and what had been started as the "Fort Garland extension" on July 27th, 1881. They had been delayed almost a year beyond the original estimate for their completion by an unusually severe winter of late snows and heavy spring rains, but once in Durango no time was lost about making it secure as an outpost of the railroad's ever crescent empire. Less than ninety days after the first train connection with the outer world, Durango saw graders pushing the line along the margin of Animas River in what was shortly to be the famous Silverton branch. At the Silverton terminus, another empire builder in the person of Otto Mears at once set about the construction of three narrow

gauge feeders, short lines that reached like fingers into the forbidding passes of the Uncomphagre Mountains and began hauling rich ore loadings out of the mines at Red Mountain, Gladstone, Eureka and Mammoth. When one of these little carriers, the Silverton Railroad, found its way blocked by the geology of the countryside to Ouray where Mears wanted it to go, the indomitable Pathfinder went back to Durango and started for Ouray all over again with another narrow gauge, the now legendary Rio Grande Southern.

When it was finished, the Rio Grande Southern accomplished in an unbelievable 160 miles of loops, trestles, snowsheds, frightening grades and every conceivable potential for disaster what the Silverton Railroad was originally planned to achieve in the six unattainable miles between Albany and Ouray.

The fourth narrow gauge operation converging on Durango was the Denver & Rio Grande's own branch extending to Farmington across the state line in New Mexico. Its trackage was originally built to standard gauge and there was talk of a Southern Pacific alliance which should see the Espee tapping the Durango coal deposits, but a concatenation of events, among them the change to oil as the dominant fuel on the Southern Pacific and the death of E. H. Harriman, put an end to this chimera and the Farmington branch was retracked to narrow gauge as the final spoke in the wheel of Durango's radiating three foot operations.

As the focus of all these comings and goings, Durango was very much metropolis. There was a daily connection with Silverton by way of the superb scenery of the Rio de las Animas Perdidas Canyon which at one time included through narrow gauge sleepers bound for Alamosa and eventually far-off Denver itself. A daily name train, *The San Juan Express,* with a parlor observation car and dining facilities ran to Alamosa where there were overnight connections with the outer world. On Mears' Rio Grande Southern passenger service was less frequent and far less dense, but tourism was in those days a ponderable factor in railroad thinking and the spectacular run through Dolores and Rico and over the trestles of Ophir was part of the "Narrow Gauge Circle" which, in the clement months, saw hundreds of tourists making the trip, picking wild flowers in the meadows of Mancos and catching their breath at the richness of ore samples from the great Smuggler Mine at Telluride.

Durango was no one-economy town. It was the entrepot for the vast agricultural activities and cattle spreads of the entire richly endowed San Juan region. Through it passed all the traffic in both freight and passengers bound for the feverish diggings that justified the existence of the Silverton branch, Mears' little three foot feeders north of Silverton and the improbable Rio Grande Southern. To the sprawling Durango Smelter came ores to be reduced from points as various as Red Mountain, Rico and the Forks of Animas. Coal was mined in the surface fields just west of town and as a cohesive agent binding all these factors into a functioning and gratifyingly profitable entity, the Denver & Rio Grande Railroad maintained shops, roundhouse and other incidentals to railroad operation there on an impressive scale.

The tempo of life in the San Juan quickened with the advent of the steamcars. Saloons and call houses flourished, the hitherto placid ranchers, many of them of Spanish descent who had taken life in their stride since first Father Escalante penetrated the region back in the eighteenth century, became aware of the fascinations of urban vice and took to playing poker for high stakes in the back room of Finch's Nose Paint Saloon and assaying the charms of the girls in the front room at Maud Lamb's, an itinerant entrepreneur of love who operated at various times at Leadville and Aspen. The cow hands heard about the conduct of their opposite numbers in the trail towns that dotted the railroad in Kansas and began shooting up the town on Saturday nights so that, in a few months from the time of the first bunting-draped passenger train's arrival, a state bordering on civil war existed between the townsfolk and the waddies.

A grand ball was announced to inaugurate the services of the West End Hotel and fashionable Durango looked forward to an evening of mannered elegance among the potted palms.

"The opening dinner will be spread in the mammoth dining hall from seven to nine p.m. when an elegant menu will be raided by Durango's elite," read a notice in the *Durango Record*. "After the royal gorge has taken place, the large force of attendants will spirit away the china and broken hearted champagne bottles, and Professor Delius and his True Fissure orchestra will take possession of one end of the room. Then sweet perfumes will greet grateful nostrils, and exquisite strains of Terpsichorean musical messages will be telephoned through the auricular drums, past palpitating hearts, to agile feet that will not rest till morn."

The Record, alas, was premature in its optimism. It wasn't the elegant menu that was raided, but the entire *mise en scène* when Saturday night cow hands shot up the premises and the ball was hastily called off while diners in evening attire stationed themselves with Winchesters behind the hotel windows and took pot shots at the raiders. The sweet perfume that greeted grateful nostrils was largely black powder smoke and when it cleared the defenders were found to have in their hands one of the guilty invaders. He was promptly strung up from the "Hanging Tree" in the Rio Grande freight yard and a week later was still dangling evidence that virtue triumphed in Durango.

"A ghastly sight it was," purred *The Record*. "A slight wind swayed the body to and fro. The pale moonlight glimmered through the rifted clouds and clothed the ghastly face with a ghastlier pallor. . . . Thus the Powers that Be have proclaimed to the world that good order, peace and quietude and safety must prevail."

Not until the grand opening of the West End Hotel had been held, its festivities unmarred by gunfire, was the body cut down.

Durango's Hanging Tree was conveniently located between the Rio Grande tracks and the front door of the European Hotel and informal executions were shared, as it were, between these two important institutions. Durango's only legal hanging, which took place several years after these still stirring events, was performed on a gallows at some remove from town but overlooking the freight yard and so managed to retain something of the flavor of railroading.

The nineteenth century had just a decade to run when N. C. Creede, prospecting above Wagon Wheel Gap thirty miles west of Del Norte, sunk his pick into a streak of near-jewelry ore and screamed, "Holy Moses, I've struck it rich!" The

Holy Moses Mine was the beginning of Creede's short but almost incredibly tumultuous annals.

It is improbable that any new mining camp was ever served by a railroad with such almost instantaneous dispatch. The Holy Moses came in in 1890. In 1891 the Rio Grande had run a stub branch line the sixty-nine miles from Alamosa and was in business as the quintessential whore house and whisky barrel railroad of all time, since these essentials of civilization rode its cars out of all proportion to more prosaic commodities.

In the first years of the Creede bonanzas, while the Holy Moses and the handily adjacent Last Chance were making their grateful owners the possessors of the silk hats, nugget watch chains and champagne tastes essential to the successful capitalists, the *Denver Republican* sent a sketch-artist reporter to Creede. He told his paper's readers, most of whom were delighted with such details of high life, that "The Rio Grande freight house at Creede is overflowing with merchandise so that whisky, billiard tables and crated bar fixtures are stacked roof-high on the platform until they shall be claimed by their owners." He then drew a pen-and-ink sketch to convince doubters which is reprinted in this book at an appropriate place.

Few diggings have taken more pleasure in their reputation for chaos than did Creede. Other mining camps in the historic pattern from Virginia City to Leadville became leaders in the howling wilderness sweepstakes but eventually got cluttered up with morality, temperance, grand opera, formal society, domesticity and other impediments to personal liberty. Book stores appeared on the Comstock before the miners on Sun Mountain had finished moving out of tents and packing cases into the more agreeably inflammable shacks and frame dwellings that were soon to burn with such glorious combustion. At Tonopah and Goldfield, two decades after Creede's finest flowering, evening attire was taken for granted in the better circles and the diggings themselves had been discovered by a prospector improbably attired in a hard derby hat and frock coat. Leadville and Central City were soon debauched by grand opera and formal cotillions, and even Telluride, comparatively immune to degenerate refinements, had a Gilbert & Sullivan Society.

Creede remained undefiled by temperance, feminism or cotillions as long as its boom lasted, and was tough and unregenerate to the end.

The Rio Grande participated wholeheartedly in the town's hilarious moral *ton*. To be sure its freight department was agreeable to trafficking in pianos and sets of Shakespeare on the same tariff schedule as Denver beer and girls for Timberline's place, but beer called for continual replacement and even the most durable furniture in the town's love stores wore out eventually. In an age innocent of the phrase, the railroad favored merchandise with built-in obsolescence.

Passenger business, of course, boomed along with the traffic in dynamite, French bevel edged mirrors, mining tools, music boxes and horse and mule shoes. The railroad in 1891 found itself in an equivocal position as a common carrier when it was necessary on the up run from Wagon Wheel Gap to augment conventional train crews with two guards who rode the engine pilot to fend off eager fortune hunters who couldn't afford the fare but found the company's right-of-way the easiest road into town.

Two of Creede's first citizens, each vaguely identified with law and order, were Bat Masterson and Bob Ford who had killed Jesse James and was immortalized as "the dirty little coward" in the familiar rhyme. Masterson was manager of the Denver Exchange and Ford was proprietor, what else? of Ford's Exchange Saloon. Arrived one day in 1892 on the up train from Alamosa a veteran assassin named Ed O. Kelley who was well connected in Old West shooting circles as the husband of a sister of Cole Younger who had been close to Jesse James. He carried a double barrel ten-gauge shotgun conveniently sawed off a foot or so beyond the chambers with which he almost immediately made a shooting gallery of Bob Ford. Ford was buried, appropriately, in Shotgun Hill and Kelley was imprisoned and soon pardoned, but between them they had put Creede on the map in a big emphatic way.

Ford's successor as Creede's most conspicuous character was Jefferson Randolph Smith, better known as Soapy Smith, King of the Thimbleriggers. Smith, who was to go on to wider destinies in Denver when the Creede diggings ran out and still later was to die violently in the Yukon, ran a gambling joint in Creede over whose entry he posted the Latin motto: *Caveat Emptor.* This, he claimed, was fair warning to greenies and suckers and that nobody could complain when he had been cleaned by so ethical a practitioner of the shell game.

Creede's foremost cyprians and bagnio queens were Lillis Lovell, a statuesque blonde whose ham-like fist was a match for the toughest Saturday night customer of her wares, Lulu Slain, "The Mormon Queen," and Rose Vastine, another Amazon whose six feet two earned her the name of "Timberline" because she was so far above sea level. All the town's madames were on good terms with the Rio Grande's train crews and their not infrequent trips to Denver and San Francisco to procure new merchandise were of great interest to everybody on the cars. When they returned, the berths of the Alamosa sleeper bulged with petticoats and chatelaine watches, and townsmen eagerly importuned the porter and conductor for clues to the most interesting additions to the dovecotes.

The traffic in handmaidens of Venus justified David Lavender's assertion that "it was not until the advent of the railroads that the orgies of the silver towns became so marked." In the case of Creede this was accomplished with a minimum of delay.

The cars of the Rio Grande came and went from Creede with a frequency that suggested the importance of this dead-end diggings during its brief season in the sun and the presence of Pullman Palace Cars indicates that there were enough arrivals and departures of means and importance to justify luxury equipment. In the summer of 1893 Train No. 465 left Alamosa for the El Moro Branch daily at 8:15, arriving at Creede at 11:40 a.m. Returning, it departed from Creede at 7 and arrived at Alamosa at 7:30 p.m. Also on a daily basis was Train No. 103 out of Pueblo at 7:30 a.m. and into Creede at 5:40 p.m. with a Pullman Palace sleeping car. The sleeper had remained at Pueblo from the evening previous where it had arrived from Denver as part of the *Colorado & New Mexico Express.* Returning, No. 104 left Creede at the ungodly hour of six in the morning, getting to Alamosa at 9:05 a.m. and Denver at 6:50 p.m. in time for dinner. It carried the Pullman Palace Car that

had come up in the capacity of a sleeper, this time in service for daytime occupancy as a parlor car.

So far as the schedules show there was never a dining car service into Creede, but plenty of time was allowed to patronize the depot lunch counters at Alamosa and Pueblo on the way.

But far and away the greatest bond between Creede and the Rio Grande Railroad and one which in turn presented these entities to the great world beyond the right-of-way, was Cy Warman, "The Railroad Poet" whose stanzas immortalized Creede itself in the lexicon of the West and whose self identification with the world of steam and steel is practically unique in the bibliography of verse.

Warman is, of course, best known for his resonant paen ending in the oft-quoted stanza:

Here's a land where all are equal —
Of high and lowly birth —
A land where men make millions
Dug from the dreary earth.
Here the meek and mild-eyed burros
On mineral mountains feed —
It's day all day in daytime
And there is no night in Creede.

No civic booster or even stockholder was a greater admirer of the railroad as an agency of wealth and commerce in the community than Soapy Smith. In Creede and in Denver, where he actually operated on the Seventeenth Street corner opposite the Union Depot, he or his henchmen kept a shrewd eye on arrivals, appraising their economic potential and degree of gullibility by those standards well known to students of human psychology and making the pitch appropriate to the individual. Well upholstered arrivals with ample luggage suggesting legitimacy of business and a degree of affluence were marked as possible candidates for a bogus stock exchange where imaginary securities were quoted by eyeshaded telegraphers over wires from nowhere. Well heeled drummers of sportive vestments and merry mein were soon invited to participate in games of chance of elevated facade such as poker or roulette from which none but the house capper ever emerged a winner. Downright bumpkins were then and there steered to a sidewalk pitch where Soapy or an assistant trimmed them at the shell game before the competition could get at them.

In an age mercifully innocent of bus depots and airports, voyagers of low mentality and obscure station arrived on the cars along with their betters in the Pullmans, and the Rio Grande functioned, in Soapy's eyes, as a recurrent and never failing source of suckers. Also the cars took away victim types once they had been trimmed to make room for new customers. The railroad giveth; the railroad taketh away.

Soapy viewed benevolently the passenger operations of all carriers into Colorado, the Santa Fe, Rock Island, Colorado & Southern, the Union Pacific, Burlington and the Fort Worth & Denver. But mostly he held in affection the Rio Grande. It went more places where money was easy to come by.

In Creede, of course, the Rio Grande was the only railroad. Soapy's admiration for it as a virtual monopoly of transient wealth was unbounded.

Soapy was regarded by the permanent residents of Creede, or those who intended to stay as long as the silver lasted, with mixed emotions. He appointed his own chief of police, an able enough gun fighter from Texas, Captain John Light. He offered the office of Mayor of Creede to Herman Straus of the famous mercantile family when he visited town and was disappointed when Straus, although he found Soapy charming, declined the honor. Creede, unlike Denver, didn't offer limitless vistas of visiting suckers and it was now and then, in the interest of remaining in business, found necessary for Smith's associates to trim some of the locals and thus incur built-in disapproval. He encouraged itinerant clergymen to stage revival meetings and thoughtfully picked their pockets as they left town, regarding godly workers in the vineyard as a sort of collection agency.

"We'll miss you the way we would the calliope at the circus," a reputable businessman told Soapy when it came time to move on from Creede. "You've been the town's greatest attraction outside the assay office."

"Fair enough," said the urbane Sapolio. "A time to work and a time to play. Now it's time for us to go."

And he did. Together with Doc Baggs and the Reverend Bowers and Judge Van Horn, he took off for gaudier destinies in Denver and an eventual date with death in Alaska. His take from the howling wilderness of Creede is unknown, but it was in the hundreds of thousands and may have topped the million mark. Almost no money left town; he had spent all on champagne and petticoats. That was one reason Creede liked Soapy.

When Creede went up the spout after producing somewhat better than $5,000,000, Soapy Smith and Judge Van Horn were not the only pioneers to board the cars for pastures new. Cy Warman folded his *Creede Chronicle* and went to work for *The Rocky Mountain News* as railroad editor, filling a position as common in the time as society editor, bicycle editor or sports editor.

Warman celebrated his change of employment in a poem which gives some insight into the life of a Denver reporter in the nineties and the importance of the railroads in the general scheme of things:

It was sometime in the p.m. in the fall of '92
I had cashed in the *Creede Chronicle* — had
    nothing much to do —
I had seen a man of leisure who was loafing
    in the street
Who had every fad and fashion from his head
    down to his feet,
And this prince was a reporter, so I shined my
    Sunday shoes,
And went down to do the railroads for *The
Rocky Mountain News.*

Now the city man was Martin from McCul-
    lagh's *Democrat,*
And he glanced over his glasses as I doffed
    my derby hat —
I had owned a daily paper in the springtime
    of the year,
That had sunk ten thousand dollars; I had
    nothing then to fear —
I had planned that in the morning I would
    dally with the Muse,
In the P. M. do the railroads for *The Rocky
Mountain News.*

The verses continued in similar vein for a considerable space, but Warman had made this point abundantly clear: the railroad man on *The Rocky Mountain News* was kept busy.

Its railhead pushed by construction gangs such as that shown below, the Rio Grande's narrow gauge tracks reached Leadville July 20, 1880, a matter of two years ahead of the competition in the form of the also narrow gauge Denver, South Park & Pacific.

In the above photograph the Rio Grande tracks are shown in the foreground of Leadville as it looked in 1899 when its mines were still in effulgent bonanza. *(Two Photos: Western Collection, Denver Public Library.)*

Dedicated archeologists can still point out the sites in the Canyon of the Arkansas of the hastily thrown together blockades from behind whose breastworks General Palmer's embattled bravoes hurled defiance, insults and whisky bottles at the advancing bully boys of the Santa Fe under the command of Bat Masterson. This was Fort De Reemer, named for the Rio Grande's chief engineer of the time, and, if the defenders appear warlike in the extreme, the record shows that what encounters they had with the enemy were something less than lethal. Having won the race for the Raton and a Southwest Passage into New Mexico, the baby railroad evened things up with the opposition when it won the Arkansas and continued on its profitable way to Leadville as shown on the page opposite. (*Western Collection, Denver Public Library.*)

Leadville, magnificently situated above the upper Arkansas Valley, became a solid gold bone of contention between three railroads, two of which eventually shared in its bonanzas when two German prospectors, George Hook and Auguste Rische, grubstaked by the local postmaster whose name was Horace A. W. Tabor, brought in the silver-rich Little Pittsburgh Mine in California Gulch and precipitated the most chaotic gold rush since the discoveries of the Comstock Lode in Nevada. The Rio Grande and the Denver, South Park & Pacific, both narrow gauge, reached Leadville within days of each other but the Santa Fe, whose original motive for its threatened route up the Arkansas had been the Leadville traffic, never got there. Here Rische and Hook are shown by the sketch artist Pranishnikoff saddling up for their historic venture, not forgetting to pack the demijohn of Bourbon which they had included in their grubstake without Tabor's knowledge. At the left: Tabor who became in turn Mr. Leadville, Lt. Governor Tabor, Senator Tabor, Bonanza Tabor and, when the wheel had come full circle, Postmaster Tabor again. Although far from being Colorado's most exemplary citizen, Horace Tabor long after his florid person had passed from the scene, enjoyed a radiant immortality as the central figure of the most durable single chapter in Rocky Mountain folklore. The archetypal parvenu, he is today one in the folk-legends of bonanza times with Uncle Dick Wootton, Soapy Smith and even the godlike General Palmer himself. None of these have had acceptable grand opera written about them, but Tabor's love affair is enshrined perpetually in "The Ballad of Baby Doe."

As elsewhere in the mines, the railroad largely put the teamsters *(above)* out of business freighting ore to the smelters of Leadville and Malta. The Rio Grande standard gauged into Leadville in 1888 and the first train in was a mixed consist with a coach for guards and passengers and high cars for bullion on the head end. *(Below: Colorado State Historical Society.)*

At the height of the Leadville boom, the Rio Grande's coaches, as suggested by the drawing at the right, teemed with low life types, roulette dealers, monte throwers, keeno tippers, green goods passers, thimbleriggers, bunco steerers and con artists, all lured by the golden bonanzas pouring from the mines of Fryer Hill. The roundhouse at Salida provided motive power in both gauges and in ample numbers to convey the just and the unjust alike to Leadville if they had the fare. (*Western Collection, Denver Public Library.*)

Sometimes the product of the Leadville smelters was in excess of the combined capacities of three railroads, the South Park, the Midland and the Rio Grande to transport it to the mint at Denver or to other destinations where it could be processed. At such times it was carelessly stacked on the Rio Grande loading platforms awaiting cars to receive it. Poured in bars of several hundred pounds each, it was beyond the capacity of thieves who abounded but were impotent in this regard. The practice of casting precious metals into ingots of such dimension as to embarrass potential thieves, unlike many other aspects of smelting and the treatment of valuable ore was not itself indigenous to Colorado. It had its origins far to the west in the brief lived tumults of Panamint, California, high in the bleak ranges surrounding Death Valley where, in the year 1873 silver recoveries sparked a momentary bonanza. So remote and inaccessible was Panamint that even Wells Fargo refused to have anything to do with it, claiming its availability to lawlessness made it no better than a "suburb of hell." With highwaymen watching Panamint's every exit, its mine owners hit upon the expedient of sending out pure silver on cannonball shapes weighing 500 pounds each. No guards were necessary. *(William H. Jackson Photo: Western Collection, Denver Public Library.)*

The mining sensation of the year 1890 in the Rockies was Creede *(opposite)* where the elements and personalities of older times and other gold rush days recapitulated the excitements of the past during the brief lifespan of the diggings. The Rio Grande, through the agency of a subsidiary corporation, the Rio Grande-Gunnison Railroad Company, arrived at Creede from Wagon Wheel Gap practically with the speed of light as is suggested by the Jackson photograph in which the Arcade Saloon has barely had time to open for business and the two facing oases up the street are still unfinished. On this page a stock extra is dwarfed by the towering cliffs as it rolls up the Creede Branch half a century after the sound of shooting had died away forever in once turbulent Creede. *(Page Opposite: Western Collection, Denver Public Library; Above: Rocky Mountain Railroad Photos: Ross Grenard.)*

A few years after the first discoveries at Creede, freight on the rails through Wagon Wheel Gap was rolling behind such Vauclain compound ten wheelers as No. 1007. The below sketch was made by a reporter from the *Denver Republican* who visited Creede in the boom year of 1891 and found the Rio Grande's freight station piled roof-high with merchandise waiting to be claimed by consignees. Lest readers should not credit his account he drew this sketch which was published along with his report in the paper. *(Above: R. H. Kindig Collection; Below: Colorado State Historical Society.)*

Forerunner of the prefabricated dwelling of a later age, saloons arrived on the Rio Grande trains knocked down and ready to assemble on short notice. One such, the Gem, arrived at ten in the morning on the same train with all its furnishings and stock of potables and was serving iced beer from a mahogany bar two hours later. Such enterprise marked Creede as a progressive community and underscored the important part played by the railroad in the regional economy of Colorado.

In upper Creede the Rio Grande's track ran down the unpaved main street in such close proximity to the false fronts that the swinging doors of such saloons as the Ouray and Switch Key could not be swung outward when a train was passing and patrons had to look both ways before emerging. Posed on the unrailed front porch of the Miner's Bank were first citizens A. L. Moses and L. C. Graves; in the foreground the town hack that met all trains. (*Colorado State Historical Society.*)

Before the coming of the Rio Grande whisky for thirsty and chaotic Creede had been packed in on mule back by Whisky Johnny, the camp dealer in the basic necessities of life. By 1956 the wheel had come full circle; passenger service was a thing of the past and a twice a week freight *(below)* served the commerce of Wagon Wheel Gap and South Fork. *(Above: Western Collection, Denver Public Library; Below: Jim Ehernberger.)*

Above is Creede station, long widowed of Bob Ford and Soapy Smith, Cy Warman and the girls from Rose Vastine's place, drowsing out the years and dreaming perhaps of the day when a reporter for the *Denver Republican* wrote: "The Rio Grande freight house at Creede is overflowing with merchandise so that whisky, billiard tables and crated bar fixtures are stacked roof high until they shall be claimed by their consignees." Below the Rio Grande's ten wheeler No. 522 posed with its passenger run at Creede in 1900 in a day when even the diminutive news butcher was as proudly uniformed as the train captain. *(Above: Everett De Golyer Collection; Below: R. H. Kindig Collection.)*

The last steam power to roll through
Wagon Wheel Gap over the unballasted right of way of the Creede
Branch and pause for water at South
Fork tank hauled stock extras in the
fall of 1956. Present with his camera
to record it was Jim Ehernberger of
Cheyenne, a devoted iconographer of
the last great years' internal expansion
on the Rio Grande.

For some months during the height of its boom, king of Creede's flamboyant and unabashed underworld was Soapy Smith, king of the thimble-riggers, whom Cy Warman was pleased to address as Sapolio Smythe. When Creede's brief candle grew dim, Smith went on to greater things in Denver and thence to the Yukon where he came to a bad and violent end. The rare photo at the right from the files of the Society of California Pioneers shows Soapy on a sleeping car, probably en route to Alaska. Soapy, black bearded and holding a bottle, was one of several passengers in relaxed attitudes similarly occupied. He was a familiar figure for many years on the cars wherever large sums of tangible wealth was reported. Below: plowing out the Rio Grande tracks under the cottonwoods in Wagon Wheel Gap was one of the annual chores on the Creede Branch in the prosperous nineties.

Although the girls and the guns and the gold had long since vanished from turbulent Creede and Soapy Smith and Bob Ford and Chief of Police John Light from Texas were only memories, a breath of romance rode the Creede Branch as long as steam remained on the head end. In this wistful pose beside the cottonwoods, No. 1136 is making its farewell run through Wagon Wheel Gap before joining the ghosts of Colorado yesterdays in the Valhalla of remembered things. *(Jim Ehernberger.)*

Twenty years after the celebrated artist Thomas Moran drew Wagon Wheel Gap, as shown below, for *Harper's,* the railroad, en route to howling Creede, built its depot against the identical cliff shown in Moran's drawing. *(Everett De Golyer Collection.)*

Nothing inspired staff artists of the illustrated press in steam heated offices in far-off New York to greater or more intense efforts at their drawing boards than the news of trains stalled in snow blockades in the Colorado Rockies. The drawings on these two pages are the pictorial version in *Leslie's Illustrated Weekly* of the catastrophic doings on the Colorado Midland during the winter of 1899 when for seventy-eight days the entire through traffic of the carrier was suspended or re-routed over the tracks of the Rio Grande. Eastern readers shivered almost as much as the management of the railroad itself did.

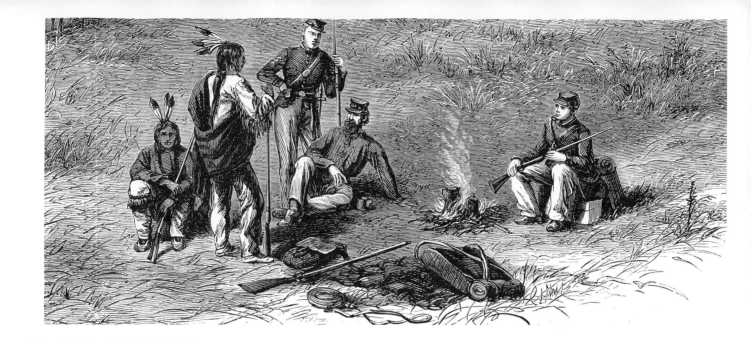

Colorado was still a Territory and scenes of Army scouts and Plains Indians such as that shown above were commonplace along its three foot right of way when the first mixed trains began running over the Denver & Rio Grande, and train crews were kept busy tossing free loaders off the platforms of the first diminutive cars, as shown below. Maintaining continuity with the now so distant past, narrow gauge mixed trains were still running on the Rio Grande's New Mexico line when Richard B. Jackson took the photographs on the page opposite, the high cars and coaches rolling tranquilly across the unballasted rails as they had done without interruption for seventy years. The detail in the upper photograph shows a bay window built into the passenger coach from which the conductor might con his train in the absence of a caboose.

On this page the Denver & Rio Grande's ten wheeler No. 524 proudly poses for its portrait with its crew in appropriate formation for the very style and archetype of the carrier's motive power at the turn of the century. *(Otto Perry Collection.)*

On the page opposite, two photographs of the vintage of 1{ from the collection of R. H. Kindig suggest the uses for wh the Rio Grande's three foot gauge was explicitly designed. Ab is the Texas Creek trestle and the branch it served leading of the main line in the foreground, while below Rio Gran No. 507 approaches a tunnel in Eagle River Canyon with town of Gilman improbably perched high on the rim of canyon as a commentary on the genius of man for digging mi in inaccessible places. Gold, silver, lead and zinc ore from Eagle Mine came down to the loading chutes by aerial tr way; passengers ascended to town by a series of stairs.

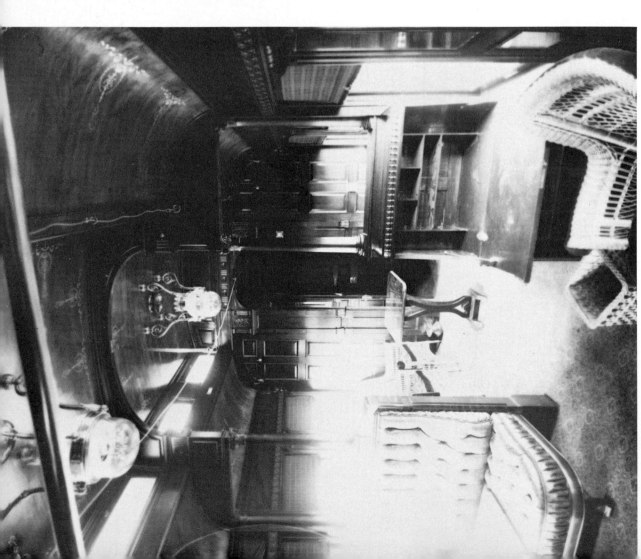

The interior arrangement of narrow gauge Pullman equipment on the Rio Grande's mainline trains followed the floor plan of coaches in the same dimension with banquettes, armchairs and table seating singly and for two staggered to provide an approximation of even weight on the trucks. *(Two Photos: Everett De Golyer Collection.)*

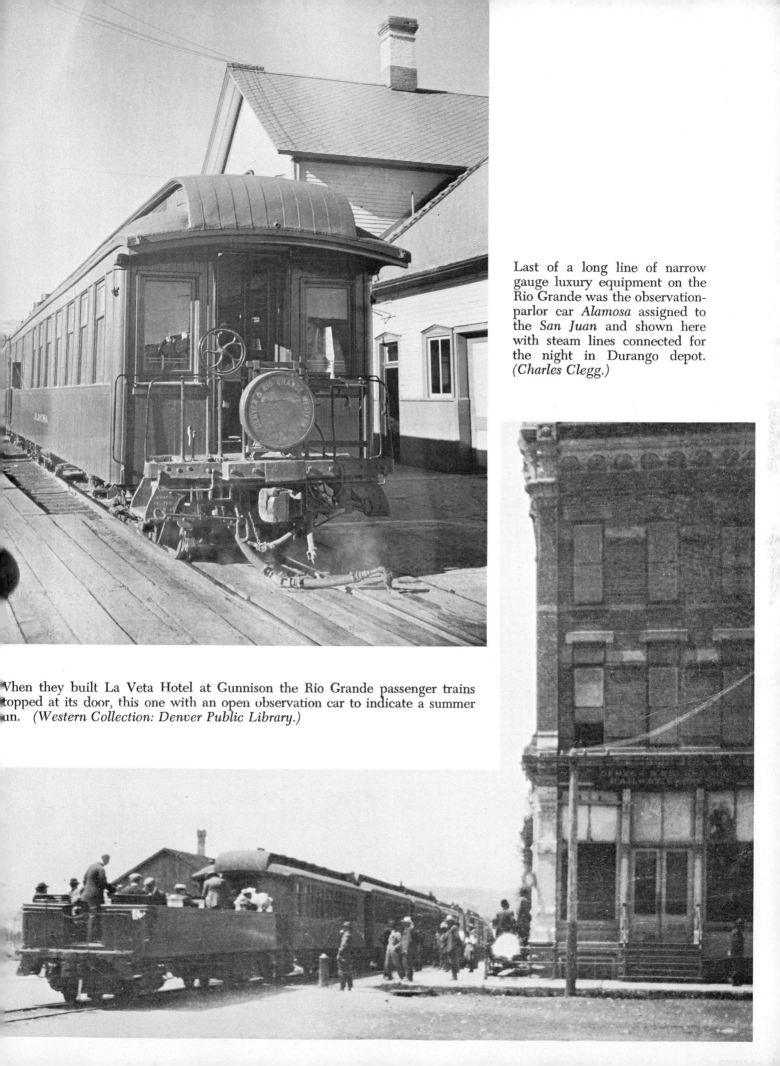

Last of a long line of narrow gauge luxury equipment on the Rio Grande was the observation-parlor car *Alamosa* assigned to the *San Juan* and shown here with steam lines connected for the night in Durango depot. *(Charles Clegg.)*

When they built La Veta Hotel at Gunnison the Rio Grande passenger trains stopped at its door, this one with an open observation car to indicate a summer run. *(Western Collection: Denver Public Library.)*

When the new right of way through Ruby Canyon near the Utah-Colorado border was built in 1929, the track at the right was the mainline of a great transcontinental carrier with eighty-pound rails spiked directly to untreated ties between which the weeds sprouted in luxurious profusion. Tie plates, heavy iron, treated ties and an improved gradient characterized the new line building at the left. *(Rio Grande Railroad.)*

In the same year the scene above was photographed, the Rio Grande's No. 782, a 4-6-0, pounded northward with Train No. 4 at Palmer Lake with seven cars in a pre-air-conditioned age. No. 782 was Class T-29, built by Brooks in 1909 and retired in 1941. *(Rio Grande Railroad.)*

Against a cheerless backdrop of winter sky, the Rio Grande's official photographer on lines west, Harry Shipler, took this photograph of a casual freight making its way over a light carpet of snow through Castle Gate on the morning of December 4, 1912. Twin steel spans have replaced the single track and wooden bridgework across the creek and the Rio Grande is becoming more of a main line every day, but nothing can relieve the grim facade of Utah geology as the shortest days of the year approach.

Three vignettes from the meticulous camera of Richard B. Jackson recreate the mood of the narrow gauge in modern times: at the right, the Ridgway depot against a cloudy background of Colorado summer; bottom left: Train No. 116 pauses by the platform at Ignacio in August 1949, while at the right engine No. 479 backs down to couple to the *Shavano* in 1938 against a background of the curiously timbered Monte Christo Hotel at Salida. Summery scenes in the long summer's afternoon of three foot steam.

The narrow gauge wasn't long on ballast or rail alignment in the eighties when No. 401 posed with a trainload of rails at Gray's Siding on Marshall Pass at the dawn of the railroad era, but the slim gauge had all the attributes of mainline railroading by 1939 when the *Shavano* rolled out of Salida and across the Arkansas River on its way to Gunnison. *(Above: Western Collection, Denver Public Library; Below: Richard B. Jackson.)*

A commonplace sight of the thirties in Salida yards was standard gauge switcher No. 1173 making up the consist of narrow gauge Train No. 315, the *Shavano*, against a backdrop of the Monte Christo Hotel. Back at the turn of the century No. 263 *(below)* had been doing the same job at the same place. *(Top: Richard B. Jackson; Below: Fred Jukes.)*

In the glory years of steam there was *The Mountaineer* with coaches and a Pullman sleeper between Montrose and Denver via Grand Junction on an overnight schedule. At the left it is shown nearing Denver on a fine June morning in 1940 with the business car of General Manager Al Perlman on the rear end. Above on the page opposite and below it appears on the wye at Montrose. Above on this page is the engine house at Montrose with one narrow gauge stall and one with three tracks for the engines to sleep in. *(Left: Otto Perry; Above: Rocky Mountain Railroad Photos: Two Photos Charles Clegg.)*

At Malta, almost to Tennessee, passengers could see the branch line leading up to Leadville and imagine in the mind's eye the wealthy excitements there when Fryer Hill was in fullest bonanza.

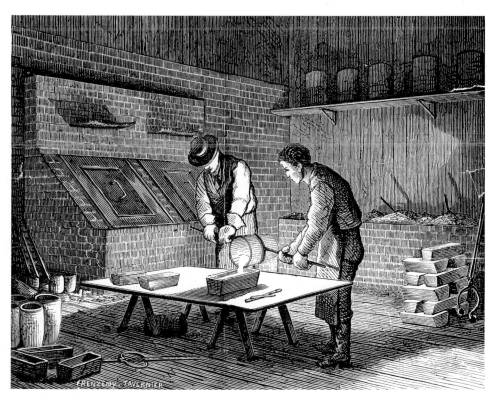

Where once the Rio Grande's patrons had rolled in Pullman plush on the first standard gauge through train in the nineties on the Salt Lake run, they traversed the same bleakly beautiful setting forty years later on the *Scenic Limited*, shown at the left double headed at Tennessee summit near Mitchell with a 2-8-8-2 as helper and 4-8-4 road engine for a portrait in smoke and glory by R. H. Kindig. Above, the *Scenic* leaves Denver with a full complement of observation platform riders in an age when no self-respecting name train but had a brass railed verandah at the rear. *(Rio Grande Railroad.)*

"Twilight on The Narrow Gauge" is a cliché that must inescapably attach to this wistful and haunting pastoral by one of the Rio Grande's foremost iconographers, Otto Perry of Denver, who caught narrow gauge engine No. 318 with the mail at Gunnison in 1944. Over the scene the shadows lengthen prophetically as the diminutive cars roll behind white flags through a mellow landscape of ancient cottonwoods beside Gunnison water.

— 191

Here is the Denver & Rio Grande Western's *Scenic Limited* of fragrant memory,
Train No. 2 on the Denver-Salt Lake run in 1938 as depicted for immortality by
Howard Fogg, dean of contemporary railroad painters. No. 2 is running late and
dawn is breaking over the Utah badlands as No. 1706 rolls its long consist of
head-end revenue cars, coaches and Pullmans out of Green River, Utah, in the
belle epoque of steam and standard passenger operations.

HERE COME THE TOURISTS

WELL AHEAD of his time in matters of promotion and publicity, General Palmer early in the game associated with his overall projects another military man whose powers of oratorical persuasion are reported by Marshall Sprague to have rivalled those of the godlike Daniel Webster and whose genius for illusion closely approximated that of Phineas Barnum. General Robert A. Cameron had first been employed as spell binder for Nathan Meeker's high minded agricultural colony at Greeley, Colorado, treacherously situated on the rival Denver and Pacific, but a lordly offer of $3,000 a year had induced him to renounce the ideologies of Uncle Horace and the devoted Meeker and throw in his lot with General Palmer's multiplicity of interlocking land companies, railroads, lotteries and other high pressure promotions.

General Cameron did not see eye to eye with General Palmer in the matter of liquor. The Springs was founded on strictest temperance principles but its hired prophet was totally unable to project his vision into the ineffable future and tell the customers what he saw on less than a tumbler of the best Bourbon. General Palmer's prejudice against the demon abated before the masterful sales talk of his red nosed associate who saw illimitable vistas of potentiality stretching into the Colorado Springs future and described his visions in a lexicon of superlatives that would have bemused the great Gladstone.

When the first stake was driven at the future corner of Pike's Peak and Cascade Avenues, General Cameron was at concert pitch, and addressed the potential customers and pioneers with such eloquence that many were close to tears. It was only when, in rounded periods, he described the future Newport of the West as destined to arise on "the margins of Noble Cache la Poudre" that his auditors realized that he was back in the groove of his pitch for the Greeley colony.

If, after communion with the bottle, General Cameron was prone to a sort of geographic schizophrenia, he was in the best of company. Buffalo Bill, the great Pahaska himself, now and then suffered from uncertainty as to his precise whereabouts at the moment and addressed audiences at his show at Cheyenne as "the fine people of Omaha, a city ever dear to my frontiersman's heart," or told the Chamber of Commerce at Minneapolis that he was enchanted once more to find himself back in "Rawlins, Wyoming, where once in his young manhood the buffalo had roamed freely."

Another spellbinder lured by General Palmer from the rascally opposition was William E. Pabor who also renounced the Greeley colony and its down to earth aspirations in favor of the more elevated prospects at The Fountain augmented by a substantial raise in salary.

Pabor, although a word artist of parts, was no match for the eloquent Cameron, although his memorial may be found today in many of the place names which General Palmer, at his suggestion, bestowed on various landmarks around the Springs. He convinced the General of the propriety of Indian and Spanish names such as Kiowa, Cimarron, Huerfano and Costilla and, presumably, named the town Manitou when Palmer would have more elegantly christened it "La Font." Pabor's triumphs of publicization, however, were his remarkable feats in discerning significant formations in the stoneyard that came to be known as The Garden of the Gods.

In General Palmer's all-inclusive scheme of a Colorado economy to support his railroad, the tourist was an important and much cherished component. Manitou and The Springs were the first of these outposts of the *bon ton* in a generation when tourists were recruited exclusively from the well to do and educated classes of Eastern society or from Europe.

We have seen elsewhere how the predominant character of Colorado Springs was English, deriving from the great number of Britons who congregated there as soon as the city had been laid out. Manitou was for valetudinarians, and when General Palmer had brought it into being in 1871 he openly expressed the hope that it might "soon become a first class watering place and spa." The customers may have been first class but the accommodations not necessarily so, and first arrivals in its early years complained that its primeval hotel had wide spaces between its wallboards through which the winds were far from therapeutic. Illness was a conversation piece and the standard salutation between newly introduced Manitou visitors was "What may be your complaint, sir?"

In a few years, however, Manitou had evolved a social facade by no means second to that shaping up in Colorado Springs. "Fashionable life here is more frivolous, not to say faster, than at similar places in the Old World," commented one English diarist. "Ladies' breakfast toilets are good enough for the dinner table, while for dinner they dress as for the opera . . . All this seems very odd among the mountains."

Chester A. Arthur, the most affluent and aristocratic of American presidents, evoked much comment because he returned to his hotel shabby and dirty after a day of roughing it in the hills. "Besides his skin hung in strips from his nose which did not improve his appearance."

As the seat of General Palmer's barony, Colorado Springs of course received the Rio Grande's most sumptuous red carpet treatment. Its first hotel of consequence, the original Antlers, was built by the railroad and for years it was the management's boast that any dish for which a patron might ask from the regional cookery of the civilized world was available from its kitchens.

The Garden of the Gods on the outskirts of town was the special joy of the railroad's publicity department, and an early travel brochure stated that "No other point of interest available by the railroad is more unique or more to be admired than this curious freak of nature." Visitors by the hundred arrived on the narrow gauge cars to see or claim they saw in stone the likeness of curious birds, serpents, an elephant attacking a lion and a seal making love to a nun. This last attraction elicited some disapproval on moral grounds, as did the name of the resort itself. There were religious tourists who felt that "something less heathenish for a name might better have befitted these Christian days." The railroad, however, sold round trip tickets out of Denver to Christian and unbeliever alike with fine impartiality and, a little later, was urging through travelers on to Salt Lake where they could explore the more superficial mysteries of Mormonism between trains.

"I had an uncontrollable desire," wrote an English visitor via the steamcars, "to ask every man I met how many wives he had and how things work out with his mothers-in-law."

More daring tourists from the East wanted to avoid the dressing for dinner circuit and took the Rio Grande's widely advertised five-day trip "Around the Narrow Gauge Circle," while those who desired altogether to throw off the restraints of city and resort life, chartered private trains of narrow gauge sleepers and business cars which were spotted on inaccessible sidings while members of the party admired the scenery, the wild flowers and the capacity for hard liquor of the miners in the neighboring diggings.

"For diversion, ma'm?" answered a sourdough to the query of a Boston visitor to Aspen in its early days. "Why for diversion, I guess we drinks whisky, ma'm. But not the way you do; we swallers it right down."

Ernest Ingersoll, who had been a member of a geological survey party to the West in 1874 took his wife and a party of friends on a ramble through the Rockies on a private train of three Rio Grande cars, finding that they provided just the right balance between effete living and positive hardship.

"Roughing it within reasonable grounds," he explained, "is the marrow of this sort of recreation."

Many visitors to Colorado were as interested in the means of transport available as they were in the natural wonders they might encounter or the social curriculum at Manitou and The Springs.

"The sleeping cars are fitted with oiled walnut, carved and gilded," wrote Boddam-Whetham after riding the infant Rio Grande, "and stained plate glass, metal trappings heavily silver-plated, seats cushioned with thick plushes, washstands of marble and walnut, damask curtains and massive mirrors in frames of gilded walnut. The floors are carpeted in the most beautiful and costly Brussels, the roof beautifully frescoed in mosaics of gold, of emerald green, crimson, sky-blue, violet, drab and black."

If invocation of the hues of rainbow seems naive to the modern traveler accustomed to railroad car interiors reminiscent of the receiving room of a creditable hospital, it must be remembered that this was an age when the national taste had yet to be debased by *moderne* decor or inhibited from pleasure by the functional. The Palace Cars of Pullman, Wagner, Mann and the other carbuilders in the grand manner were the first experience of luxury for thousands, and the satisfaction engendered by plush, ormolu and gilding was warm and universal.

More than any other single agency, the Palace Cars were to shape American taste for splendor and luxury in the final decades of the nineteenth century. Largely they took their cue from the rococo and Gothic of the Mississippi River steamers which they were to an overwhelming degree relegating to the discard, but whereas the ample grandeurs of the *Robert E. Lee, Great Republic* and *J. M. White* were available, comparatively, to hundreds, the cars which went everywhere were influencing the minds and ambitions of thousands.

A familiar American superlative of the days before the Civil War had been "beautiful as a steamboat." Now the ultimate in splendor was suggested by "beautiful as a Palace Car."

As the novelty of the Pacific Railroad wore off and riding the Overland Route to California became a commonplace, more adventurous travelers sought out the Rio Grande as the ultimate expression of railroad adventure, providing mountain assaults and seemingly bottomless abysses where the Union Pacific could offer nothing more thrilling than Sherman Hill.

"What a fierce wild pleasure," wrote Walt Whitman of a trip through the Rockies in 1879, "to lie in my berth at night in the luxurious Palace Car, drawn by the mighty Baldwin embodying, and filling me, too, full of the swiftest motion, and most resistless strength! . . . The element of dan-

ger adds zest to it all. On we go, rumbling and flashing, with our loud whinnies thrown out from time to time, or trumpet blasts into the darkness."

Lord Dunraven, an inveterate traveler and articulate peer, recalled that when he stepped out of his Pullman in a desolate way station, "we found ourselves plunged suddenly into the wild and woolly West . . . On the tracks the magnificent Palace Cars shone forth in all their pristine grandeur of plate glass, polished metal, highly varnished wood, luxurious velvet, mahogany and silver-mounted interior" in unflattering contrast to the shack towns, tent cities and false fronts of the trackside communities where they paused.

G. A. Sala, a British journalist in the best deerstalker hat and astonished monocle tradition was amazed to find Pullmans in the American West so similar to Pullmans on English trains, it never having occurred to him that they were an article of American export. The dining car menus were more profusely studded with luxury fare, he discovered, too.

Generally speaking, the Rio Grande took a dim view of the Colorado Indians as promotional material, preferring instead the Spanish-Mexican motif when naming points of interest in the landscape as Lover's Leap, Devil's Gate and Coronado Canyon, and it remained for the Santa Fe to capitalize to the fullest extent on the Navajo and Pueblo tribal artifacts, names, customs and folklore that are to this day the standard promotional pitch of that carrier. "A good Indian legend can be attached to any locality with a little care and attention," the late Lee Lyles, vice president in charge of Santa Fe advertising, once remarked to one of the authors of this book. "Nothing adds to the appeal of a desolate mesa more than knowing that a beautiful Navajo maiden sought refuge from worse than death at the hands of a brutal ravisher by leaping from it . . . All it takes to create a tradition is a little imagination."

If it missed the boat in the matter of the aboriginal interest in Colorado and Utah, the Rio Grande was at least not victimized as was Henry Villard's Northern Pacific when he hired a delegation of Crows to perform tribal dances at its gold spike ceremony in 1883. The Crows sold their brass bracelets and ornamental beads to Villard's guests at substantial gain over what they had cost Villard when he gave them to them before the ceremony.

Well in advance of the best modern promotional technique, the Rio Grande early in the game realized the value of good pictorial publicity and retained to depict their railroad and the countryside through which it passed a top-notch professional photographer in the person of the talented William Henry Jackson. Jackson had been attached to the Hayden expedition that certified the wonders of the Yellowstone and was one of the most prolific and painstaking regional photographers in an age when photography was a physical, as well as intellectual, occupation.

The great weight and bulk of the equipment involved, the nice timing of shots to coincide with the short and sensitive life of the plate emulsion and the fragility of the glass plates that were universal before cellulose roll film, all required a rare combination of energy and know-how. The Rio Grande provided Jackson with a succession of special studio cars, often with a locomotive assigned to their transport and spotting, that enormously simplified the photographic problems of his time. Over the years Jackson exposed literally thousands of square feet of glass plates, some of them more than twenty inches square, in his huge view cameras, developing them within a few minutes of their exposure to make a matchless record of Colorado in the railroad age. His pictures today constitute the durable foundation of all Colorado regional photography and are the cherished backbones of picture collections both at the Western Collection, Denver Public Library, and at the Colorado State Historical Society.

Other Western railroads were quick to perceive the value of their own photographic exploration and the Great Northern, improving on Jackson's makeshift but effective camera trains, provided Haynes with a formal studio car complete with dark room and a photographic *atelier* where its products might be purchased that toured the Northwest in the interest of the Villard road. The Union Pacific had long ago, of course, retained Colonel Charles Savage of Salt Lake as part time employee and official recorder of the epic ceremony at Promontory. Some of the earliest photographs in the Rio Grande archives, notably the few depicting operations on the Rio Grande Western

in Utah, are by the same cameraman who made the most celebrated of all photographs of the Old West, the engines "touching head to head" and the grouped dignitaries at Promontory on May 10, 1869.

One exception to its general disregard for Indians as inspiration for travel was made by the Rio Grande publicity department in 1905 when it was found profitable to build reproductions of the Mesa Verde cliff dwellings near Manitou and people them with genuine Indians who made and sold pottery and posed with the tourists to be photographed in the Brownie cameras of the age. The reproductions, if not exactly indigenous to the suburbs of Manitou, possessed at least one aspect of authenticity: they were built from prehistoric material freighted in from a less accessible region.

The tourist sleepers which were part of Rio Grande passenger equipment almost until the time of the 1914 War came into vogue in the eighties on all Western railroads as a variation of the Palace Car or otherwise "the poor man's Pullman," many of them having actually been built by the Pullman Company at its Detroit and Chicago works. The tourist car was neither as luxurious nor as ornate as the Palace Cars and evoked patronizing glances from first class passengers riding in torrents of plush, ormolu and marquetry, but they opened the West to thousands of pleasant people who could never have afforded the extra fare luxury runs. The tourist car was remembered by occupants for its cane seats "that put bunyons and a beautiful basket weave impression on the backs of one's legs — the brooding, lingering smells of stale food with the lusty odor of garlic predominating." Many tourist cars provided a modified galley at the end of the car where passengers cooked their own meals, berths were made down by a porter and on some trains guides rode the cars to make themselves agreeable to the cut rate passengers and tell them tall tales about the regions traversed. Often the guides were college boys from the East who made a good thing out of vacations spent riding back and forth on the second class cars.

"Whole families bound for Rocky Mountain resorts loll about on the wicker or leather seats," wrote a reporter for *World's Work* in describing life on the tourist Pullman in 1902. "One or two people are heating coffee on the range at the end of the car . . . heads project from the open windows: everybody is happy. In porter service and plush these people are not so well provided as the parlor car passengers, but to discomfort they will not own. They contend that their berths are as snug as those in the first class car behind."

Everywhere in the Rockies, both on the cars of the Rio Grande, the Santa Fe and the Colorado Midland, the "heads projecting from open windows" in a pre-air-conditioned age were a problem at which the carriers shuddered. The multiplicity of tunnels with critically narrow clearances provided liberal opportunities for decapitation, but the numbers of such fatalities seem to have been small. Apparently the modest speeds of the age afforded ample time to withdraw enquiring faces at Plainview or Ute Canyon.

At Glenwood Springs, the railroad built its celebrated outdoor swimming pool filled with thermal water only a few feet removed from its mainline tracks and passengers in dead of winter could look out of their drawing room windows at daring bathers splashing around in its therapeutic depths during a snowstorm.

Another of the Rio Grande's promotional swimming pools, that at Manitou, achieved at least local immortality on the basis of an epic witticism of Eugene Field concerning Kemp Cooper, the glacial and supremely aloof managing director of the *Denver Republican*. "Colonel G. K. Cooper," wrote Field, "went swimming on Sunday afternoon in the hot water pool at Manitou and the place was used as a skating rink in the evening."

While it might be mistaken to remark that the Rio Grande Railroad single handed brought the region, which the *Denver Post* today delights to call "The Rocky Mountain Empire," into being as a tourist attraction in the nineteenth century, it assuredly was the most puissant agency in its exploitation and publicization. One has but to leaf through the enormous amount of promotional literature bearing the railroad imprimatur in the files of the Denver Public Library to realize the attention that was lavished on seasonal passenger business in a day and age when only the very well-to-do could afford Paris and London and when even they were increasingly aware of the

attractions of their native country, especially the part of it that lay west of the Missouri River.

Even before the coming of the railroad the therapeutic powers of various Colorado hot springs and mountain elevations were widely recognized in the East so that valetudinarians arrived overland by carriage and horseback before a foot of rail had been spiked in the Centennial State, but the Rio Grande put health on a commercial basis and may well have been surprised if the health seeking trade brought upper case fashion and the socially elect in its wake.

By the nineties it was possible to find first class hotel accommodations wherever the narrow gauge iron found its way, at Silverton, Gunnison, Leadville, Ouray, Glenwood Springs, Aspen and even Durango. Of course, better than first class was the rule at Colorado Springs, although The Springs had by now ceased to be a sort of evening dress company town owned and administered by the Rio Grande. There were other railroads by now, but General Palmer's road still dominated the scene and, until the coming of the Broadmoor, well after the turn of the century, the Antlers possessed a close monopoly on carriage trade tourism.

If Colorado got a good press in the East, it was in large measure a good press invoked by the Rio Grande Railroad, for although the up and coming Santa Fe was also uncommonly tourist-minded, its purview lay more properly in Arizona, New Mexico and the then booming citrus vistas of Southern California where such a notable resort town as Pasadena was practically an extension of the railroad itself.

In its February 4 issue for 1888 that highly influential periodical, *Harper's Weekly*, "The Journal of Civilization," devoted ample letterpress to the Rio Grande and it is worth reproducing its account in extenso for the flavor of travel reporting of the period.

> It is hard for the Eastern mind to take the narrow-gauge railway seriously. The unrivalled railway equipment of the East which sends its passengers from New York to Chicago in a single day, without change of cars, has done much to fix the belief, already half formed by certain unpretentious little roads east of the Mississippi, that the narrow gauge system is necessarily slow, unreliable, and trifling — a sort of juvenile imitation, in fact, of what a full-grown, serious-minded

railway ought to be. The American fondness for something big has for many years worked to the disadvantage of the narrow-gauge idea in railroad building; but it has remained for the West, wherein this tendency toward bigness is most fully developed, to build a narrow-gauge line that in point of size and business ability will compare favorably with the best of the wide-track roads of the country.

It was somewhere south of Colorado Springs that I first saw a train on the Denver and Rio Grande Railway. The Atchison, Topeka, and Santa Fe's through express, the "Cannon-ball" train of the West, which had come all the way across the Kansas plains, had side-tracked at the foot of a curve to let something pass. I stood on the rear steps of the Pullman car, watching a cloud float across the dull gray dome of Pike's Peak. "She's coming," said the conductor, as he half mechanically looked at his watch, "and on time to a dot."

"What's coming?" I asked.

"The Denver and Rio Grande's Pacific Express."

I swung out from the lower step and looked up the track. Over beyond a sand-hill I caught a glimpse of a wisp of steam and a puff of smoke. A moment later a locomotive, all fresh and bright and glistening, its driving-wheels whirling like so many indistinct blurs, and its pitman-rods flashing up and down like rays of sunlight, shot out from behind the hill, at the head of a long train of cars, and came roaring down the curve. The compact, well-proportioned locomotive and the gently swaying cars, each window and panel gilded with the fervent Colorado sun, made one forget for a moment that the track was narrow, or that the rolling-stock was of less than usual size. When it had gone rushing past at the rate of fifty miles an hour, I suggested to the conductor that it seemed strange that the huge bulk of the Santa Fe's "Cannon-ball" should wait meekly on the side track while the lordly little Pacific Express went its way.

"Yes," said the conductor, in an aggrieved tone of voice; "she goes right through, an' never stops for nothing."

In more presentable English this sentiment would represent in a fair measure the spirit that built the road in 1871 and the policy that operates it now. The builders of the system had only $10,000 in money with which to give their project life, but they had plenty of pluck, determination and hope. The original design was to build a main line from Denver to the city of Mexico, with branches to all the important mining districts along the way. With their $10,000 the founders began work on July 28, 1871. Three miles of track were laid by August 16th and the first narrow-gauge train run over it. During the closing days of October the line was opened as far as Colorado Springs. From that time on there was plenty of money to work with, for investors saw that the venture was a success. By the middle of the following June the road got as far as Pueblo, and there its original purpose was checked and turned aside. Instead of going south to the city of Mexico, it went west to the mining camps in the mountains, where it has done a giant's share in working out the destinies of the State. Since the first spike was driven in 1871 there has been no cessation of building. Even now, when the main line and branches, with about 1400 miles of track, touch nearly every point of commercial value in Colorado, extensions are being made to new fields of mining activity. It is likely that so long as there is a new mine to be developed or a valley opened for settlement the road-builders will continue their work. In time they may make the system a part of a new through broad-gauge line from the Pacific to the Atlantic. All that is needed is the laying of the third rail, which has already been found necessary on the eastern part of the main line. As it now is, the passenger can take a through train from Denver to Ogden, Utah, by way of the Denver and Rio Grande's main line and the Denver and Rio Grande Western, which continues on through Utah from the western boundary of Colorado.

It is not as a commercial line, however, that the Denver and Rio Grande is best known in this country. In carrying the venturesome road westward through the mountains, the engineers, by no design of their own, laid out a route that has since become known as the "scenic line of the world." The surveys were made on a purely economical basis, yet they passed through some of the grandest scenery on the North American continent. It would naturally be supposed that a road with such a profusion of scenery along every mile of its track — towering mountains, lofty passes, or narrow gorges — would have secured, almost at its completion, a large passenger travel; but as a matter of fact it was not until a few years since, when a change of management of the passenger department made practical use of the scenery, that the road had anything except local traffic. So great are the natural attractions of the line, and so skilfully have they been laid before the public, that under the present direction of affairs the tourist travel has become, in summer at least, many times larger than the local business. What with the literary excellence and the wide distribution of the company's advertising matter, the Colorado scenic route has become so well known that not even the foreign observer can have any excuse for omitting the Rocky Mountains from his book on America.

To one who has made the tour of the Denver and Rio Grande system it is wellnigh impossible to say which point of interest is best worth seeing. The Marshall Pass is high and hard to climb, and the views from its summit are wide and varied; yet one might not venture to assert that in the matter of general attraction it is superior to the rugged depths of the Royal Gorge or the sombre windings of the Black Cañon. The road over La Veta Pass, with its wonderful muleshoe curve and its twistings and turnings, is a sufficiently curious sight to repay a journey over the range; but few will contend that the chasm of the Toltec Gorge or the landscape wonder of the ride up Animas Cañon to Silverton is not worth fully as much.

The Marshall Pass is perhaps better known than any other point by reason of its great height, its magnificent scenery, and the difficulty with which it is climbed, to say nothing of the fact that it is on the through line of the road between Denver and Ogden, and that it is practically the backbone of the continent. Its 10,820 feet of height, seemingly impassable to anything other than the pack-mule, was hardly an obstacle to construction engineers who laugh at grades and speak lightly of elevations. When these men were told to go over into the Gunnison country, they went. There was only one thing to do when they reached the continental divide at the Marshall Pass, and that was to go over it. With them it was not a great engineering problem, as it would have been with a broad-gauge road, but merely a practical question of how many twists and turns they would have to make, at a maximum grade of 220 feet to the mile, to reach the summit from each side.

Old-time mining operators yet marvel much at the rapid advance of a civilization that enables them to sit at ease in a Pullman car and ride over the Marshall and La Veta passes, and through the Royal and Toltec gorges, or over the rough country to Leadville or Silverton, when only a few years ago they made the same journeys with a pack train, or a slow-moving freighting wagon. The ride from Denver to the San Juan mining regions, which only a short time ago

required a month of perilous travel, is now made in a day, and the trip to Leadville, once beset with the most annoying of difficulties, is in this new era of Colorado's wonderful progress a matter of only a few hours. The Gunnison country, for a long time the mysterious, Indian-haunted region of the State, has of late years been transformed into one of the best known stretches of territory along the through line to Utah.

The summer wayfarer, who seeks the mountains for his health, or for the fish and game with which a bountiful nature has been so lavish, is prone to regard the road as a picturesque adjunct to America's grandest scenery, or perhaps as a convenience for fishermen and hunters. This impression is unwittingly given a semblance of probability by the practice, on all except the main lines, of stopping trains at any telegraph pole to let passengers on or off. Tourist fishermen and settlers who live at a distance from stations know what a great convenience this is. Yet even the vacation traveller, be he ever so unobservant, cannot fail to note how thoroughly in earnest, and how business-like and dignified, is this little giant of the West. I know of no road in the country that has a better system of management, or that conducts its affairs with greater regularity and precision.

Appropriately enough, as long as there was to be profit in the tourist trade via the medium of railroad travel, the Rio Grande that had done such notable pioneering in this field, was its beneficiary to the end. As late as 1961 the little narrow gauge *Silverton Train* running in summer months from Durango to Silverton over the storied route up Animas Canyon continued to be a profitable operation and one of the most celebrated tourist attractions in all the Rocky Mountain region. When narrow gauge operations everywhere else had disappeared from the passenger schedules of *The Official Guide*, the *Silverton Train* was running filled to capacity and with waiting lines of applicants for space on its decrepit yellow wooden coaches and combines. Per passenger mile in terms of revenue, it was the most profitable railroad operation in the United States.

Throughout the early years of the Rio Grande when all but a microscopic fraction of travel to and from the Queen City of the Plains was accomplished aboard the steamcars, Denver's Windsor Hotel marked the end of the trail for countless thousands of travelers who arrived aboard the Burlington, the Santa Fe, the Union Pacific, the Colorado & Southern, the South Park, the Fort Worth & Denver, the Rock Island and, of course, the Rio Grande. The Windsor, until it was surpassed in elegance by the sumptuous onyx paneled lobby and towering rotunda of the Brown Palace further uptown, was Denver's most celebrated landmark and its diamond dust mirrors, tesselated marble floors and its bar where Buffalo Bill Cody could be en-

countered in converse with Lord Dunraven were institutional throughout the Rocky Mountains. Passengers getting down from the cars eagerly directed cabbies to hasten toward its ample suites, and departing notables invariably paused for a last quick one at the Windsor before returning to Leadville or San Francisco. Throughout the golden age of Colorado railroading, the Windsor was a world renowned symbol of Western hospitality, and here a staff artist for *Leslie's* in the course of the Leslie Expedition to report on the Far West, recreates its lobby in the Windsor's hour of splendor when H. A. W. Tabor was the town's most magnificent spender and the Matchless was still producing.

From the day of wooden Pullmans, Saratoga trunks and rolling news stands on the platforms to the age of stainless steel and high speed trucks, Denver's Union Depot has maintained a continuity with yesterday when it was still part of the old West. *(Below: Colorado State Historical Society.)*

In the year 1890 Rio Grande patrons sipped the medicinal waters at the railroad owned springs at Manitou while other constituents took pictures of the scenery with primeval box cameras as depicted below in a drawing for *Harper's* by Charles Graham entitled "Over the Rockies in an Observation Car." *(Above: Western Collection, Denver Public Library; Below: Bancroft Library.*

General Palmer's vision of empire embraced not only the heavy industry of Pueblo, the coal mines of the San Juan and the ore shipments from bonanzas in Leadville and Silverton as sources of traffic and revenue to the Rio Grande, but agriculture as well. Company towns mushroomed wherever the soil beckoned, none more profitably than that of Alamosa, for a time the terminal of the Fort Garland Extension, whose surrounding ranches in the fertile Sangre de Cristo Valley were planted to barley, oats, potatoes, alfalfa and wheat, all of which went out to the great world aboard the cars. Alamosa was founded by the Rio Grande Construction Company, a railroad subsidiary of which Ex-Governor A. C. Hunt was president and whose land office is shown here populated with local rustics and products of the regional economy. It was drawn for *Harper's* by the celebrated artist team of Paul Frenzeny and Jules Tavernier.

— 203

As an authentic tycoon of his generation, General Palmer rode free over every carrier of consequence in America. A partial collection of his annual passes occupied a dozen montages such as this at the Pioneer Museum, Colorado Springs.

The first Antlers Hotel at Colorado Springs, built in 1883 by General Palmer as an adjunct to his railway, overnight became established in the lore of the West as a resort of socially acceptable worldliness, sharing the charm and distinction of the similarly elegant Southern Pacific hotel, the Del Monte at Monterey, California. When Willa Cather, in one of her novels, wanted to identify a character as to the manor born, she depicted her as always wintering in a combination of gaiety and propriety at the Antlers, sipping old fashioned cocktails on the terrace and dancing far into the night in its ornate ballroom. *(Pioneer Museum, Colorado Springs.)*

The first Antlers, destined to be destroyed by fire in 1898, was famous for its luxurious furnishing supplied by Arnold Constable in New York, its Turkish baths, billiard room, central heating and gas light, but mostly for its cuisine of which it was boasted that no dish known to the classical repertory of food anywhere in the world but could be supplied by its chefs on demand. The Antlers, then and later, was located within handy walking distance of the Rio Grande depot at The Springs, shown below. *(Pioneer Museum, Colorado Springs.)*

Until the construction of the cogwheel tramway out of Manitou to its summit in 1890, Pike's Peak was virtually a tourist attraction and property of the Rio Grande Railroad. While their elders played croquet, drank brandy smashes and discussed the validity of visiting European titles, children were dispatched under the escort of competent guides and packmasters in burro trains for a day's outing and picnic at the summit. Like everything else, Pike's Peak was part of the railroad's apparatus of promotion and this charming scene, "A Burro Party, Pike's Peak" was drawn for *Harper's Weekly* in 1888 by Charles Graham at the suggestion of the Rio Grande's publicity department. Less enviable are the altitudes achieved by the Rio Grande on this page: at the right flagging in winter in the high passes, and below, plowing out Cumbres Pass in the narrow gauge nineties by the legendary Fred Jukes.

During the great waves of migration from Europe and Ireland, the Rio Grande brought in thousands of workers for the smelters at Pueblo and the mines of Durango and Crested Butte, but by 1900 immigrant cars had largely been replaced by the more comfortable tourist Pullmans shown on the opposite page. (*Right: Pullman Standard.*)

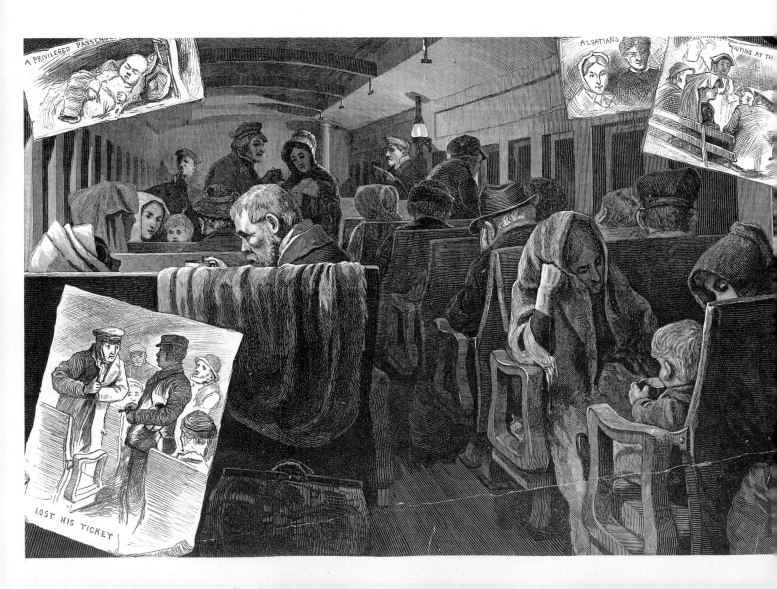

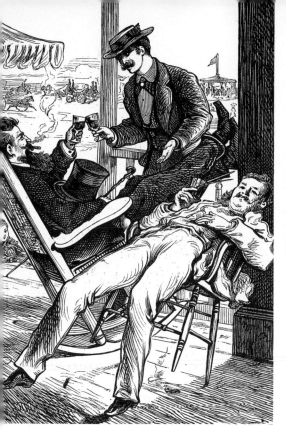

The first tourists brought to Manitou and Colorado Springs by the Rio Grande were well-to-do Easterners and Englishmen described by a contemporary as in search of "gossip, cobblers, romance, flirting and croquet," as shown here on the porch of the Count Pourtales elegant Broadmoor Casino.

By the turn of the century Pullman tourist cars with most of the comforts of the Palace Cars but less ornate of decor were carrying thousands of students, school teachers and tourists of modest means through the summer months in the Rockies. *(Santa Fe Railroad.)*

From the river to the rim of the Royal Gorge of the Arkansas is 1550 feet straight up, and for many years the Rio Grande included open observation cars in its trains at this point because from no angle could passengers see clear to the top through the windows of conventional coaches or Pullmans. *(Rio Grande.)*

More, perhaps, than any other railroad on the continent, the Rio Grande's operations have been conducted against a backdrop of perpendicular landscape, rushing torrents and in a series of parks, passes, canyons and river-carved ravines that have been ballrooms for the elements. Much of its trackage is, seemingly, straight up, and its trains snake their way along mountain shelves and above abysses that would dizzy the proverbial mountain goat. One of the identifying landfalls of the Rio Grande for many years was Castle Gate, a straightened hatchway into Utah, shown at the left in morning mists and as a double header freight breasts its neatly ballasted iron. Below: Train No. 5, the *Exposition Flyer* with nine cars and No. 1205 running helper emerges from Tunnel 29 on the eastern approach to the Moffat. The Rio Grande tunnels between Denver and the summit have been compared to a monstrous arch of flying buttresses holding in its place the escarpment of the continental cordillera. *(Left: Rio Grande; Below: R. H. Kindig.)*

Rolling smoothly for a classic portrait of merchandise transport behind articulated No. 3614 is the Rio Grande's westbound *Ute*, one of the oldest of name freights, as it whistles off from Pine Cliff, Colorado, in the summer of 1941. Below is the silhouette of Tunnel No. 2 at Plainview as seen from the rear platform of one of the carrier's black painted all-steel cabooses bound downgrade toward Denver. *(Above: Henry R. Griffiths, Jr.; Below: Rocky Mountain Railroad Photos: Richard F. Lind.)*

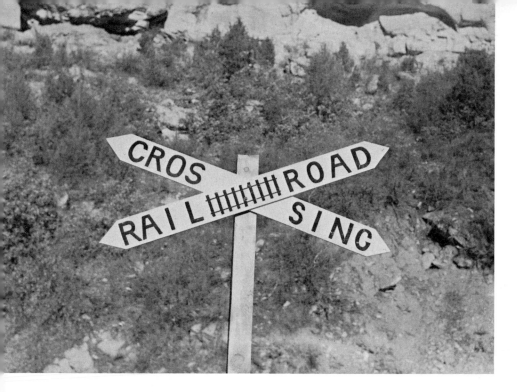

For the benefit of illiterate peasants in southwestern Colorado and those who read no English, Rio Grande crossing signs contain a pictured track as well as the conventional written legend. *(Charles Clegg.)*

Framed between signals controlling traffic through the Moffat Tunnel, Rio Grande No. 1512 pauses at East Portal while the tallowpot sands his flues after a helper run up the hill. *(Rocky Mountain Railroad Photos: Neal Miller.)*

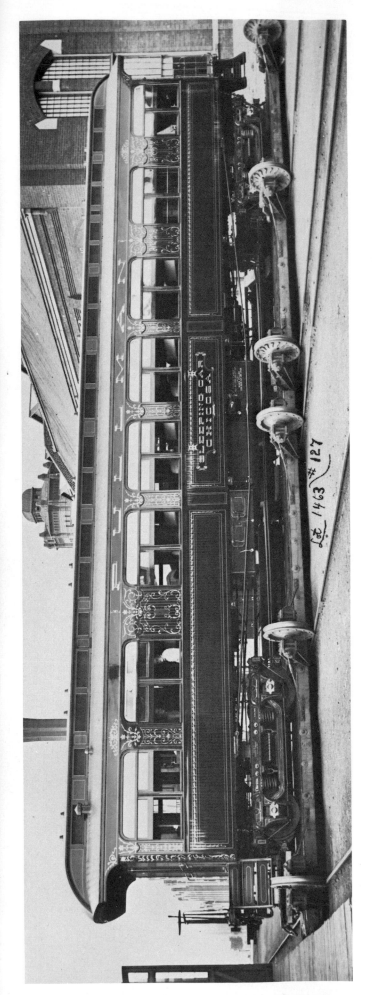

Dating from the *belle epoque* of carbuilding in the nineties were the open end Pullman sleeper *Chicosa* and the gleaming diner *San Juan* assigned to the earliest standard gauge runs between Denver and Salt Lake in the nineties. *(Above: Pullman Standard; Below: Arthur D. Dubin Collection.)*

In the heyday of the ten wheelers, the year 1900 saw the Rio Grande's No. 534 pose in Denver yards with its crew, whose persons might or might not inspire confidence in passengers, while below No. 536 in the same year awaits a highball to move out with *The Trans-Continental, San Francisco, Butte & Portland Express*, surely one of the longest train names ever to appear in *The Official Guide*. *(Two Photos: R. H. Kindig Collection.)*

This superb shot of narrow gauge steam in action against a theatrical backdrop of summer clouds was made of Train No. 425 headed by No. 475 by Richard B. Jackson on the Santa Fe run just south of Espanola in 1940. Amateurs of narrow gauge operations were specially fond of the Chili Line for its small trains and atmosphere of day before yesterday, here admirably captured by a dedicated photographer.

The Rio Grande's narrow gauge Chili Line between Antonito and Santa Fe, so-called for the brilliant hued chili beans dried by the natives along the right of way, was a magnificent and picturesque archaism as long as it lasted. A daily mixed ran each way over its 126 miles of rugged terrain pausing at mid-point at Embudo, whose depot, shown above, was a landmark in the countryside. It was famous as the handiwork of a station agent who, displeased by its original frame construction, had been moved to build an entire new facade of river stones before the management learned of his esthetic improvements. The revised structure proved so substantial, however, that the Rio Grande was happy to let it stand as a permanent memorial to the man of train orders and waybills. Below, No. 475 appears again, this time meeting its opposite number at Embudo in 1940. (*Two Photos: Otto C. Perry.*)

The downgrading that was the inevitable fate of even the finest luxury equipment is suggested by the beautiful Rio Grande Western diner *Colorado* as it came from the builder and a dining car of coeval vintage assigned to the Salt Lake City wrecking train many years later. *(Above: Pullman Standard; Below: Everett L. DeGolyer Collection.)*

By the opening years of the nineties, dining on the steamcars in the Far West was an event in the lives of travelers who, barely twenty years earlier, had been obliged to accept the dubious fare and non-extant service at eating houses along the stage routes. When the Rio Grande standard gauge diners from Pullman and Barney & Smith went into service between Denver and Salt Lake, eating, as is suggested from this animated drawing, was serious business and the diner patrons showed small sign of malnutrition. Game was still abundant in the West; prairie chicken, quail, venison and antelope appeared on all menus; champagne and claret were the suggested breakfast wines, and the Rio Grande was already famed for its fresh mountain trout that have been the hallmark of its diners ever since. No contemporary artist for the picture press of the time could resist having an Indian aboard his train.

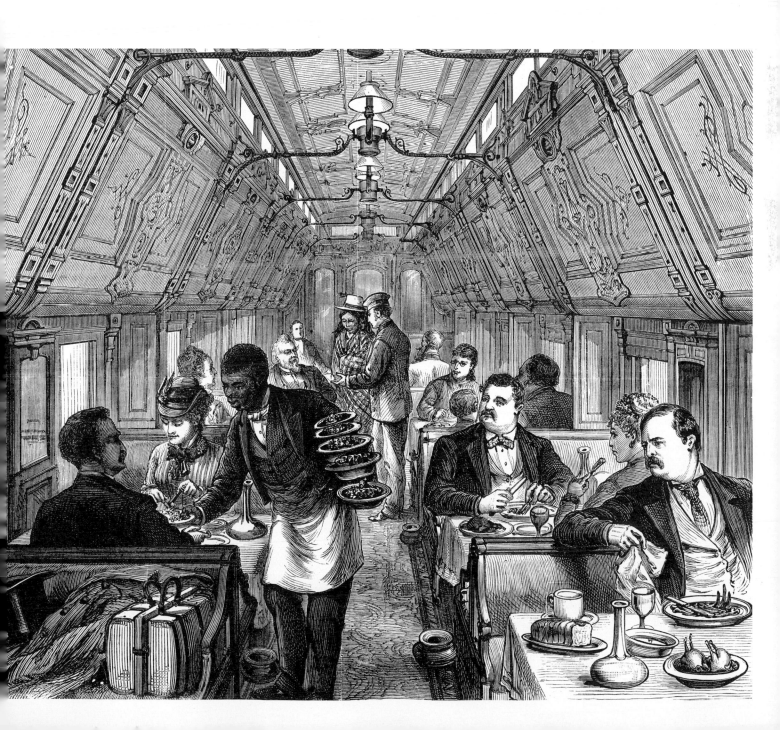

Perhaps the most photographed of all trains in The West of steam was the narrow gauge *San Juan* on the Alamosa-Durango run in its final years. On this page it is shown *(top)* topping Cumbres Pass westbound; *(center)* running combined with the Santa Fe train out of Antonito in 1939, and *(bottom)* up Cumbres Pass near Cresco, June 1950.

A
Portfolio
of
Portraits
by
Otto Perry

Here again the *San Juan* runs
down Toltec Gorge *(top);*
poses pastorally near Lobato,
New Mexico, and *(bottom)*
rolls off the waterlevel miles
in the same vicinage in 1941.
All the photographs on both
these pages are from the camera of Otto Perry, a devoted
chronicler of the cars and
engines in their every Colorado aspect.

"Now I lay me down to sleep."

"Boys," said Mr. Douglass, "the porters will soon make up the beds, and I want you to see how ingeniously everything is arranged."

Here is what the porter did:

He stood straddling on two seats, turned a handle in the top of a panel, and pulled down the upper berth. It moved on hinges, and was supported after the manner of a book-shelf by two chains that ran on spring pulleys.

Then he fastened two strong wire ropes from the upper to the lower berths.

"What's that for?" asked Harry.

"To prevent passengers from being smashed flat by the shutting up of the berth," Philip answered, after a moment's puzzling over the question.

"You can have the upper berth, Philip," said Harry, impressively. "It's better ventilated than the lower, they say; but I don't mind that."

Meanwhile the porter took from the upper berth two pieces of mahogany, cut to almost fill the space between the tops of the seats and the side roofs of the car. The edges were grooved, and slid along upon and closely fitted the top of the seat and a molding on the roof. These side-pieces were next fastened by a brass bolt pushed up from the end of the seat-back.

Then the bed-clothing (kept by day in the lower seats and behind the upper panel) was spread on the upper berth, and the mattress of the lower berth was made up from the seat-cushions, supported upon short slats set from seat to seat. . . .

To finish his work, the porter hung a thick pair of curtains on hooks along a horizontal pole, and then affixed a long plush strip to which were fastened large gilt figures four inches high — the number of the section. (*"The Century World's Fair Book For Boys and Girls,"* by Tudor Jenks. 1893.)

By the mid-eighties through service on the diminutive sleepers between Denver and Salt Lake was so accepted a mode of travel that an artist assigned to depict interesting aspects of life on the cars could come up with nothing more sensational for *Harper's* than the drawings opposite depicting life in the wash rooms, by now a recognized hazard of American travel, and a little girl saying her prayers before going to sleep in a narrow gauge berth.

ourists to the American West in the nineteenth century were there in large measure to experience the aspects of nature so widely advertised by earlier pioneers and by the guide books whose multiplicity testified to their demand. Visitors to Colorado before the coming of the motor car wanted to experience the soaring mountains, the yawning abysses, the foaming rivers and broad mountain uplands which Coloradoans called "parks" at first hand. To the carriers of the time, the tourist trade was solicited as an important element of railroad economy. Many through trains and all excursion specials of the time and place carried open observation cars of one sort or another, and as nice a one as could be asked could be fashioned (*left*) simply by cutting off a conventional coach at the window level.

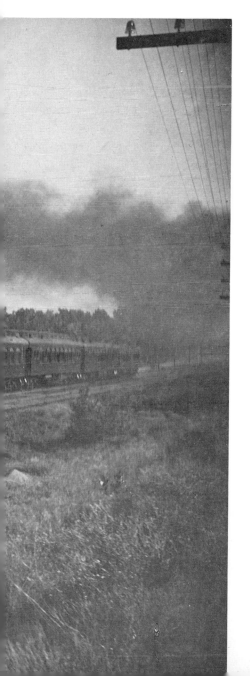

In the heyday of the tourist trade, the Rio Grande made a fine thing out of the scenery and setting along its right of way with the ascent over Marshall Pass as the starred attraction in this somewhat idealized drawing. When the *Scenic Limited* started its first run out of Denver, westbound it was powered by a Vauclain compound as depicted at the left. (*Two Photos: Robert Le Massena Collection.*)

— 225

The all-Pullman *Scenic Limited* as it posed outside the Burnham shops in 1906 *(above and opposite)* included the combine *Probus*, dining car *St. Charles*, coach *Greenfield*, sleeper *Los Gatos* and observation car *Tryphosa* and was the pride of the road, despite the mutations of time as evidenced by a cracked plate. *(Two Photos: Rio Grande Railroad.)*

Below is a rare action shot of No. 701 at speed in 1900 near Littleton on the head end of the Rio Grande's overnight run from Denver with sleepers for Creede, Grand Junction and the connections at Ogden for the Northwest. *(Western Collection, Denver Public Library.)*

The beautiful dining car *St. Charles* reflected the sumptuous taste of the first decade of the century when passengers admired fine food on the cars and the most elegant surroundings in which to consume it while passing through the Rockies. *(Arthur D. Dubin Collection.)*

Sometime in the mid-twenties, No. 779, a 4-6-0 smokes its way up the grade along the banks of Arkansas with four cars on its drawbar while (below) somewhere about 1910 an open air observation car, apparently cut down from an outmoded business car or other vehicle with an ornate platform grille, pauses for the conventional ten minutes at Hanging Bridge while the passengers absorb the majestic implications of the Royal Gorge. (Two Photos: Rio Grande Railroad.)

The year 1910, with the end of any appreciable social order still four years in the future, found the depot platform *(above)* at Grand Junction well populated with travelers awaiting an eastbound train. The uptown ticket office *(below)* in the Albany Hotel at Seventeenth and Stout, shared with the Missouri Pacific, in the same year suggested prosperity in an era of ornate architecture and bowler hats as the only thinkable attire of urban usage. Gene Fowler was a reporter on the *Denver Post*, call whisky at the Brown Palace was two bits. All was right with the world. *(Rio Grande Railroad.)*

Here is how, if you were a granddaughter of Jay Gould and married to an English title of the most exalted antiquity, you might have toured the American West on your wedding trip in 1911. The romance between Vivien Gould and plain sporting Jack Beresford of London had been the talk of two continents but Beresford, a great gentleman in his own right, but without a fortune to match the Goulds refused to press his suit until, in romantic storybook manner, he unexpectedly fell heir at once to some money and more magnificence as Lord Decies. Their wedding at St. Bartholomew's in New York on February 6, 1911 assumed near riot proportions, especially since an American patriot who resented foreign alliances had challenged Decies to a duel with a challenge beginning: "Cad that you are . . ." To recover from what was undeniably some of the most strenuous nuptials in the record, Lord and Lady Decies toured the West aboard a special train that included Missouri Pacific official car No. 2 and two head-end cars for their personal entourage. Naturally they traveled over Gould lines, the Mopac, Rio Grande and Western Pacific. In the group above Lord Decies is in the center, his Lady stands between her husband and Frank A. Wadleigh, Passenger Traffic Manager of the Rio Grande. *(Two Photos: Rio Grande Railroad; George L. Beam.)*

Although the photographic files of the Rio Grande fail to disclose the specific occasion upon which this picture was taken at the Hanging Bridge in the Royal Gorge of the Arkansas in 1911 of a group around the platform of the Rio Grande business car *Frederick*, the identity of two of its members suggest finance at its most exalted imaginable level. In the cloth hat, black mustache and high stiff collar in the center is Otto H. Kahn, a rising young partner in the all-powerful Wall Street firm of Kuhn-Loeb, much interested in Western railroad securities in the post-Harriman era, and in the beard and long traveling coat is the no lesser magnifico, Commodore Arthur Curtiss James, heavily involved in the railroads of James J. Hill, President of the Western Pacific, and an immense investor in the Utah copper resources being at the time exploited by Colonel Daniel C. Jackling and the various Brothers Guggenheim. The train was routed over the Rio Grande as "The Kahn Special" as is attested by the marker flags on *Frederick* and it is safe to venture that the conversations aboard it were in nine figures and would have rocked foundations of banking houses in two continents had they been available to repetition. At Kahn's right, in charge of the multi-million dollar cargo is Frank A. Wadleigh, the railroad's passenger representative and envoy on occasions of such epic import. (*Rio Grande Railroad: George L. Beam.*)

The Gunnison Diversion Tunnel, 5.8 miles in length and said at the time it was constructed in 1909 to be the longest irrigation tunnel in the world, was built by the U. S. Reclamation Service at a cost of $3,000,000 as part of the Uncompahgre Reclamation Project. It diverts 1,300 cubic feet of water from the Gunnison River a second under Vernal Mesa to the Uncompahgre Valley. Above is a view of the narrow gauge Presidential Special which, in 1909, brought President Taft to open the tunnel itself. About to leave eastbound for Salida, the engine is No. 168 followed by a coach and three business cars "P," "B," and "N." (U. S. Bureau of Reclamation, John W. Maxwell.)

In 1903 President Theodore Roosevelt made safari throughout the American West with special emphasis on Colorado where, at various times, his Presidential Special rolled over the Rio Grande, the Colorado Midland and the Colorado Springs & Cripple Creek District. Here he is shown during a pause at Pueblo where he spied a Civil War veteran in the crowd and hailed him: "You who wear the button . . ." (*Lorraine Dexter Collection.*)

232 —

In the below photograph the Presidential Special with the observation car *Rocket* is spotted at Glenwood Springs where an age of electronic sophistication might view with amusement the communications between the chief executive and the outer world when a single telegraphic circuit sufficed to keep the pulse of an unhurried and well ordered era. At the left, a little old lady achieves celluloid immortality by facing the camera as the Roosevelt train is pulling out of Colorado Springs. (*Above: Lorraine Dexter Collection; Below: Western Collection, Denver Public Library.*)

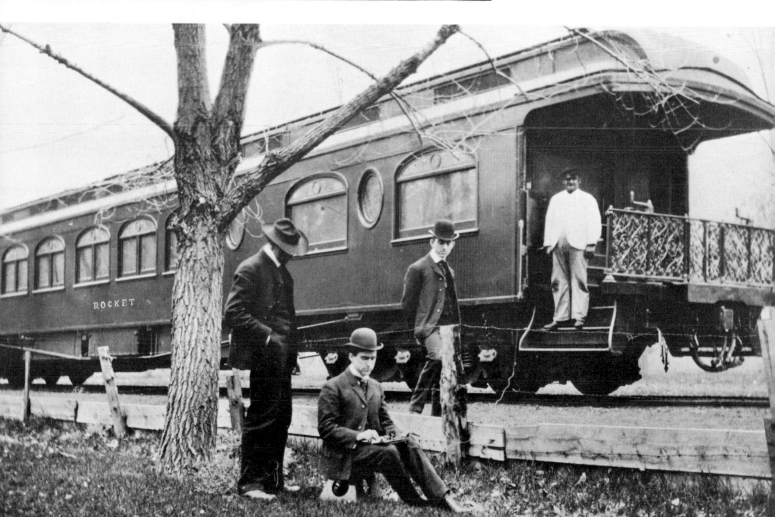

About the year 1910 this Rio Grande diner was elaborately decorated for some special run or festival occasion and its interior preserved as a souvenir of good times aboard the cars in years gone by. On the page opposite are the front and rear ends of the *Panoramic Limited* as it was about to leave Salt Lake on June 2, 1924 and recorded for posterity by the lens of Harry Shipler. *(Above: Rio Grande Railroad; Opposite, Two Photos: Shipler, Salt Lake.)*

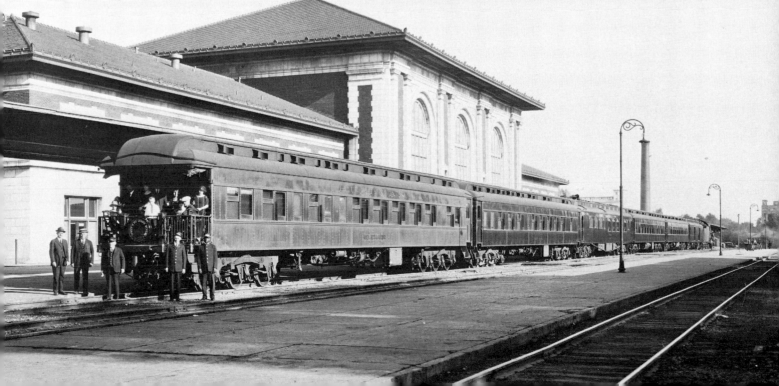

At Tunnel No. 29 on the Denver & Salt Lake section of the run, the *Panoramic* lived up to the implications of its name rolling smokily behind a Rio Grande 4-6-4 as helper and a 2-8-2 road engine. (*R. H. Kindig.*)

Forerunner of the *Exposition Flyer* on the Denver-Ogden run in the thirties was the crack *Panoramic,* Trains No. 4 and 5, with coaches, sleepers, diner and open platform observation-lounge car. It carried a San Francisco Pullman for interchange with the Western Pacific at Salt Lake and another for the Southern Pacific's *Overland Limited* at Ogden. Landscape at Pine Cliff *(below)* lives up to the road's slogan: "Through the Rockies, Not Around Them." *(Two Photos: Rio Grande Railroad.)*

As the *Scenic Limited* rolled down the Colorado years to become one of the great train names of the West, its observation cars changed with the times. Above is one of them with all the amenities of the thirties including a radio on which passengers might hear "Amos an' Andy" and other classics of the period. Below, a somewhat earlier car *Eagle Canyon* is switched in Denver yards. On the page opposite the *Limited* gets into its stride double headed for Tennessee Pass over the profile of a venerable favorite on the observation end, *Royal Gorge*, here shown with the drumhead insigne of the *Panoramic* on its platform rail. (*Above and lower opposite: Rio Grande Railroad; Right: Otto Perry; Below: R. H. Kindig Collection.*)

Comparatively modern operations out of Durango are embodied in the photographs on these two pages, that at the left showing the Rio Grande's venerable No. 476, fitted with an old time oil headlight for appearance in a film with a railroad setting, emerging from the deep cut at Rockwood on the Silverton run, and No. 453 doing routine switching in Durango yards for its portrait in light and shadow against the flawless backdrop of a summer sky in the San Juans. *(Left: Johnny Krause; Below: Gordon S. Crowell.)*

Posed at milepost 333 on the Cerro Grade May 27, 1949 is the last train of Crested Butte coal. Engine No. 361 is hauling its maximum rated tonnage, three gondolas of eleven tons each with twenty-five ton loads plus a fourteen ton caboose. *(John W. Maxwell Photo; Below: Otto Perry.)*

When subjects were not available to his special train, shown with its photographic studio and darkroom car on Mule Shoe Curve, the Rio Grande's photographer William H. Jackson ventured into the wilderness with a horse-drawn darkroom in which to sensitize his glass plate negatives. *(Two Photos: Western Collection, Denver Public Library.)*

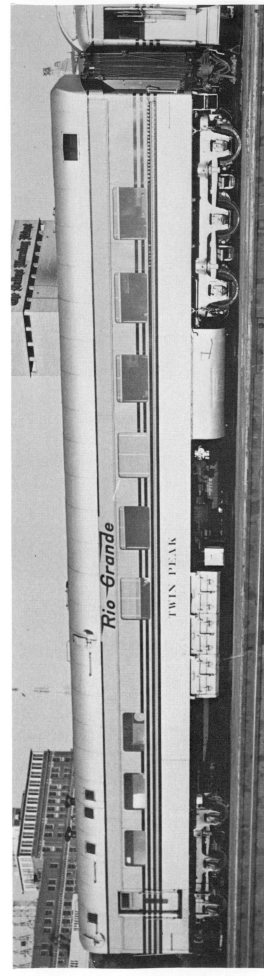

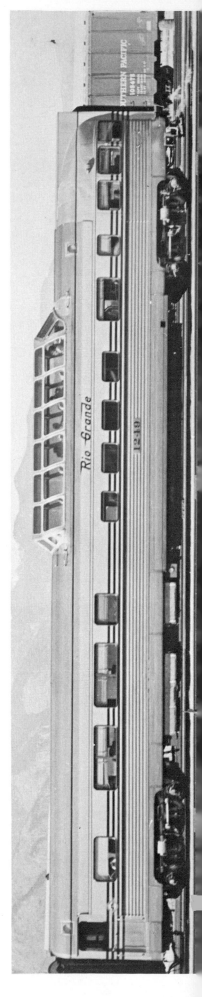

The Pullman-built standard open section and drawing room sleeping car *Penalosa* was assigned to the second version of the Denver–Salt Lake overnight *Prospector*. The streamlined diner *Twin Peaks* was photographed against a background of Dallas, Texas, by Everett De Golyer when it ran south over the Forth Worth line with an Air Force Academy special out of Colorado Springs in 1960. *(Three Photos: Everett De Golyer.)*

Originally built for the Chesapeake & Ohio's ill-fated *Chessie*, the vista dome observation-chair car No. 1249 was purchased in 1949 for the *Royal Gorge*.

In sunshine and in storm the standard construction observation car *Granite Cañon* embodied the grand manner of another time and was a favorite with the membership of the Rocky Mountain Railroad Club whenever a fan trip was mounted. Above, it braves the elements at Boulder during an excursion in February 1951; below, every prospect pleases as the long train pauses and poses at the East Portal of the Moffat under summer suns a year later. *(Two Photos: Everett De Golyer Collection.)*

Although, as on railroads everywhere, unusual or exotic equipment is increasingly rare around Salt Lake, special equipment now and then makes an appearance as in the case of the tool car of the Rio Grande's wrecking train shown above and the private car *The Virginia City,* owned and occupied by the authors of this book on their editorial occasions in its preparation. *The Virginia City* is shown attached to *The Prospector* ready to roll to Denver behind the business car of General Manager L. H. Hale. The tool car, a symbol of fallen greatness, was once the private varnish of tycoon Harry Blackmer and won by him from a former owner in a poker game. It was partially destroyed by fire after passing to the estate of a Rio Grande business car and remains as probably the only tool car extant with high speed passenger trucks. *(Above: Everett De Golyer; Below: Lucius Beebe.)*

When this photograph of a Spartan track inspection motor car was unearthed from pre-Cambrian deposits in the Rio Grande's files at Denver, it was disowned, and that instanter, by the office of the superintendent of motive power and the denial followed by further repudiation by operations officials confronted with the roadbed it occupies. Its baling wire improvisation, however, primitive braking system and running board tank for extra water for the radiator speak for a Yankee genius at its most effulgent, probably at a time when the railroad's finances could stand improvement. (*Rio Grande Railroad.*)

On June 16, 1934, the Denver & Rio Grande Western Railroad achieved what had long been the dream of Denver people, only partly fulfilled by the original Arkansas River route, a direct line to Salt Lake and an outlet thereby to all points of the Pacific coast. The means was the completion of the so-called Dotsero Cutoff running from the Denver & Salt Lake mainline at Bond and joining the Rio Grande rails across Tennessee Pass at Dot-sero, a thirty-six mile short line that relegated the Arkansas River route to a secondary position and saved 175 miles detour. To celebrate the opening of the life-saving cutoff, the Rio Grande sent three twelve-car, double-headed specials up from Denver and here, glad with bunting and carrying white on its smoke-box, is one of them with No. 1161 specially scoured and silvered with graphite running as helper. *(Otto C. Perry.)*

Another special with No. 1177 on the head end and twelve cars on the road engine's drawbar carried a contingent of railroad executives, civic dignitaries, newspapermen and the conventional free-loaders with white flags at the smoke-boxes of its coupled motive power, while below is a general view of the gala crowds which turned out for the occasion in holiday attire to hear spellbinders praise "the last major railroad construction in the continental United States." *(Above: Otto C. Perry; Below: Rio Grande Railroad.)*

THE DENVER & SALT LAKE RAILROAD

LTHOUGH THE combined trackage of the Denver & Rio Grande and the Rio Grande Western provided Denver with its own, home-owned railroad connection to the West, the Royal Gorge route was fantastically indirect, and empire builders in the Queen City of the Plains still dreamed of one that might eliminate the Rio Grande's 175 mile detour to the south. One of these empire builders was David Moffat, a gold rush pioneer of '59 who had parlayed modest success as a small shopkeeper into a considerable fortune from the mines of Creede, Leadville and Cripple Creek. "A dull, patient, acquisitive man," as David Lavender has called him, Moffat had been President of the Denver & Rio Grande to give him railroading experience and, in 1902, he went on record with a resolve to head straight across the mountains to Salt Lake with something he called the Denver, Northwestern & Pacific Railroad. Nobody else wanted to share the financial risk and there was even active opposition from the Union Pacific, so Moffat swore he would sink his last dime in the project if necessary. It proved to be and he died broke.

The Denver & Salt Lake, as was the road's name by the time, although nobody ever called it anything but The Moffat Line, headed up the escarpment of the Front Range at Coal Creek and ran through thirty-one tunnels of varying depth in a single twenty mile stretch on the way to James Peak. Moffat planned a two and a half mile tunnel under James Peak, but by this time his resources were running dry and the four percent grades were surveyed over Rollins protected by two solid miles of snowsheds under which the rails ran and entire communities of railroaders lived during the winter.

Within a few months of each other in 1911, three major events affected the destinies of the Moffat: the end of track reached the mountain community of Craig, Colorado, 232 miles west of Denver but less than half way to its proposed Utah terminal, David Moffat ran out of money and then David Moffat fell down dead. The railroad stopped dead in its tracks and to this day has never gone a foot farther west.

But in 1922 Denver's perpetual water shortage reached crisis dimensions and engineers proposed a tunnel to tap the vast resources of the Western Slope. To enlarge the tunnel project to include the by now staggering railroad was no great step and the two combined tunnels, one for water and the other for rails, were named for David Moffat. The six mile bore cost $18,000,000 but it eliminated for all time the Corona crossing and twenty-three miles of its track. The running time of passenger trains over the Rollins was seven hours; through the new tunnel was twelve minutes.

This massive achievement in the bowels of James Peak gave the management of the Rio Grande ideas, and surveys were commenced to run a new line from west of the Moffat to a point on the old mainline that should eliminate the long and bothersome jog down to Pueblo and its 175 additional miles. The so-called Dotsero Cutoff running from Bond on the Moffat to Dotsero near Glenwood Springs did just this and, beginning in 1935 the Rio Grande began routing its fastest passenger trains and freight via the direct line over the once inconsequential Moffat. Over its rails ran the old *Panoramic*, then the *Exposition Flyer* and finally the *California Zephyr* and the *Prospector* of today.

A generation has come into being that never saw David Moffat and knows him only as a name, but sentimental Coloradoans remember the original Moffat Line with affection and it is enshrined in the Rocky Mountain Valhalla of departed railroads, one with the South Park, the Colorado Midland, the Uinta and the Rio Grande Southern.

No other Rocky Mountain railroad, not even the South Park at Boreas or the Colorado Midland at Hagerman had greater snowfall to overcome and combat than the Moffat encountered at the 11,660 foot elevation of Rollins Pass at Corona where snowsheds, roundhouses and every other installation of the railroad sometimes disappeared under the snow for weeks on end in bad winters. A sketch artist's version of one of the Corona sheds appears above; below, one of the Denver & Salt Lake's celebrated Mallets-of-all-work crosses the Coal Creek road below Tunnel No. 1 in a snowfall unmarred by wheels on the highway surface. (*Rocky Mountain Railroad Photos: Neal Miller.*)

In 1905 the town of Arrow was the end of track for the Salt Lake line and construction workers were the most admired and admiring patrons of the saloons, gaming rooms and bagnios which were the town's only appreciable industries. Later there was a brisk trade in lumber, but in 1905 it was a howling wilderness of frontier tumults which experts in such matters said compared favorably with the town of Grants when the South Park was building and which challenged all comers in the wickedness sweepstakes. Before the dining room shown in this photograph was built, its site was occupied by a vast mud-

hole and drunks tossed out of the saloons on the crest of the hill could always attract an audience if they rolled far enough to be engulfed in it. By the time this photograph was taken with Dave Moffat's private car at the end of the train and a group of polite ladies by the track, the end of track had gone on and Arrow basked in comparative respectability. Edward Bollinger in his full dress biography of the Moffat, "Rails That Climb," devotes an entire chapter to the gaudy iniquities of Arrow in its gunfighting days. (*Western Collection, Denver Public Library.*)

The Moffat road in various aspects: at the top No. 406 and 209 cross Coal Creek bridge with a westbound freight of fifty-three cars; center: No. 409 heads up Train No. 12, the overnight mixed from Craig to Denver, with an express car, baggage car, tourist Pullman sleeper and assortment of merchandise cars ahead of the caboose; bottom: a short way above Coal Creek No. 302 hauls the westbound daily passenger run from Denver to Craig in the summer of 1939. (*Three Photos: R. H. Kindig.*)

Back in the year 1910 when action photography was less common than it was to become, No. 300 running with a single coach still bore the lettering on its tender of the original Denver, North-Western & Pacific. Thirty years later (*right*) Denver & Salt Lake motive power was still characteristically compact and angular. (*Below: Buchwalter Collection: Colorado State Historical Society; Right: Lucius Beebe.*)

Railroad conscious Colorado moppets took a more sanguinary view of the D&SL than some financiers and admired to place pennies on the track for No. 300 to flatten.

Rarely in 1910 was a photographer on the scene of an accident in a matter of moments after its occurrence, but when Denver, North-Western & Pacific's No. 302 was derailed on the helper end of a double-headed passenger run above Plainview someone was on hand with a camera even before the passengers had gone away. "This is a hell of a way to run a railroad" are the obvious sentiments of the patron in the foreground, making his way from the scene of disaster luggage in hand. *(Buchwalter Collection, Colorado State Historical Society.)*

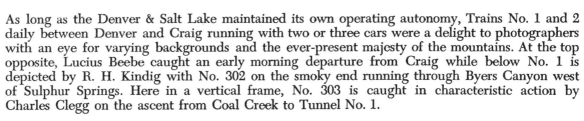

As long as the Denver & Salt Lake maintained its own operating autonomy, Trains No. 1 and 2 daily between Denver and Craig running with two or three cars were a delight to photographers with an eye for varying backgrounds and the ever-present majesty of the mountains. At the top opposite, Lucius Beebe caught an early morning departure from Craig while below No. 1 is depicted by R. H. Kindig with No. 302 on the smoky end running through Byers Canyon west of Sulphur Springs. Here in a vertical frame, No. 303 is caught in characteristic action by Charles Clegg on the ascent from Coal Creek to Tunnel No. 1.

— 257

In 1906 Pullman outshopped the car *Marcia* for the Denver, Northwestern & Pacific from Plan 2185B, and there went into service an official car that was to know the tread of Colorado railroad names from its original owner David Moffat, to the occupancy of Al Perlman, the Rio Grande's brilliant general manager at the time of the 1941 war. Far from elaborate in decor, *Marcia* provided a snug retreat from Rocky Mountain winters and slept and fed its occupants in a single salon of general assembly instead of the separate dining and observation rooms of more elaborate practice. While many *aficionados* of carbuilding regard *Marcia's* period as the *belle epoque* of leaded window gothic and graceful elegance of decor, there is no doubt that the Rio Grande's No. 100 dating from the Pullman twenties was better adapted both to privacy and the higher speeds of a more mature age of railroading. It was the favorite business car of Judge Wilson McCarthy. *(Four Photos: Pullman Standard.)*

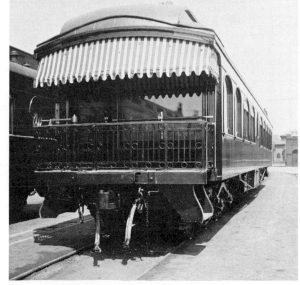

— 259

As recently as 1907 a snow blockade on the Denver, Northwestern & Pacific was important enough to make the front cover of *Leslie's* as shown opposite. On this page two photographs by Colorado's most devoted historian, R. H. Kindig, depict *(above)* the Denver and Salt Lake's No. 404 as it appeared after the line's merger as Rio Grande No. 1224, while below the *Rocky Mountain New's* snow excursion in 1939 chuffs through Sulphur Springs with D. & S. L. Mallet No. 203 for motive power. *(Page Opposite: Western Collection, Denver Public Library.)*

LESLIE'S
ILLUSTRATED
WEEKLY

A MIDWINTER BLOCKADE IN THE ROCKY MOUNTAINS.

HARDY RESCUERS BEARING FOOD SUPPLIES UP RUGGED AND SLIPPERY SLOPES TO THE STARVING PASSENGERS OF A
TRAIN STALLED FOR DAYS BY A TREMENDOUS SNOW-STORM.—*Drawn by G. W. Peters.*

Here No. 204 with headlight burning emerges at prudent speed from tunnel No. 4 bound downgrade to Denver in 1941. (R. H. Kindig)

Opposite is an action photograph from the Early Ordovician era of operations on the Salt Lake Line when it took two engines working steam to the limit of their boiler capacities to hike four cars over the grade around Yankee Doodle Lake with the snowy slopes of James Peak for an identifying background of a scene that could be nowhere but in the high places of the Shining Mountains. *(Rio Grande Railroad.)*

Before the Moffat road achieved access to Denver Union Station, it was forced to maintain its own terminal in downtown Denver where, on parallel stub tracks No. 1 and a special excursion train are shown loading passengers while a van for Adams Express is drawn up at the left. *(Western Collection: Denver Public Library.)*

The eerie subterranean quality of life at the Moffat line's route over Rollins Pass is suggested below by Corona station completely covered with snowsheds where a troglodyte dog and cavedwelling passengers await a down train to Denver beside the main line. At the right is a map of the Moffat road projecting westward off the margin although it stopped in fact for good at Craig. (*Two Pictures: Western Collection, Denver Public Library.*)

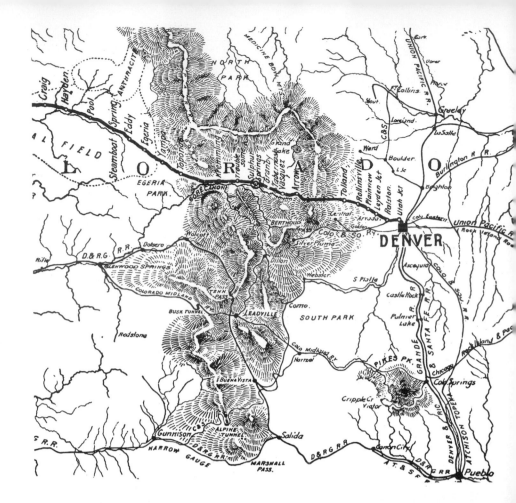

The Denver & Salt Lake had the distinction in its years of independent operations of being one of the few short lines in the record to maintain sleeper service, let alone own Pullman equipment. The tourist sleeper shown below was for a time maintained in overnight service in the Denver-Craig mixed train where, although its Pullman antecedents were undeniable, it could scarcely be termed a luxury conveyance. "I rode the sleeper once and recall that it was uncommonly noisy," recalls Richard Kindig. "There was considerable coach traffic getting on and off at all hours of the night with doors slamming, people talking, clumping around in heavy boots and the inevitable jerk every time the engine took up slack to start the mixed train." More aristocratic was the daytime run shown above in Byers Canyon west of Sulphur Springs with somebody's scrupulously maintained business car on the rear end. *(Above: R. H. Kindig; Below: Arthur D. Dubin Collection.)*

On September 2, 1904 and bearing on its tender the insigne of the Denver, Northwestern & Pacific, the Moffat Road's No. 300 *(below)* had been on the head end of the first three car passenger train over Rollins Pass. George Barnes, later destined to be a local celebrity in railroad circles, was conductor, A. F. Norburry engineer on that distant date and memorable day. Here it poses for its portrait forty years and many miles later. *(Two Photos: Everett De Golyer Collection.)*

The Moffat Road's venerable No. 303, shown at the top of the opposite page paused on line to take on passengers, rolled down the years as a familiar institution to residents at Pine Cliff, Tolland, Tabernash and Steamboat Springs. Here it is shown making easy work of the stiff grade between Coal Creek and Tunnel No. 1 early on a June morning in 1945. No. 303 is gone now, swept away in the universal calamity of Diesel and changing times, but to the perceptive ear of true believers, the sparkling sound of its passing can still be heard in Gore Canyon or at Plainview, its remembered whistle one with the ghostly sound of Roland's horn in the pass at Roncevalles. *(Lucius Beebe.)*

From the time when the Moffat road's construction into the howling wilderness of the high passes engaged the attention of sketch artists to the frontier shack towns that followed in its wake *(above)* down to the closing years of the carrier's independent existence, runs on the road were characterized by a special and resolute chunki-ness of motive power designed for slow ascents over staggering grades. In the below frame No. 118, a 2-8-0, and No. 207, a 2-6-6-0 true Mallet work steam for a west-bound extra at Ralston with twenty-six cars in 1947. *(R. H. Kindig.)*

Once it became part of the operating economy of the Rio Grande, traces of the Moffat road as a once autonomous carrier rapidly disappeared. Cars, motive power and other properties soon carried the insigne of the all-pervading Rio Grande and the last connecting link with the Salt Lake's past was the *Yampa Valley Mail* on the Denver-Craig run in Diesel, shown here against a mountain backdrop to dwarf the mobile occasions of man. *(Rocky Mountain Railroad Photos: Richard F. Lind.)*

Riding the right hand cushions of No. 3604, the Rio Grande's eagle eye controlled 131,800 pounds of tractive force riding on sixty-seven inch drivers activated by 200 pounds of steam pressure exerted through 21 x 36 inch cylinders. Massive, versatile and superbly utilitarian, the engines of its class ran in freight and passenger service, with or without a wide variety of helper engines, in sleet and storm, sunshine and darkness, at elevations never less than the mile above sea level of Denver yards. Godlike at the throttles, their drivers rode always at Olympian altitudes. *(Rio Grande Railroad.)*

MAINLINE OF THE ROCKIES

HE TWO great and determining factors in the character of the Denver & Rio Grande Western Railroad, as it was eventually to be known, were its failure to achieve the Southwest through Raton Pass and, of course, the Rocky Mountains themselves. The success of the Santa Fe in the Raton accomplished two things at once, a toughening of the baby railroad's will to live in a competitive world, and its diversion in a westerly direction. It had nowhere else to go.

Only a few weeks had elapsed from the fracas around Trinidad and there was still an odor of arnica and bandages about the Rio Grande when it was involved in another and even bloodier contretemps with that old debbil Santa Fe. Swollen with confidence, the State Street moguls building out of Kansas announced that they were going to continue aggression in Rio Grande territory by building through Pueblo and up the narrow Canyon of the Arkansas to the rich traffic of Leadville. Had it succeeded in this patently piratical adventure into the Colorado heartland, the Rio Grande would be today no more than a memory, one with the Gilpin County Tram, the Georgetown Loop, the Rio Grande Southern's trestles at Ophir and all the other ghosts of Colorado's transport yesterdays.

For a time it looked as though the cards again favored mutton-chopped Cyrus Holliday. Cañon City, up-river from Pueblo, had also been jilted by General Palmer when it had wooed the narrow gauge and was willing to welcome anybody at all who would survey and grade a railroad into its midst. Cañon City merchants, savoring the double pleasure of aiding the Santa Fe and discomfiting, as they thought, the rascally General Palmer, turned out in force with shovels and mule teams to help Ray Morley and the myrmidons of the Santa Fe.

Legend holds that Morley, apprised of the news that General Palmer's men had been alerted to the peril and were already grading west out of Pueblo, leapfrogged ahead of their railhead by a desperate Message-to-Garcia ride to Cañon City in which he rode a blooded horse to death and finished the anabasis, panting and near collapse, on foot just in time to alert the citizens and sound the tocsin of alarm. David Lavender, official historian of the time, made shrewd inquiry into the matter and established that Morley had ridden a fine black stallion (the only point on which the two versions of the saga agree) at prudent pace and achieved Cañon City mounted and in good wind.

So much for the stuff of legend. The Rio Grande and the Santa Fe were again joined in battle and this time the baby railroad's survival was at stake. It may be, too, that the Santa Fe was overconfident. Part of the charm of the railroad wars of the nineteenth century was the moral fervor which characterized embattled tycoons bent on stealing everything in sight. Contestants for a promising franchise smote the opposition hip and thigh while calling on God to vindicate their larceny like medieval barons in a boundary dispute. Both the Santa Fe and the Rio Grande called on heaven to witness the righteousness of their causes.

General Palmer did better. He called on the courts of Colorado and eventually the United States.

The battle for the Canyon of the Arkansas will not bear detailed recital here. The legal marches and countermarches of the opponents, their cavalry charges and courtroom ambuscades fill voluminous bales and packing cases in Denver's halls of justice to this day. All through the Rocky Mountain region it snowed summonses, and writs and judgments achieved blizzard proportions. An entire generation of lawyers retired in affluence on the pickings.

Incense to the old Gods of The Mountain and a thunder of adulation to The Manitou arise from the stacks of Rio Grande motive power on the head end of a C.C.C. seventeen car special on Tennessee Pass near Malta in 1940. (R. H. Kindig.)

In the Arkansas Valley the contest assumed overtones of violence which were to provide the basis for television programs in years to come. Each side hired armies of professional plug-uglies whose zeal in a righteous cause was inflamed with every visit to the saloons where company funds flowed like water to purchase something a good deal more effective. The Santa Fe invoked pure melodrama by hiring the notorious Bat Masterson to command its army of pot-valiants who, sixty strong and recruited from the best deadfalls in Dodge City, arrived by Santa Fe special on a tight schedule that was only interrupted while Masterson paused at telegraph points to issue edicts of defiance and forecast doom and discomfiture for the enemy.

That there was a good deal of powder burned is attested by the subsequent court record where the Pueblo & Arkansas Valley Company, which was in fact the Santa Fe of Colorado, showed expenses for May, June and July of 1879 that included such items as

Cartridges furnished	$ 20.00
Colt Revolvers & Ammunition .	112.30
Arms & Ammunition,	
Miscellaneous	94.50
Payroll for W. R. Morley's Gang	$6,018.00

The newspapers of the time are full of references to the armed insurrection of the Santa Fe Railroad and the *Rocky Mountain News* commented editorially that "the only private army to be maintained in the United States was that of a Boston corporation in Colorado."

The battle was full of surprises. At one point General Palmer seemed to admit defeat and leased the entire Rio Grande system to the Santa Fe, but the deal was rescinded when a sneak court ruling appeared which awarded the rights to the Royal Gorge to the baby railroad. Court decisions mounted in favor of General Palmer and probably were reflections of the general feeling in Colorado which to a marked degree supported the Rio Grande and viewed the Santa Fe with disapprobation. Folklore flourished amidst a fine jungle growth of rumor and propaganda. A delightful fable still current to this day maintains that a loyal Rio Grande conductor charged with getting vital court evidence to Denver with a minimum of delay and lacking an engine to transport him, seized a handcar, spread the tails of his frock coat of office and was wafted down the Divide by winds favorable to General Palmer's cause.

In the end, and despite the ruffling and strutting of heavily armed badmen in the streets and saloons of Pueblo, the Santa Fe lost out on the battle front as well as in the courts when Bat Masterson, in a moment of complete duplicity, sold out to General Palmer and the Rio Grande armed forces were allowed to seize a number of depots and roundhouses which the occupying Kansas toughs failed to defend. A final blow to the Santa Fe's hopes came when Jay Gould, who at the moment was at the height of his predatory power and at war with the Union Pacific, bought heavily into General Palmer's Rio Grande holdings. What General Palmer thought of having the foremost man of disaster of his time as partner is not on record, but so powerful was Gould in the money markets of the East that the Santa Fe was unwilling to offend him and retired from the contest for control of Colorado.

By the terms of the enforced settlement between the two roads, the Rio Grande paid the Santa Fe $1,400,000 for construction already accomplished in the Royal Gorge, including the celebrated Hanging Bridge along the north wall, and promised to undertake no ventures into New Mexico. In return the Santa Fe withdrew from the Upper Arkansas Valley and with this its threat to the Leadville traffic which, while ample at the moment, would not have sufficed for another aggressively operated railroad. The Santa Fe went on to positively effulgent destinies in the direction of California and speculation is profitless as to what would have been its history had it succeeded in penetrating the Rocky Mountain area instead of the high plains of the Southwest.

The opening years of the eighties witnessed a spate of construction and negotiations in the Utah mountains and their far western slope which was to result in the ultimate achievement by the Rio Grande of a through route between Denver and Salt Lake over Marshall Pass and the Canyon of the Gunnison. In July of 1881 there was incorporated in Utah a railroad whose title rather than its geographic location held premonitions of things to come. This was the Denver & Rio Grande Western Railway, the first of several corporate entities of this approximate name, but the D. & R. G. W. of 1881 had little in common with the far-flung carrier that was ultimately to assume its nominal mantle. It was, in actual fact, a holding company incorporated to acquire a number of small, disconnected carriers in the Valley of Deseret that were already in uncoordinated operation. One of these was the Bingham Canyon & Camp Floyd Railroad which had been built to narrow gauge in 1873. Another was the Wasatch & Jordan Valley Railway, also built to three-foot gauge. The aggregate line of these two diminutive carriers was thirty-five miles and extended from Alta in the Little Cottonwood Mining District on the east of Jordan River Valley through Sandy to the Bingham Mining District to the west. Contracts were at the same time let for the construction of a line from Salt Lake City south and east toward the Colorado border, utilizing as a part of the route still a third narrow gauge short line running the fifty miles from Springville in a southeasterly direction over the Wasatch Mountains to the coal fields in Pleasant Valley. The Utah & Pleasant Valley Railway was acquired in 1882 and there began to shape up the pattern of rails, division points and location of facilities that was to constitute, in the fullness of time, an entry to Salt Lake and the entire state of Utah.

Construction connecting with the Pleasant Valley line shortly added 155 miles of rail extending from Salt Lake City to Pleasant Valley Junction, later changed to Colton, over the tough grades of Soldier Summit. This entire mileage was operated under lease to the Denver & Rio Grande Western as a detached property and shortly thereafter it was decided to build a branch from Pleasant Valley Junction along Fish Creek to a point on the original survey of the Pleasant Valley Railroad two miles north of Scofield, abandoning that portion of the U. & P. V. between the point of connection near Scofield and Clear Creek Station and thus eliminating one of the two lines over the Wasatch itself.

The following year rails were laid for a distance of an additional 175 miles from Pleasant Valley Junction to the Colorado border and north from Salt Lake City to Ogden, a distance of thirty-seven miles, which established direct connections with the Union Pacific at its Utah terminal and thence westward to California over the Central Pacific. This construction of 1883 brought to virtual completion the grand design for a through route all the way from Denver to Ogden, a distance of 772 miles and through trains were immediately placed in service over the first of the several transcontinental main lines of the Denver & Rio Grande Western Railroad. It was operated, however, as two separate companies, the Denver & Rio Grande and the Rio Grande Western, an arrangement which was to obtain for some years to come.

In the mid-eighties events conspired to force a far reaching change in the form of broadening the gauge of its main lines everywhere on the Rio Grande. Other railroads were building into the Colorado picture. The Burlington had come to Denver. The Denver, Texas & Gulf contemplated a line from Denver to Pueblo, along the very lifeline of the Rio Grande itself, and at Pueblo began building an extension that was to connect at Trinidad with the Denver & Fort Worth to form a through line connection to Texas. The Santa Fe was planning to extend its Pueblo and Arkansas Valley branch from Florence to Cañon City and also from Pueblo into Denver. The Missouri Pacific, backed by Gould financing, was racing across the Great Plains toward Pueblo from the East, and the Rock Island was building through Kansas and Nebraska and it was obvious would soon be finding a Colorado terminal. The Colorado Midland, also in the very heartland of Rio Grande territory, was building up Ute Pass out of Colorado Springs and would soon be in Buena Vista, Leadville and even Aspen. The South Park, still another rival for the mining traffic, had achieved Leadville in 1884 and was building toward Baldwin and the Crested Butte country. Another narrow gauge, the Texas & Santa Fe Northern had completed a line from Santa Fe to Espanola where it connected with the Rio Grande. With the exception of this last, all the competition was standard gauge and the time had obviously come for the Palmer road to start thinking in terms of four feet, eight and a half inches if it were to survive.

The year 1881 saw the first standard gauge construction that was eventually to extend to all the Rio Grande main line and all but a few miles of its most remote branches in the San Juan country. The trackage selected for revision was, appropriately enough, between Denver and Pueblo where the emerging competition was most dangerous and where, at the Pueblo end, the Colorado Coal & Iron smelters were fast becoming the most important single industry in the complex of heavy manufacture that was the basis of the railroad's future. The Santa Fe was already tapping the rich traffic from these furnaces when the Rio Grande undertook the experiment of laying three rails where only two had been before. The roadbed was widened, heavy curves reduced, carrying structures reinforced and new and longer cross ties were ordered and, finally, new forty pound rails were laid to produce a combined narrow and standard gauge track. The entire 119 miles to Pueblo was finished by the end of 1881 and, when placed in operation, pronounced a huge success. Standard gauge locomotives were at once ordered, the Burnham Shops largely rebuilt to accommodate their repair and servicing, and the Rio Grande emerged from its original status as the Baby Railroad into the world of broad gauge operations.

The final mileage of what was to eventually become the new mainline of the Rio Grande via Tennessee Pass and so to Red Cliff and Grand Junction was built in 1889 and 1890 and was the keystone which bound together the whole project of a standard gauge operation from Denver to the road's western terminal in Utah. It was to bypass the Gunnison route with its uncommonly picturesque landscape and narrow gauge and to contribute the final touch to making the railroad a big time carrier.

In December 1889 the rival Colorado Midland reached New Castle and the tracks of the Denver & Rio Grande for a common outlet to Grand Junction and The Rio Grande Western. Joint trackage rights were set up for the Midland and the Rio Grande rails to Rifle Creek and the Rio Grande Junction Railway Company was formed in the best tradition of railroad construction to lay the standard gauge iron from Rifle Creek to Grand Junction and it was then leased to the two proprietary companies.

From Malta west what amounted to an all-new line was laid to Red Cliff involving a tunnel 2,572 feet long at Tennessee Pass which effected a saving of 4.5 miles over the old narrow gauge survey.

The track west of Red Cliff, then three foot, was converted to standard to connect with the now existing standard gauge rails of the Rio Grande Junction Railway at Rifle Creek, and the entire stretch of track into Grand Junction was thus made available to standard operations, to remain the carrier's mainline and principal artery of traffic until the completion of the Moffat route years later.

Far to the west the standard gauging of the Rio Grande Western trackage in Utah as a preliminary to a new right of way all the way to Denver was begun in the spring of 1889. It involved extensive revision of the original survey in Price Canyon to avoid excessive curvature as well as in the desert to improve gradients and alignment. The new line required the construction of well over 100 miles of new roadbed and shortened the overall mileage between Denver and Ogden by eighteen miles.

The year 1890 saw the completion of this very considerable undertaking and the commencement of standard gauge operations between the carrier's two major terminals. It marked the dividing line in the railroad's history between pioneer days and the era of its maturity.

Gould influence in Western railroading which had already touched the Rio Grande with the kiss of operational death, did not end with the departure of Jay Gould from the scene in 1892, but was maintained at great cost to the Gould fortune by George Gould, Jay's son and principal heir, after the turn of the century.

Upon the death in 1900 of Collis Huntington, George Gould was afforded by his heirs an opportunity to purchase the Huntington, and controlling interest in what was then the greatest railroad system in the West. Gould had ample resources to have swung the deal but refrained from doing so because he felt it would be an affront to "his friend" Edward H. Harriman, a scruple his father would not for a moment have entertained and which proved almost with the speed of light to have been a misconstruction of the word friendship. The Gould-Harriman friendship existed only in George Gould's imagination as was demonstrated when Harriman picked up the control of the Southern Pacific for himself and was shortly engaged in integrating it together with Union Pacific and Oregon Steam Navigation into the magnificent property it was to become under his management.

Disillusioned and as pigheaded as they came, Gould now determined on a transcontinental railroad of his own and one that should elevate him to the club of empire builders hitherto exclusively populated by Hill, Villard, Cyrus K. Holliday and the Big Four of the Southern Pacific. Even better men than Gould, notably the Pennsylvania's boldly ambitious Tom Scott who had sold out his Texas & Pacific and with it eligibility, had found membership requirements too stiff, but George Gould was undismayed.

Already the Gould writ ran as far as Pueblo, Colorado, through the agency of the Missouri Pacific, whence its extension to the shores of Great Salt Lake was the Rio Grande. A new Gould line, the Western Pacific, would be the completing link from Salt Lake City to San Francisco that would finish an unbroken line of Gould affiliates all the way from tidewater Maryland to the Golden Gate.

When Gould told Harriman of his plan Harriman's reaction was explicit. "If you build that railroad I'll kill you."

Gould went ahead with the Western Pacific, but he had already overextended his credit in an attempt to get the Wabash into Pittsburgh over the entrenched hostility of the Pennsylvania Railroad and J. P. Morgan, and when the panic of 1907 came to a head, the Gould railroads were thrown into receivership. The New York banking firm of Kuhn-Loeb and Rockefeller interests took over the Western Pacific and the Rio Grande, and George Gould's dream of a personal transcontinental disappeared forever.

No railroad in the record of steam transport ever had so many branches as did the Rio Grande in the time of its most miscellaneous flowering, a circumstance which, in later years, was to fascinate rail fans and amateurs with the multiplicity of its operations, their inaccessible destinations and variety of motive power and rolling stock involved. The three-foot iron, selected in the original planning of General Palmer for its versatility, reached into every draw and canyon where profitable carloadings could be solicited. Often enough laid to serve a single mine or industry, they sometimes found themselves, when its economic life span was run, serving ghost towns and haunted hamlets of

yesteryear, a discovery which drew cries of admiration from antiquarians but furrowed brows in the auditing department. Nothing so quickens the pulse of the railroad amateur as a weed grown branch line to practically nowhere with a weekly mixed consist scheduled to serve the ghosts of miners and prospectors long gone and forgotten save by the archivists of the Western Collection, Denver Public Library. These impractical excursions into history endeared the Rio Grande beyond all other railroads to fans and collectors and sometimes, ironically, the operation of a ghost train to nowhere such as the Silverton run proved the best paying operation per passenger mile on the carrier's time card, dwarfing, in proportion, the revenues deriving from the lordly *California Zephyr*.

This sort of paradox enchanted the beholders but vexed the operating department.

Sometimes, as in the case of the so-called Fort Garland Extension, what started as a branch of modest ambitions, a branch became in effect a secondary operation of importance in the overall economy of the road. Branches came in all sizes, ranging from the O'Brien's Quarry branch out of Castle Rock, 2.3 miles and the Rock Creek branch, 2.8 miles, to the Silverton run out of Durango, 46 miles and the Westcliffe branch, 30 miles. A connection 20 miles long was spiked to the Crested Butte branch at the mouth of Taylor River with an eye to possible continuation into the Taylor River region, while such stub lines as those to Lake City, Anthracite and Aspen were of truly formidable dimensions.

All the Rio Grande branches hauled freight of one sort or another. Many carried passengers in mixed consists; a few in regularly scheduled passenger runs such as those to Lake City and Aspen, and two, the Silverton and Creede branches with Pullman sleepers.

Throughout the eighties the Rio Grande's light iron was spiked wherever a carloading promised. Track was laid from Red Cliff to Rock Creek in the Eagle River to provide loading facilities for the mines at Belden. The branch from Castle Rock to O'Brien's Quarry was extended a further two miles. The Blue River branch was completed to Dillon. There was the Strawberry branch connecting with the Aspen branch. The Chama lumber spur was completed on a roadbed provided by the lumber company that was conducting timber operations there. At Tres Piedras another lumber spur was laid down. A three rail operation was inaugurated from Littleton to Fort Logan. On the Rio Grande Southern, whose destinies were by now closely involved in the Rio Grande economy, the main line was laid connecting Telluride with the Rio Grande Ouray spur, a distance of 45 miles.

In 1889 the State of Colorado undertook the building of a new capitol at Denver and, when the Board of Managers decided on the use of local granite for the structure, a branch 4.50 miles long was laid from a point near Hierro on the main line a few miles west of Gunnison to the Aberdeen Quarry in the southern part of Gunnison County and all the vast quantities of stone used in the construction came out on the creaking flatcars to be ponderously conveyed to the Queen City of the Plains.

Many aspects of the Rio Grande's mountain operations aroused wonder and admiration in visitors, none more so than the heavy grades of the Calumet branch near Salida.

"Nobody has ever well described this wonderful little feeder of the Leadville division which leaves the main line at Brown's Canyon and ascends the mountain gulches to the east with the steepest grades and heaviest curves in the world that are overcome with the ordinary drive-wheel locomotive," wrote one observer in 1891. "Afar up in this range of mountains, seven miles away and nearly three thousand feet higher than the bed of the canyon, is the famous Calumet mine from which is extracted the hematite ore that keeps in blast the furnaces of the Bessemer works at Pueblo. Every morning of the year a ponderous locomotive and small train of cars toils up this steep, and every afternoon they make their perilous descent to the valley, loaded with iron, with the steam brakes on the cars, the water pressure on the locomotive drivers, and a man standing at the brake wheel of each car.

"This is the most wonderful piece of railroading in the universe. The maximum grade is four hundred and six feet to the mile, or nearly eight per cent, and the maximum curvature, twenty-five degrees. The terminal of the branch is half a mile higher than the commencement. Imagine, then,

the difficulty in ascending with empty cars, and the danger of descending with loaded ones. Still, strange though it may seem, a locomotive cannot make the descent unless at least five cars are attached. They are essential to provide the power for the steam brakes . . .

"Some few years ago when the operation of the line was commenced, runaway accidents were an almost daily occurrence. The seven miles were within a brief period strewn with the wrecks of cars and locomotives and iron ore . . .

"Finally, extremely heavy locomotives were built and a force of exceptionally brave trainmen secured. The latter were instructed to cling to their post·at every hazard, and never to flinch in the moment of danger. Not a serious wreck has been recorded since. Starting from the mine, every brake is manned so that should the steam fail, the train could still be checked. While there have been several runaways in two years, there has not been a wreck. The sight of these trains descending is one of thrilling interest, the sparks from the car wheels cutting a pathway of light down the mountains, which can best be described as having the appearance of a molten stream of fire rolling down to the river bed of the canyon.

"In Switzerland there are grades as steep as those of the Calumet branch, but they are equipped for operation with the cable and cogwheels."

The last of the Rio Grande's acquisitions of operative or geographic importance was the Denver & Salt Lake, characterized by David Lavender as "the hard luck short line of all time" that had started in business in 1902 as the Denver, Northwestern & Pacific. The road was the dream child of David Moffat, a highly successful speculator in Colorado mining ventures at Leadville, Creede and Cripple Creek who himself had been President of the Rio Grande at the period that saw its greatest expansion and changeover from narrow to standard gauge.

At the time that David Moffat was moved to undertake what was to prove the last of the transcontinentals, there were two sources of money in the dimension required for this sort of thing available to American entrepreneurs. One was Drexel Morgan & Company, that is to say the firm of J. P. Morgan, and the other was Kuhn - Loeb whose guiding genius was a pious, shifty, orthodox Jew named Jacob Schiff who was not above making his religion a convenience to banking as had been discovered back in 1901 during the great railroad war between the James J. Hill - J. P. Morgan interests and those of Edward H. Harriman. At a crucial point in the engagement, Harriman left an order for Schiff to purchase a pivotal 40,000 shares of Northern Pacific, but Schiff, fearful of the wrath of Morgan, and the order having been given on a Saturday, retired to his synagogue and claimed complete ignorance of the commission.

By now, however, Morgan and Kuhn - Loeb were seeing eye to eye in a community of interests where railroads were concerned and nobody, but nobody was going to offend Edward H. Harriman. Harriman, a transcendent genius for organization, and his superbly coordinated hatchet man Julius Kruttschnitt, were actively engaged in making the Union Pacific-Southern Pacific-Oregon Steam Navigation Company complex of railroads into the biggest thing west of the Missouri. Harriman, whose droopy moustaches and Caspar Milquetoast facade concealed a will of vanadium, had a way of getting rid of opposition. When Stuyvesant Fish, President of the Illinois Central and a swaggering social magnifico, offended Harriman in a minor matter of Newport protocol, he was in the ranks of the unemployed in a matter of hours. With the Union Pacific, Harriman's baby of the moment, nobody was going to advance so much as a thin dime to any old gentleman from Colorado who had delusions of main line railroading on an east-west axis.

Moffat and William Evans, President of the Denver Tramway Company, had for some years been considering the possibility of an electric route over the Rockies. Electrification was in the air, the interurban movement that swept the United States in the years prior to the 1914 war was just getting under way. It was to see all sorts of electrically powered long hauls in successful operation with sleepers, diners, Railway Post Offices and all the amenities of big time steam railroading on long distance runs, and an outsize interurban through the Shining Mountains was not as chimerical as it sounds today.

On one of his trips east in an attempt to raise funds in Wall Street, however, something happened to jar Moffat out of his catenary thinking. He wired his Denver associates, "I have decided to build a steam railroad," and the first person singular was entirely appropriate. Moffat was to undertake the Salt Lake line on his own, was to sink his personal fortune in it and die in harness in its service, but despite all his efforts the road had come to a halt at Craig, 232 miles out of Denver and never moved a foot past Craig station.

The Rio Grande did all in its power to impede progress on the Moffat line and nearly succeeded in having it fatally bogged down in Gore Canyon on the western slope of The Divide. The canyon that is today the most spectacular of all the countrysides traversed by *The California Zephyr* had been named for Sir St. George Gore, the first of a long line of noble nimrods to invade the Shining Mountains in the first half of the nineteenth century when he had hired Jim Bridger as guide and headed into the wilderness with the most magnificent entourage yet seen in America. The Rio Grande, or perhaps it was Harriman, undertook to have the United States Department of the Interior forbid Gore Canyon to the Moffat road on grounds that it was a future reservoir site, and might have been successful if President Roosevelt hadn't cut himself in on the hassle and sided with the railroad.

Before the great tunnel that was to make Moffat's name immortal in Colorado was dreamed of, the railroad survey went over the very crest of the Rockies by way of Yankee Doodle Lake and vast snowsheds at Rollins Pass where, at Corona, an entire urban community existed under a deep blanket of snow for five months of the year. At Yankee Doodle Lake the track ascended 1000 feet in only three loops and on the escarpment of the mountains, almost within view of Denver, it burrowed through no fewer than thirty tunnels.

But David Moffat and his fortune came to the end of the road almost at the same time and Craig remained, as it does today, the western terminal of a railroad running essentially to nowhere.

What saved the Moffat line, temporarily at least, and was to give the Rio Grande a new mainline of its own was the growing need of more water for the City of Denver. It could only be brought from the western slope and the proposal was made to tunnel under James Peak for an aqueduct and a new, lower grade for the Moffat line at the same time. The Moffat Tunnel was eventually built at a cost of $18,000,000 and saved half a mile in elevation and twenty-three miles of track for the Denver & Salt Lake, making it the smallest railroad in the record to have at its disposal such a monumental feat of engineering. A six mile tunnel for the accommodation of microscopic car loadings and a single train each way every twenty-four hours was a patent absurdity, and eventually a deal was made with the bondholders of the tunnel, who were in fact the Denver taxpayers, to permit the Rio Grande to share trackage rights with the Salt Lake line. At one point the Rio Grande's main line over Tennessee Pass and down the Eagle River passed only thirty-four miles from the Moffat iron, and to bridge this gap and save 175 miles of the then main line via Pueblo, the Rio Grande built the Dotsero Cutoff, since hailed as the last major piece of railroad construction in the United States.

Moffat partisans, and they were vocal and persistent if not numerous, opposed the Rio Grande at every possible opportunity and made nasty references when chance permitted to the Rio Grande as a "foreign" and, therefore, presumably, heartless and unworthy corporation whose management was vested in the Burlington, Missouri Pacific, Western Pacific and other tag ends of the Gould railroad empire. Somehow the idea of a successful enterprise built by out-of-state capital is immoral, whereas failure with local financing is admirable. It's part of the provincial mentality everywhere. No matter.

For a few years after its lease agreement with the Rio Grande the Denver & Salt Lake retained its own corporate and operating identity and maintained freight service and a daily passenger train each way between Denver and Craig where it made a living at subsistence level from a lean traffic in coal, hay, livestock and timber, but its affairs were dominated by the lessor Rio Grande which gradually absorbed its once highly individual locomotives and cars and rebuilt its faltering right of way into a mainline of continental implications, well ballasted track, 160 pound rail and centralized traffic control. At long last the D & S L disappeared entirely and its Trains No. 1 and 2 emerged to serve Craig in the stylish guise of the *Yampa Valley Mail*.

The great day when the Rio Grande should commence operations was not without incident.

A number of special train movements out of Denver with business cars and specially assigned equipment loaded to the guards with railroad brass, state and civic dignitaries and all the accustomed free loaders necessary to moments of public rejoicing headed for Bond where a monster barbecue had been spread and a nationwide radio hookup, something new and portentous in those days, had been arranged. But the specials were badly off-schedule. None of the Rio Grande head end crews had ever been allowed to make the run in the days of the Moffat's authority and the Moffat engineers and firemen assigned as pilots had never encountered anything even resembling the splendid Rio Grande motive power or the yet stranger Diesels which were just coming into vogue.

Then to pile disaster atop chaos, a sudden snow squall, a commonplace in the Rockies but rough on bunting and caterers' tables, made a shambles of the festival scene. Paper plates took off like veritable flying saucers, wind-fed flames in the barbecue pits threatened not merely to roast the sacrificial oxen but to incinerate them. Raindrops marred the gloss on silk top hats and dignitaries wished they had been possessed of the foresight to wear bearskin coats instead of cutaways.

Worst of all, as radio time approached, the Governor of Colorado, the Governor of Wyoming, the Governor of Utah and countless poobahs of earnest mein who were due at the microphone at Bond were still crawling along at Plainview while motive power superintendents ventured ahead to see if the engines would clear the tunnels. Radio technicians glanced at their watches, the master of ceremonies clutched at his throat and made choking noises. It was obvious (a) that the dignitaries wouldn't be on time, and (b) that when they did get there, some would be the worse for wear on the hospitality of the business cars. Ruin loomed.

In this pass a veritable Casabianca of the high iron in the person of Carlton Sills, the Rio Grande manager of passenger traffic, emerged amidst the reviewing stand chaos whence all but he and a wilted master of ceremonies had fled.

As the second hand indicated that the Rio Grande was on the air from coast to coast and, perhaps, from pole to pole, the high priced announcer spoke into the microphone words to the effect that it was his pleasure and his privilege on this auspicious occasion to introduce the Governor of the Centennial State, His Excellency the first citizen of Colorado who would now go on the air. Having written the governor's speech, Carlton Sills had a transcript of the great man's words and was able to impersonate a politician's platitudes with sonorous dignity. Next the Governor of Utah spoke to the listening millions, then the Receiver for the Rio Grande Railroad, Judge Wilson McCarthy who was able to listen to himself from the vantage point of his business car at Tunnel No. 10. Judge Mc-Carthy found Judge McCarthy admirable and applauded freely as he yielded the microphone to William Jeffers, President of the rival Union Pacific. Bill Jeffers spoke graciously of the esteem in which he held the engineering, the acumen and the determination of the Rio Grande and in the U. P.'s business car No. 100, crawling along at Tolland, Bill Jeffers applauded his sentiments and a chorus of executive vice presidents raised their glasses to shout "Hear! Hear!"

Altogether Sills impersonated no fewer than ten bigwigs of assorted dimensions, representing state and industry, banks, bondholders, and other orators in absentia. As a grand finale he fairly outdid himself as the Episcopal Archbishop of Denver on whose behalf, before collapsing, he delivered a swinging benediction on the Moffat. The Archbishop himself, by this time somewhere above Pine Cliff, looked stunned and made notes on his starched shirt cuffs against the next time he had to invoke Divine approbation on a railroad.

As the Rio Grande went off the air, the first of the specials ground to a halt at Bond. The sun was shining brightly and caterers' men were retrieving paper plates and restoring order amongst the bunting. Skilled chefs were having at the roast oxen with gleaming butcher's tools and bottles were circulating among the distinguished invitees. It was a splendid occasion and Carlton Sills was as good as new in less than a week.

The opening to through traffic of the Moffat Tunnel route had its immediate and obvious effect on the pattern of Rio Grande operations of making the Moffat the carrier's transcontinental mainline and relegating the old trackage through Pueblo and up the Valley of the Arkansas to an operation of secondary importance. On-line industries and other interested parties viewed the change with dismay, although, with competition in the form of the Colorado & Southern, the Santa Fe, the Rock Island and the Missouri Pacific all serving the complex of communities south of Denver, the effect was by no means as cataclysmic as it would have been had the Rio Grande been the only railroad in the region.

Passenger traffic via the Royal Gorge continued in diminishing volume save in the tourist season and the Pueblo route train was named *The Royal Gorge* in place of *The Scenic Limited* of glorious memory. On the Moffat run, *The Panoramic* gave way to a fine new train run in connection with the Burlington and Western Pacific and named *The Exposition Flyer* in honor of the Pacific Exposition which arose on Treasure Island in San Francisco. *The Flyer* had its counterpart over the Union-Southern Pacific a hundred miles to the north in *The Forty-niner* which was also inaugurated with an eye to the tourist traffic attracted by the Fair and whose memory is still green more than twenty years after its disappearance from the time card. The majestic passage of *The Exposition Flyer* alternated with the scheduling over the Moffat of the nameless Salt Lake Line run to Craig which, after the Rio Grande took over the Salt Lake Line in its entirety, was dignified with the title of *Yampa Valley Mail*. For a time, too, the Craig train carried a sleeper and ran eastbound on a night schedule with a tourist Pullman tagging behind head end cars and coaches. It was the nearest thing to the big time the Moffat road ever came.

The coming of the 1941 war was, in operating terms if not in terms of personnel and management, the turning point which decreed a bright future for the Rio Grande and its firm establishment in the traffic pattern of the Western States where, over the years, there had always been elements that foresaw the eventual abandonment of the entire Rio Grande system. In January 1942 the Rio Grande's net operating income had soared a whacking 161 per cent over that for the same period in 1940. By mid-summer of 1942 it had reached an astronomical 900 per cent over a twelve-month previous. Vast defense industries had been located, largely through the efforts of Judge Wilson McCarthy, along the rights of way in Colorado and Utah and an extremely helpful $5,500,000 was derived from hauling munitions in and out of on-line plants in a single year. As the theater of war shifted from Europe to the Pacific and the surge of transcontinental traffic reversed itself, the other and hitherto adequate mid-continental mainlines of the Union Pacific and Santa Fe proved grossly inadequate for the task of moving more than 95 per cent of all passenger traffic routed toward California, and the Rio Grande came into its own as a military railroad to a degree that bemused even Denver.

All along the Dotsero Cutoff where single track operations had been possible by the use of the most modern devices, including Centralized Traffic Control under the administration as chief engineer and later general manager of Alfred Perlman, it was found necessary to lay out passing tracks wherever the right of way permitted. Troop trains ground their way up through the tunnels of the East Approach practically on smoke signals powered by the widest imaginable variety of locomotives including the Diesels which had already become a commonplace in freight but not passenger operations on the road. Double headers with twenty Pullmans on the drawbar of the most improbable arrangements of motive power took siding at Plainview and East Portal while *The Exposition Flyer* inched by on its downhill run to Denver. Venerable true Mallets from the Salt Lake Line showered soot on the Rio Grande's own formidable articulateds running as helpers to the latest Diesels from General Motors. On-line telegraph operators at one room depots experienced the eerie sensation of witnessing the almost soundless passage beyond their telegraph bays of specials carrying an entire regiment equipped for battle that emerged like ghosts from the falling snow and disappeared like spectres with only diminishing marker lights to mark where they had been. At night the high passes of the Shining Mountains were alive with the coming and going of such a multitude of trains and men that the spirits of the Long Hunters in Gore Canyon were alarmed and took to the higher hills above timberline.

All along the Rio Grande far flung mainline threading the continental cordillera from the Great Plains to Great Salt Lake the 400 rebuilt bridges shook under accelerated tonnage, 4,000,000 new tie plates absorbed the augment of pounding rod assemblies and the 240 miles of all-new and for-

midably heavier steel that Judge McCarthy had forethoughtfully purchased got scant chance to acquire even the thinnest film of rust between the long extras whose smoke exhaust from West Denver to Roper Yard resembled a smoke curtain across the Rockies.

The 1941 war was a great day for the Rio Grande, perhaps the greatest in all its long record of borrasca and bonanza.

The years following the excitements and commotions of the 1941 war saw many changes in the operational scheme of the Rio Grande, not all of them for the better and some not calculated to enhance good public relations with those Coloradoans who viewed their home railroad not only as a corporate entity but as an extension of the Rocky Mountain personality and a vehicle for continuity with the heroic past.

In 1948 abandonment was announced of the twenty-six miles of narrow gauge rails running from Sapinero to Cedar Creek that had been laid in 1882 as part of the original main line, and a short time later permission was asked to take up the Baldwin and Crested Butte Branches. The railroad pointed out, more or less reasonably, that from 1950 to 1952 the Crested Butte operations had put the management in the hole for more than half a million dollars, and since no passenger service was involved, the abandonment, while universally regretted, was viewed as inevitable. A year later the road announced the termination of through train service between Salt Lake and Ogden on the grounds it was costing the Rio Grande $80,000 and could be easily absorbed by the existing trains of the Union Pacific without hardship to anyone.

The most serious blow to the railroad's public image, to use a Madison Avenue cliché, was the determination on the part of the management in the person of General Manager Al Perlman to do away with the *San Juan,* the last regularly scheduled narrow gauge passenger operation of a name train anywhere in the United States. Under one name or another — it had originally been *The San Juan Express* — this atmospheric varnish run had been in picturesque operation since the opening of the Durango line in the eighties. When winter cut off communications via Wolf Creek pass, which was not infrequently, the daily train was the sole tangible communication between the San Juan region and the outer world. Admittedly, it was one of the most celebrated and highly regarded tourist attractions in Colorado, but unhappily the tourists only rode it in summer and its overall annual balance sheet showed a deficit.

On grounds of purely operational statistics and the revenue involved, *The San Juan* was a liability. In terms of good will and fair repute it was the Rio Grande's greatest promotional and sentimental asset and its abandonment, after months of hearings and mounting bad feeling that asserted itself even in Denver and attracted highly unfavorable attention to the railroad everywhere, Mr. Perlman was able to discontinue its services. In a business that is celebrated for its almost total lack of any least comprehension of public relations, it was a towering example of callous disregard for public sentiment. It confirmed the suspicions, not entirely allayed by the Rio Grande's repudiation of its obligations on frequent occasions over the years, that the management was as hard hearted as it was inept and Mr. Perlman left to assume more exalted duties as President of the New York Central leaving behind him a name for being "the butcher boy of the passenger business."

Of his departure, A. M. Camp, senior banker and grand man of the San Juan, wrote, "It was fortunate that it occurred while our railroads in Colorado were left with a wheel turning."

This may not have been entirely fair to Mr. Perlman, a scientific student of railroad engineering and its technical aspects of wide dimensions, and one whose activities may very well have been viewed as benevolent in the accounting department, but Mr. Perlman's heart was in carloadings and fast freight schedules and he shared the prevailing railroader's cynicism about passenger runs that lost money. There are those who say that the untimely taking off of *The San Juan* has haunted his professional career even in the board room of the mighty New York Central, but that of course is mere superstitious talk among mountain folk.

On the credit side of the Rio Grande's post war ledger is the radiant fact of its participation in the *California Zephyr*, a through transcontinental de luxe streamliner between Chicago and San Francisco over the connecting Burlington and Western Pacific. The *Zephyr* from the very begin-

ning proved to be an inspiration of the first chop. Scheduled to traverse the most picturesque portions of its run along the Feather River in California and through the entire depth of the Rockies by daylight, it became an instantaneous sell-out in summer and maintained an enviable record of occupancy all the year round. It was the first train in the Far West to incorporate vista dome cars in its consist, an innovation that has been copied widely on other carriers and which brought the train's three proprietor railroads many kudos as pioneers. The Rio Grande's pro-rata participation in the *Zephyr's* mileage is only a little over twenty-two per cent of its total run, but they are far and away the most spectacular and memorable miles and, morally speaking, did wonders for the railroad.

In addition to the *California Zephyr* and what remains of the *Royal Gorge*, the Rio Grande maintains an overnight streamliner between Salt Lake and Denver called *The Prospector* whose operation and maintenance may be envied, and appropriately, by any railroad in the land. *The Prospector* had its beginnings under melancholy auspices in a two-car Budd-built makeshift of the same name that was tried out just before the 1941 war. A little jewel-box train with head-end revenue, coach space, sleeping accommodations and a microscopic dining compartment all comprised in two stainless steel units, *The Prospector* had everything except the ability to get revenue matter from here to there. It simply didn't work.

"It ran in steam more often than under its own motive power," recalls Carlton Sills, hero of the Moffat dedication and head of the railroad's passenger department today. "It was a charmer and everything about it was wrong. We had too much coach space and not enough berths and the motor units were incapable of getting it uptown to the Brown Palace Hotel. It went back to the builder without thanks, but it gave us the idea for today's *Prospector*."

Today's *Prospector* is a fine thing to see, discounting Diesel on the head end, in its livery of orange and black, rolling up Soldier Summit in the sunset and meeting the sun again in Colorado the next morning as it emerges from the Moffat for the long, spectacular descent to the Queen City of the Plains. The bottles in its club compartment would be of more than passing interest to Uncle Dick Wootton were he around and might have persuaded him to sell out to the Rio Grande instead of the scoundrelly Santa Fe. There is usually fresh Rocky Mountain trout on the menu, lineal descendants through countless trout generations of ancestors served for breakfast on the narrow gauge cars when first they ran through the Canyon of the Gunnison as part of one of the great railroad adventures of the continent.

The trout will do as well as anything to establish the long and wonderfully romantic continuity of the railroad that is in truth the Mainline of the Shining Mountains. Like the mountains themselves they have been there all the time and, should cataclysm one day overtake the human race, there are scientists who foretell that the fish of its oceans and rivers alone may carry on the continuity of life on a planet whence all else has vanished. Perhaps the trout, then, may be an omen of longevity for the Rio Grande, too. They, too, are a part of the high passes and the great adventure under various skies and share what The Book says is the everlasting character of the hills.

Nearing the end of steam at Palmer Lake where once the Rocky Mountain zephyrs blew Rio Grande trains from the narrow gauge track, freight still double headed with white flags for an extra with No. 1207, a 2-8-2 as helper and No. 1523, a 4-8-2 as road engine. *(Everett De Golyer Collection; Joseph Schick.)*

Nearing the end of the trail, too, the narrow gauge trains with which the Rio Grande had begun operations still, in the fifties, rolled ore cars on the three foot rail against a background of snowy peaks as they had in the golden times of the bonanzas when it all began. The continuity of steam maintained a mystic communion with the past. *(Jim Shaughnessy.)*

Following page: With high cars of preferred merchandise for interchange with the Southern Pacific at Ogden and the Western Pacific at Salt Lake, the Rio Grande's redball hotshot, *The California Fast Freight* mounts toward Soldier Summit with forty-four cars in the summer of 1939. Motive power was 2-8-8-2 articulated No. 3507 and 4-6-6-4 No. 3709 to form a massive tandem of horsepower in the long afternoon of steam. The photograph was taken by R. H. Kindig.

The pillar of cloud against the Colorado skyline that marked the going of the Rio Grande's articulated motive power is caught in three photographs by Jim Ehernberger near Frazer, Colorado, two of them with the monsters cut into the trainline as helpers, one on the head end as road engine.

The views of behemoth on these pages are by two of the ranking and recognized practitioners of railroad photography in the years of steam. On the page opposite, Richard Steinheimer shows a Rio Grande coal extra at the top of Soldier Summit in December 1951 with a 4-6-6-4 on the head end and a 2-8-8-2 still visibly working steam as the cars grind to a halt at the rear. Below in an action shot by Henry R. Griffiths, Jr., an identical arrangement of motive power with No. 3707 ahead and No. 3501 out of sight behind sixty-five cars eastbound over Soldier in the summer of '41. The rising sun device on the smokebox of Rio Grande articulateds was evolved by the railroad's engineering department to make approaching trains more visible at grade crossings.

The apotheosis of Rio Grande motive power and the thundering hallmark of its operations has been its Mallets, true Mallets in their original redactions, simple articulated locomotives in their later perfection. For the photographer bent on capturing the railroad's inner character through the linements of outer form, these locomotives surging like dawn animals in a Paleozoic world through the high passes have been the quintessence of mountain conquest, behemoth out of the Book of Job: "Lo, now his strength is in his loins, and his force is in the navel of his belly. . . . His bones are as strong pieces of brass; his bones are like bars of iron. . . . Behold he drinketh up a river and hasteth not." On the page opposite behemoth moves under a pillar of cloud with *The Royal Gorge* out of Minturn in 1949; here behemoth lurches out of Wolhurst, Colorado, in the same year with a mile of merchandise on his drawbar. *(Two Photos: Rocky Mountain Railroad Photos: Ross Grenard.)*

The seven true Mallets or other types of articulated locomotive on these two pages suggest the origin of the Rio Grande's fame as a carrier of matchless and diversified motive power for its mountain runs. No. 3554 shown above at Minturn *(Everett De Golyer Collection)* was purchased from the Norfolk & Western during the 1941 war. Nos. 3404 and 3410, shown below in a photograph by R. H. Kindig, are hiking *The Ute* up the two percent grade on the Moffat run west of Plainview with forty-four cars in 1939. On the page opposite the profiles of motive power in uneasy repose at top and bottom are by R. H. Kindig, No. 3410 in the center is from the collection of Everett De Golyer.

The Rio Grande's first articulated locomotives were true Mallets and comprised eight 2-6-6-0 engines built by American Locomotive in 1910, assigned to helper service and heavy drags on Soldier Summit in Utah. Here one of the road's primordial monsters of a later series acquired in 1913 squats on its tracks in the roundhouse at Salt Lake in its first year of service, primal ancestor of a long race of beautiful and useful engines to come that were to make the Rio Grande's mountain operations synonymous with articulated power as long as steam lasted in the high passes of the Shining Mountains. (*Rio Grande Railroad.*)

The look of Colorado railroading in the grand manner is explicit in this fine painting by the celebrated artist-designer Otto Kuhler, himself a resident of Pine, who has depicted Mallet No. 3713 leaning into a curve on sand-drenched rails with a time freight and smoke enough to vex the operating department and delight the eye. A 4-8-4 heading an invisible passenger train is drifting off the summit of the hill westbound. In the background, the highest peak in the artist's composition is Maple Mountain, while to the right is Little Diamond, so named for the abundance of diamond-back rattlesnakes on its rocky slopes.

In 1944 the Silverton Mixed on the page opposite ran twice a week out of Durango at nine in the morning, often not returning until after midnight. When the end of the 1941 war revived tourism it posed at Rockwood with half a dozen high cars for ore, a caboose, three coaches, the open solarium car *Silverton* and the business car B-7 occupied by General Manager Al Perlman and the authors of this book. Below the meadows of Rockwood nearly hide the three foot iron. *(Above, below: Lucius Beebe.)*

In many cities, the traditional pensioner serving as crossing tender in a picturesque trackside pagoda from which he emerged to crank down manually activated gates or pose with lantern and flag, gradually yielded to automatic signal lights or the elimination of grade crossings altogether. But in Salt Lake City, the crossing tender was institutional into comparatively recent times at a multiplicity of downtown crossings of both the Denver & Rio Grande Western and the Union Pacific. *(Three Photos: Lucius Beebe.)*

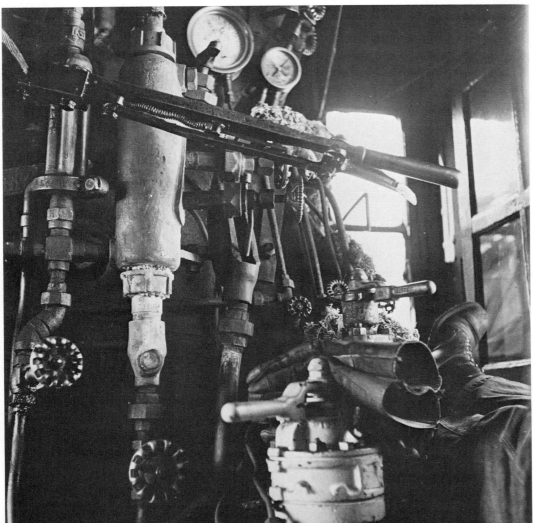

At the top on the page opposite is a chilly glance forward into the gathering Colorado storm from the head end of a narrow gauge freight on Toltec siding at three o'clock one morning in April 1953 as the rails of the mainline whiten and the crew speculates if the eastbound train they were to meet is going to make it. Below is lunchtime in the snug cab of narrow gauge No. 491 at Farmington, New Mexico. Shown here and running across the fold is the casual progress of a cut of empty narrow gauge high cars and their accompanying caboose just north of Aztec, New Mexico, on the Durango-Farmington Branch. *(Above, Opposite: Philip R. Hastings; Below, Opposite and Above Here: Richard Steinheimer.)*

Freight hogs of varying pedigree and estate throng these pages, all with the Rio Grande's ensign and all going somewhere. Below: 4-8-2 No. 1520 carrying white teams up with articulated No. 3709 on a fast stretch of tangent out of Grand Junction. At the top on the page opposite No. 1607 rolls thirty-eight cars of merchandise west of Cisco, Utah; in the center, No. 1517 heads up a redball just west of Tunnel No. 1, while at the bottom, Nos. 1600 and 3706 are applying the air as they whistle for the yard at Grand Junction in 1942. All four photographs are by Otto Perry. At the right, switcher No. 1198 poses face-on at Alamosa on a three rail track for a portrait by Forest Crossen of Rocky Mountain Railroad Photos.

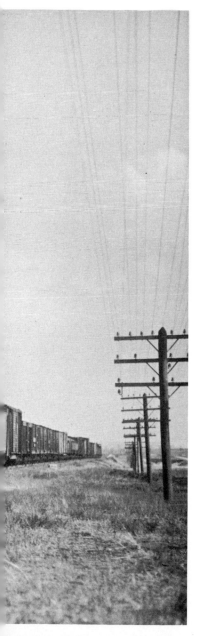

Long barreled, versatile and durable, the Rio Grande's 1500 series Mountain Type 4-8-2s brought 66,640 pounds tractive force with each unit when they came from American Locomotive Company in 1922 and 1923 and remained in active service in both freight and passenger hauls as long as steam lasted. On the page opposite No. 1501 double heads the *Scenic Limited* on Tennessee Pass; below, No. 1519 powers a red-ball freight out of Denver. On this page, one of them is being lifted from its wheels by a 120-ton crane at Burnham Shops and *(below)* No. 1517 drifts downgrade near Keeldar with Second No. 36 in 1941. *(Opposite: Two Photos: R. H. Kindig; Above: Rio Grande Railroad; Below: Otto Perry.)*

The big picture at the left is a study of steam in its last days as two switchers go about their duties under an early morning sun at Salida. On this page Rio Grande articulated No. 3603 on the smoky end of *The Ute* grumbles up the grade on the Moffat Route near Scenic with thirty-three cars at fifteen miles an hour. In the lower frame, another Silurian monster, No. 3501 is cut into the middle of a merchandise westbound near Gilluly, Utah, on the ascent to Soldier Summit. The time is June 1941. *(Left: Jim Shaughnessy; Above: R. H. Kindig.)*

In the days when the *Scenic Limited* carried through Pullmans for Salt Lake it made a fine showing as it stormed up Tennessee Pass on a late summer's afternoon with all the attributes of a limited train in the grand manner of old: head-end revenue cars, coaches, Pullman sleepers, diner, observation club car and No. 1802 up ahead to show what railroading on a mountain run should be. (*Above: Henry R. Griffiths, Jr.; Below: Graphic House.*)

308 —

Early morning finds Salida yards' activities halted until the passing of the eastbound *Scenic Limited,* narrow gauge Mike No. 483 bound for the Monarch Branch run *(above)* and 2-8-0 No. 1138 awaiting assignment. The main line is at the far right, over which, until the Moffat, ran the entire traffic of a transcontinental carrier.   *(Above: Otto Perry; Below: Jim Shaughnessy.)*

Three vintages of Rio Grande dining cars are shown on these two pages: below is a handsome interior in the elaborate age before air conditioning about 1915, while opposite is the diner *Twin Peaks* built by American Car & Foundry in May 1927 topped by *Mt. Massive* at the car wash between runs in today's *Prospector*. *(Page Opposite: Everett De Golyer Collection, Arthur D. Dubin Collection; Below: Kaufmann & Fabry.)*

Most of the Rio Grande's 1100 series of 2-8-0 locomotives, Consolidations, were built by Alco in 1908 and 1910 and many of them remained in service as the carrier's workhorse engines for as long as steam lasted on the Rocky Mountain main lines. They were given all and any assignments, singly on branch line hauls to Creede and in Provo Canyon, double headed with other motive power with a mile of redball snaking out behind. During the 1941 war they knew final moments of glory when they breasted the high passes as helpers on the head end of troop and munition trains in the great parade westward. Here the Consolidations are bedded down for the night in Grand Junction roundhouse. On the page opposite at the top, one of them runs tandem with a Burlington 2-8-2 during the urgency and pooled operations of wartime, while below No. 1193 picks them up and sets them out in Provo Canyon. (*Above: Neal Miller, Rocky Mountain Railroad Photos; Opposite: Otto Perry, Everett De Golyer Collection.*)

The Rio Grande's articulated locomotive No. 3613, a 2-8-8-4 shown below climbing the three percent grade at Tennessee Pass with an extra of perishable fruit from the Sacramento Valley in May 1949, is one of ten Class L-132 engines purchased from Alco in 1930. They were identical in specifications with Class L-131 No. 3605 shown above purchased from the same builder three years earlier, and so satisfactory that the first order for ten was repeated. (Above: Everett De Golyer Collection; Below: R. H. Kindig.)

This atmospheric nocturne by Howard Fogg depicts an eastbound articulated No. 3607 taking fuel at Minturn coal chute preparatory to heading up Eagle River Canyon and Tennessee Pass. "It may be assumed," says Fogg, who prepared the painting with the assistance of R. H. Kindig, "that a second and perhaps even a third 3600 are on the far end of the manifest. The year is 1930."

The Rio Grande's 3400 series of articulated locomotives of 1913, of which sixteen were ordered from the American Locomotive Company, were true Mallets, using saturated steam controlled by piston valves on the high pressure cylinders and slide valves on the low. On the opposite page at the top the prototypal No. 3400 is shown with seventy-five cars south of Castle Rock, while below No. 3413 runs as helper on a double header in Lincoln Hills. (Above: Otto C. Perry; Below: Rocky Mountain Railroad Photos: John Maxwell.)

For some reason not immediately apparent to historians of the carrier, the Rio Grande's 2-6-6-2 articulated locomotives of the 3300 series were among the most infrequently photographed of all engines. The one above was photographed at Helper, Utah, by Joseph Schick and is in the Everett De Golyer collection at Dallas. Below, No. 1052, also a true Mallet with the same wheel arrangement and part of an earlier consignment from the same builder, poses as it was delivered to its new owner in 1910. (Rio Grande Railroad.)

As every photographer knows, night action shots of railroad operations are out of the question without special equipment and great effort, but an approximation of them has been achieved by Otto Perry of Denver on these two pages with action shots taken at twilight and so processed as to enhance the gathering shadows. Above: three Rio Grande narrow gauge engines Nos. 488, 489 and 484 hike a long train of tanks and cut lumber up the four percent grade to the Cumbres at Creslo, Colorado. Below and at the top of the page opposite, a heavy drag freight tops Tennessee Pass in the face of a gathering summer thunderstorm at dusk, and, below, the *Colorado-New Mexico Express* pulls out of Denver on a summer evening just at nightfall.

light Over The High Passes Of The Rio Grande

On these two pages the Rio Grande's merchandise rolls in a rich variety of consists against the equally various backgrounds of the Colorado countryside. Here a brace of 4-8-2s move westward out of Salida with a long tail of eighty-five cars in October of 1939, while below at the extreme left *The Ute*, a daily fast merchandise haul in the thirties between Denver and Salt Lake, emerges from Tunnel No. 8 on the Moffat run behind No. 1177, a 2-8-0 and No. 3410, a 2-8-8-2 articulated with thirty cars on their drawbars. In the center No. 3707, a 4-6-6-4 winds up Soldier Summit near Gilluly, Utah, with First No. 30, and at the far right No. 1403, a 2-10-2 drifts down the eastbound grade from Soldier into Thistle with fifty cars in the spring of 1914. All four photographs were taken by R. H. Kindig.

An exception to the gallery of Kindig portraits of freight on its way on these two pages is the triple header with three massive Rio Grande locomotives earning their keep on Tennessee Pass in the summer of 1949. A 2-8-8-2 No. 3613 is helper, road engine is a 4-8-2 No. 1503 while No. 3610 is cut into the middle of the train.   (*Rocky Mountain Railroad Photos: Ross Grenard.*)

The Colorado winters with twenty below temperatures and drifts of legendary dimensions still blew down from the peaks of the Shining Mountains in the last years of steam as they had when they blew the *Montezuma* off the track at Palmer Lake so long ago. Opposite: a 3600 articulated drops down grade from Soldier Summit with an extra water tank on its drawbar after a helper job, while on this page steam exhaust attests a gelid morning as an eastbound extra pants its way into Thistle. *(Two Photos: Richard Steinheimer.)*

Nocturne Over the Shining Iron
At the Headwaters of Arkansas

Come as a Silurian from the dawn-world of shallow waters and the meres and mystic marshes of primeval times, the Rio Grande's articulated 4-6-6-4 No. 3703 climbs Tennessee Pass where the Arkansas has its beginnings to establish a tangible continuity between the age of steam and the dinosaur. The time is April 1938 above Malta and the consist a Civilian Conservation Corps special of fifteen cars. *(R. H. Kindig.)*

Throughout its history the Rio Grande's most relentless enemy has been snow, but snow on the level tangents in modern times presented only a fraction of the herculean problem of shoveling out by hand a deep slide on the Silverton branch in the eighties suggested by the drawing on the opposite page. In the winter vignette shown below, Richard Steinheimer has caught for all time one of the Rio Grande's utilitarian 2-10-2 heavy duty freight hogs barking its way out of Thistle, Utah, for the assault on Soldier Summit on the head end of a train of coal empties. The time was December 1951. The temperature twenty-eight degrees below zero.

Once, in the great Harriman era on the Southern Pacific, Farmington, New Mexico, bid fair to importance on a projected Southern Pacific mainline to penetrate the San Juan Basin from the south but Harriman's death relegated the project to the discard and today Farmington is the terminus of one of the Rio Grande's last narrow gauge branches and the scene of this switching operation. The date is 1961, the photographer Richard Steinheimer.

Night in the remote high passes of the Western Continent finds the Rio Grande's No. 487 breathing deeply in the thin air at Cumbres Summit while the train crew turn up retainers for the descent to Chama. *(Jim Shaughnessy.)*

On these two pages, a distinguished railroad photographer, Richard Steinheimer turns his lens on engaging aspects of the Rio Grande's operations in the age before Diesel. On the page opposite No. 1403, its cylinder heads neatly silvered for all its humble assignment, arrives at Thistle on a December morning eastbound with a load of coal empties. At the left here, a fireboy contemplates the cameraman from his elevated station, in more clement season, as is suggested by the water bag, while below, in Roper Yards, Salt Lake City, a track repair gang relines a switch against a background of conventional yard activities accomplished by both steam and Diesel.

On the page opposite, the narrow gauge is seen operating in its final twilight, at the top a pair of freight engines in tandem head south out of Alamosa on their way to Durango; below: a helper on "the hill" nudges a string of ore cars over Cumbres Summit in the summer of 1959. *(Above: Robert Hale; Below: Richard Steinheimer.)*

With green flags fluttering feebly at its smokebox, narrow gauge No. 483 brakes a string of ore cars against the pull of gravity down the grade on the Monarch branch, one of the last slim gauge operations of the Rio Grande to possess overtones of mining on a railroad whose early days and most of whose original feeder lines had been predicated on precious metals or the transport of iron and the components of its manufacture. *(Richard Steinheimer.)*

So many wistful properties of the narrow gauge in one photograph: Cumbres depot, the water plug and faithful No. 492 against a timberline growth of Colorado pine and lonely hillside. Below: the longest narrow gauge tangent, fifty-four miles in the San Luis Valley reaches endlessly north out of Moffat. *(Above: Jim Shaughnessy; Below: Richard B. Jackson.)*

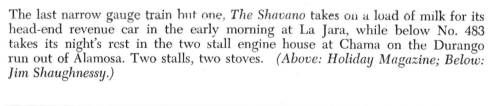

The last narrow gauge train but one, *The Shavano* takes on a load of milk for its head-end revenue car in the early morning at La Jara, while below No. 483 takes its night's rest in the two stall engine house at Chama on the Durango run out of Alamosa. Two stalls, two stoves. *(Above: Holiday Magazine; Below: Jim Shaughnessy.)*

Until the coming of the still larger and more puissant 1800 class, the Rio Grande's 1700 class Northern 4-8-4s were the most stylish pacers on its motive power roster. Built by the American Locomotive Company in 1928-29, they were conventionally assigned to fast passenger runs and one of them, No. 1702 is shown here on the head end of the *Scenic Limited* fifteen miles out of Denver in 1937 loping through fields of wildflowers for a railroad pastoral of rare charm. At the top opposite another 1700 puffs through Denver yards on the same train, while below is a study of the valve gear and side motion of the archetypal No. 1700 as it came from the factory in 1929. *(Above: Henry R. Griffiths, Jr.; Opposite: Lucius Beebe, the Rio Grande Railroad.)*

In the great tradition of mountain railroading in its operational noontide was the Rio Grande's well remembered *Scenic Limited* shown on these two pages in attitudes typical of its spectacular run. Opposite, with No. 1200 as helper and No. 1707 as road engine, it heads up Tennessee Pass near Pando for a recorded image of splendor high in the secret places of Colorado remoteness. Here, a few years earlier, without benefit of a helper engine, it sparkles in the morning freshness of its early departure hour just south of Denver. *(Opposite: R. H. Kindig; Below: Lucius Beebe.)*

On the overleaf is a full dress study by Richard Steinheimer of a Rio Grande champion, a Challenger type locomotive backing down in Provo yards in December 1951 to pick up a northbound merchandise for Salt Lake and Ogden.

The end came for the Rio Grande's long line of Mallets and giant articulated
motive power late in the fall of 1956. The two views on these pages were taken
in October of that year by Jim Ehernberger who got these penultimate action
shots of No. 3613, a 2-8-8-2 working freight at Tabernash at the west portal of
the Moffat. Tabernash is famed as the coldest spot in Colorado when the mercury
plunges but Tabernash was no colder than the fires of the Rio Grande by the   — 343
year's end.

Bright and early on the morning of June 11, 1939, the first section of the Chicago, Burlington & Quincy's Train No. 39 with an all-Pullman consist pulled into Denver from Chicago on the first run of the transcontinental *Exposition Flyer* behind a Burlington 4-8-4 No. 5624 as shown below. A second section followed with head-end business, tourist sleepers and coaches and the *Flyer* was in business. Half a century earlier, the Burlington had advertised the advantages of sixteen wheel Pullmans on its Colorado overnight runs as is depicted at the right. *(Below: R. H. Kindig; Right: Arthur D. Dubin Collection.)*

RAND-M°NALLY-CO.

INTERIOR VIEW OF THE PULLMAN
(16 WHEEL) SLEEPERS RUNNING
ONLY ON THE BURLINGTON ROUTE

Named for the San Francisco Golden Gate International Exposition of fragrant memory at Treasure Island, the *Exposition Flyer* was jointly operated by the Burlington, Rio Grande and Western Pacific Railroads between Chicago and California from 1939 until after the 1941 war.

Here it is shown at Plainview, Colorado, on its first run, June 11, 1939 in two photographs by R. H. Kindig. Its ten cars were powered by Rio Grande 2-8-2 Nos. 1210 and 1209 and a Burlington lounge-observation car with enclosed platform brought up at the rear end.

The *Exposition Flyer's* second section westbound in wartime boasted a less classic consist than usually made up the first train and ran with a rag-tag assortment of equipment pressed into service for the emergency. Here it has picked up Pullman standard sleepers left over from the first section and lacks the panache of an open platform observation club car which the train maintained as a symbol of railroading style as long as it was listed in the pages of the *Official Guide*. (Charles Clegg.)

Inspired by the stylish competition for the San Francisco Exposition trade placed in the running by the Union Pacific in the *Forty-niner* on the Overland haul the *Exposition Flyer* was a train of classic dimensions until the 1941 war saw it running often in two sections with downgraded equipment to suit necessitous times. Here, although a wartime run in July 1942, it still retains vestiges of elegance west of Fireclay with No. 1804 on the business end. Below is one of the pool of six fine dining cars maintained by the Burlington and Rio Grande jointly for this train. *(Above: R. H. Kindig; Below: Burlington Lines.)*

All unaware that the greatest boom in passenger traffic in the history of rail transport was just around the corner, the Rio Grande in 1941 ordered from the Edward G. Budd Manufacturing Company two stainless steel Diesel-electric rail motor car units of two cars each for overnight service between Denver and Salt Lake via the Moffat Tunnel route. The two units of Train No. 1 were named *John Evans* and *David Moffat*, those of No. 2 *Brigham Young* and *Heber C. Kimball*, thus evenly dividing honors between the Mormon saints to the west and Colorado gentiles to the east. Each seated forty-four in its coach, slept eight in Pullman sections and two in a stateroom called a cabinette. There was also a miniature galley and dining alcove accommodating eight and the cars were promised for a speed of seventy-five miles an hour. Although *The Prospectors*, as the little trains were named, were miniature jewel boxes in design, almost nothing was right about them in practical fact. They were underpowered and the motors flatly refused to function with anything resembling satisfaction on the carrier's mountain grades so that a steam locomotive was frequently assigned to take them over the run. The proportion of coach seats to sleeper space was incorrectly appraised so that the Pullman space was invariably overcrowded and the coach half empty. The fantastic surge of wartime traffic shortly gave an embarrassed management an excuse for retiring them and eventually they were returned to Budd to be credited against the cost of the *California Zephyr*. The little trains were, alas, prospectors that never found color in the pan, let alone bonanza. *(Three Photos: Rio Grande Railroad.)*

Caught in an all-too-characteristic moment of pause near Golden, while two members of the crew probe its mechanical innards and the rear brakeman flags out behind, *Prospector I* is shown above in a pose it assumed too often to gratify its owners. The motive power ran hot on the least provocation and was insufficient for the Rio Grande's heavy mountain grades. "It ran in steam as much of the time as it did under its own motive power," recalls the railroad's Carlton Sills. "We were determined to get mileage out of it even if it required a steam locomotive that could as well have hauled fifteen standard Pullmans." Only a few months after its acquisition, the approaching clouds of the 1941 war relegated *Prospector I* to the discard and Rio Grande operating officials breathed more freely. (*Above: Otto Perry; Below: Rio Grande Railroad.*)

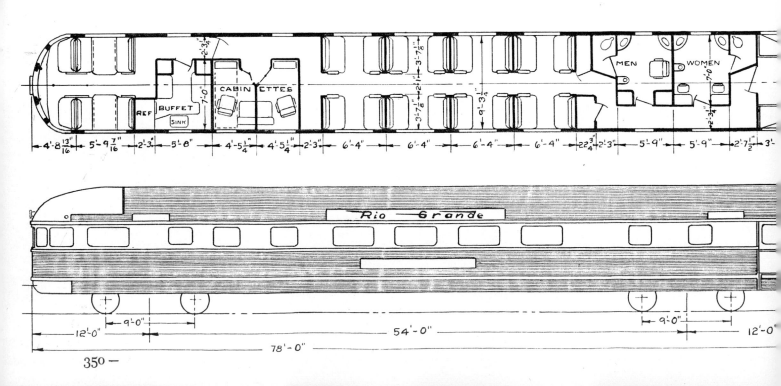

Devotees of the steam tradition in railroading did not look with favor on the motor driven stream-lining of *Prospector I,* but in the light of the later desolation of Diesel that was to sweep steam into oblivion, they now incline to view the little trains in retro-spect with something like affec-tion. The vignettes at the right were taken by Lucius Beebe on the occasion of *Prospector I's* first run when it came from the Budd plant over the rails of the Central Railroad of New Jersey, far away and long ago.

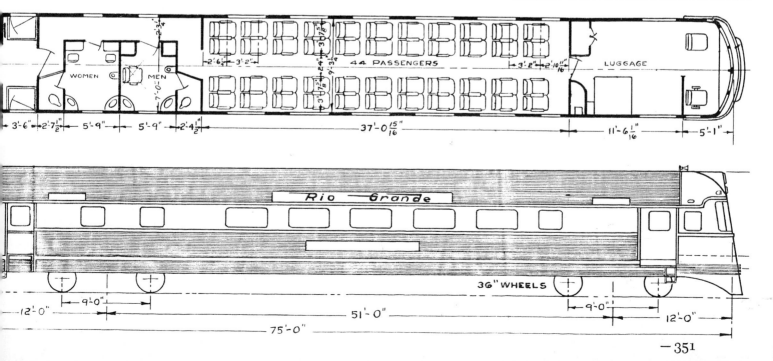

One of the most successful and physically enchanting overnight runs anywhere, the Rio Grande's second *Prospector* fulfilled all the hopes the carrier had had for the original and ill-advised train with the same magic name. On the Salt Lake-Denver run between dusk and dawn over the Moffat Route, its consist varies with the season but invariably includes Pullman sleepers, coaches, an uncommonly handsome dining-lounge car unit and head-end revenue cars. On the page opposite, under a drawing symbolizing the origin of its name, *The Prospector* barrels downhill near Plainview on a summer's morning within sight of the Denver of its destination. Here it is shown a few minutes later on the same run at Coal Creek across the valley from tunnel No. 1. *(Opposite: Rio Grande Railroad; Above: Rocky Mountain Railroad Photos: Richard F. Lind.)*

As regal as its name, *The Royal Gorge* is perpetuated on these pages in three characteristic poses: opposite at the top, as it pulls out of Denver Union Station with No. 1803 on the smoky end and, below, double headed streaking southward out of Littleton. Above: still double headed it shows to vertical advantage with No. 122 and No. 1802 climbing Tennessee Pass east of Minturn in 1949 with flags on the smokebox to show that this is the first of two sections. *(Three Photos: R. H. Kindig.)*

Transition in the Valley of the Arkansas: *The Scenic Limited* in steam and its successor, *The Royal Gorge* in Diesel at Palmer Lake in 1961. *(Above: Otto Perry; Below: Rocky Mountain Railroad Photos: Richard F. Lind.)*

Gone but not forgotten is the Rio Grande's atmospheric depot atop Tennessee Pass from which were handed up how many train orders in the long parade of steam, sometimes when the snow drifted up to its eaves. In the below frame, *The Scenic Limited* pauses on a winter afternoon amidst the snows and silence on Tennessee Pass for its rear end portrait in a day when well conducted trains still ended in an open observation car. *(Above: Rocky Mountain Railroad Photos: Richard F. Lind; Below: Rio Grande Railroad.)*

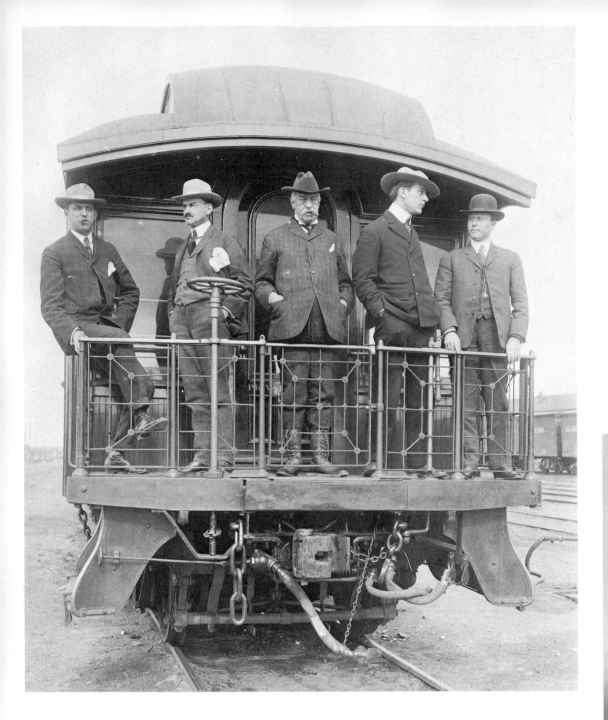

The look of the empire builders clings to the last of their tribe in the grand manner of the transcontinentals in this group of moguls in the course of a tour of inspection of the Rio Grande's western connection, the Western Pacific Railroad, during its construction in 1905. Front and center and obviously Mr. President on the observation platform of one of the Gould business cars is President of the W. P. Charles Elsey with wing collar, cigar and presidential mein of the time. Seated on the rail is Virgil G. Bogue, vice president and chief engineer of the road, while between them is Eastern Capital as represented by Kingdon Gould whose ancestor Jay Gould, in his brief but energetic lifetime, had built the railroad realm of which the Rio Grande as well as its connections, the Missouri Pacific and finally the Western Pacific were components.

The evil but fascinating genius of Jay Gould, who in the late seventies had conspicuously identified himself as a man of disaster by his looting of Erie, turned westward toward the obvious potentialities of Colorado railroading. In 1877, the Rio Grande was experiencing extreme financial embarrassment and it shortly was announced that Jay Gould had come up with half the sum needed to continue construction as far as Albuquerque en route to the Rio Grande River. The Rio Grande's earnings leaped; back wages were paid up and interest payment due in November 1878 was in the bank in September. Thereafter until his death in 1892 Gould was influential, through bondholding in the Rio Grande's affairs, although it was never considered a "Gould railroad" to the extent that its Pueblo connection, the Missouri Pacific was a wholly dominated property. When the Rio Grande's eventual western connection, the Western Pacific, was undertaken after the turn of the century, Gould interests through his sons, were prominently involved. Below is the *Exposition Flyer* as a Western Pacific train at Portola in 1940, photographed by Guy L. Dunscomb; at the right Jay Gould himself.

The night scenes on these two pages were taken in Alamosa yards when standard gauge steam was only a memory on Veta Pass by Jim Shaughnessy, a photographer skilled in the technique of night lighting and the massive effects of black and white. The water tower is the last to be found in service anywhere beside the Rio Grande's standard tracks and is for the service of narrow gauge steam on the Durango run, a lonely reminder of the great days that are past and the glory that once rode the iron everywhere.

Black engines span the years in this study of Rio Grande motive power by Dick Steinheimer depicting an engineman coming off duty at Roper Yard in Salt Lake City in 1952 framed by a pair of 2-8-2s in steam and a Diesel yard goat.

Destined to become one of the most popular and profitable long haul luxury trains in the land, the *California Zephyr* was inaugurated as successor to the *Exposition Flyer* in 1948 as the joint Chicago-San Francisco operation of the Burlington, Rio Grande and Western Pacific carriers. Its 2,532 miles of scenic run filled it to eighty percent capacity in winter *(above)* and found it sold out for weeks in advance during the vacation months as below. *(Two Photos: Rio Grande Railroad.)*

While the first factual vista dome cars on an operative scale were indeed part of the equipment of the *California Zephyr* and were soon to spread to other name trains everywhere, the idea was nothing new, as is suggested by the primeval version of a vista dome car shown at the left. This one was proposed in the eighties, but the idea was destined to lie fallow for half a century before being translated into reality on the Rio Grande. In the below scene the *California Zephyr* breasts the grade at Coal Creek just before entering Tunnel No. 1 on its westward passage. *(Rocky Mountain Railroad Photos: Richard F. Lind.)*

Diesels come in all shapes and sizes to form pousse cafes of motive power. Above: two unmatched units put a shoulder behind the caboose at Tunnel No. 2 on the Moffat approach; below: ten units decorate the head end at Plainview. *(Two Photos: Rocky Mountain Railroad Photos: Richard F. Lind.)*

Changing of the guard: while old timer No. 1138 is still partly in the shadow of the water tower at Salida yards and the rising sun is still low, four GP-7 units with screaming blowers on their dynamic brakes roll down from Tennessee Pass to pause briefly for a crew change before following the once narrow gauge trail down to Pueblo. *(Jim Shaughnessy.)*

Following page: The end of a Denver & Rio Grande Western merchandise run provides the end of the book in a superb study of Colorado railroading by Richard H. Kindig.

APPENDIX

THE DENVER AND RIO GRANDE RAILROAD
AND CONSTITUENT LINES

| JANUARY 1ST | MILES OF LINE | | | |
	Narrow Gauge	Standard Gauge	Three Rail	Total
1872	76			76
1873	155			155
1874	155			155
1875	164			164
1876	164			164
1877	275			275
1878	304			304
1879	337			337
1880	337			337
1881	684			684
1882	977		123	1190
1883	1314		123	1437
1884	1562		123	1685
1885	1562		123	1685
1886	1562		123	1685
1887	1562		123	1685
1888	1673		160	1833
1889	1574	16	265	1855
1890	1635	64	226	1925
1891	1013	681	296	1990
1892	965	805	296	2066
1893	965	822	296	2083
1894	961	825	296	2082
1895	961	825	296	2082
1896	995	825	296	2116
1897	995	861	296	2152
1898	995	856	296	2147
1899	1035	852	300	2187
1900	976	966	300	2242
1901	957	1024	317	2298
1902	918	1042	360	2320
1903	916	1243	203	2362
1904	911	1273	203	2387
1905	906	1285	203	2394
1906	904	1353	205	2462
1907	787	1470	208	2475
1908	787	1522	208	2517
1909	787	1522	208	2517
1910	787	1522	208	2517
1911	787	1522	208	2517
1912	787	1617	113	2517
1913	787	1621	113	2521
1914	783	1631	117	2531
1915	789	1630	106	2534
1916	789	1630	106	2534
1917	789	1630	106	2534
1918	792	1675	102	2569
1919	792	1664	102	2558
1920	792	1666	102	2560

Year by Year Outline

Corporate and Physical History of
THE DENVER AND RIO GRANDE WESTERN
RAILROAD COMPANY
AND ITS PREDECESSOR COMPANIES

1870 to 1954

Compiled by Hugh T. Glen May 20, 1954

1870

THE DENVER AND RIO GRANDE RAILWAY COMPANY incorporated October 27, 1870 in the Territory of Colorado and the Territory of New Mexico.

1871

CONSTRUCTION:

Denver to Colorado Springs completed NG (Grades between Louviers and Husted not compensated for curvature.)

1872

CORPORATIONS:

WASATCH AND JORDAN VALLEY RAILROAD COMPANY incorporated October 24, 1872 in the Territory of Utah. Sandy to Alta, Utah.

THE CANON COAL RAILWAY COMPANY incorporated August 17, 1872 in the Territory of Colorado. 2 miles of track near Florence, Colo.

BINGHAM CANYON AND CAMP FLOYD RAILROAD COMPANY incorporated September 10, 1872 in the Territory of Utah. Sandy to Bingham, Utah.

CONSTRUCTION:

Colorado Springs to Pueblo NG
Pueblo to Florence NG
Coal Creek Branch NG

1873

CONSTRUCTION:

Bingham Branch NG by Bingham Canyon and Camp Floyd Railroad Company.

1874

CORPORATIONS:

SAN PETE VALLEY RAILWAY COMPANY incorporated June 29, 1874 in the Territory of Utah. Nephi to Morrison, Utah.

CONSTRUCTION:

Florence to Cañon City, Colo. NG

1875

CORPORATIONS:

UTAH AND PLEASANT VALLEY RAILWAY COMPANY incorporated December 11, 1875 in the Territory of Utah. Provo to Pleasant Valley, Utah.

CONSTRUCTION:

None during the year.

1876

CONSTRUCTION:

Pueblo to La Veta NG
Cuchara Junction to Engleville NG
COLORADO admitted to the United States as a state August 1, 1876.

1877

CONSTRUCTION:

La Veta to Russell NG Original line over Veta Pass.
Engleville Junction to Engleville NG

1878

CONSTRUCTION:

Russell to Alamosa NG

1879

CONSTRUCTION:

None during the year.

1880

CORPORATIONS:

TEXAS, SANTA FE AND NORTHERN RAILROAD COMPANY incorporated December 10, 1880 in the Territory of New Mexico. Espanola to Santa Fe, N. M.

CONSTRUCTION:

Cañon City to Leadville NG
California Gulch Branch NG
Alamosa to Chama NG
Castle Rock to Hathaway NG
Leadville to Kokomo NG
Colorado Springs to Manitou NG

1881

CORPORATIONS:

THE DENVER AND RIO GRANDE WESTERN RAILWAY COMPANY, CONSOLIDATED, incorporated July 21, 1881 in the Territory of Utah.

THE SALT LAKE AND PARK CITY RAILWAY COMPANY incorporated May 26, 1881 in the Territory of Utah.

CONSTRUCTION:

Third Rail Denver to Pueblo
Third Rail Pueblo to Minnequa
Malta to Rock Creek NG

Salida to Gunnison NG
Poncha Junction to Maysville NG
Gunnison to Crested Butte NG
Alamosa to South Fork NG
Chama to Durango NG
Douglas Quarry Branch NG Douglas to Madge Quarry near Castle Rock.
Oak Creek Branch NG near Florence
Grape Creek Branch NG Cañon City to Westcliffe
Orient Branch NG Villa Grove to Orient
Calumet Branch Hecla Jct. to Calumet NG near Brown Canyon.
Blue River Branch Kokomo to Wheeler's NG
Crevasse to Helper NG Construction begun.
Springville to Provo NG
Provo to Ogden NG Construction begun.
Colton to Scofield NG
Bingham Branch purchased from Bingham Canyon and Camp Floyd R R Co. NG

1882

CORPORATIONS:
  CALIFORNIA SHORT LINE RAILROAD COMPANY incorporated June 12, 1882 in the Territory of Utah. Sold to San Pete Valley Railway Company August 31, 1889.
CONSTRUCTION:
  Grand Junction to Crevasse NG
  Gunnison to Grand Junction NG as part of NG main line Denver to Salt Lake
  Crested Butte to Anthracite NG
  Durango to Silverton NG
  Wheeler's to Dillon NG
  Parlin to Quartz NG constructed by Colorado and Southern Railway Company as part of its main line Denver to Gunnison via Alpine Tunnel.
  Detour to Springville NG Purchased from Utah and Pleasant Valley Railway Company.

1883

CONSTRUCTION:
  Hathaway to O'Brien's Quarry NG
  Lehigh Branch near Louviers NG to Lehigh Coal Mines
  Kubler Branch NG constructed by predecessor of the Colorado and Southern Railway Company.
  Maysville to Monarch NG
  South Fork to Wagon Wheel Gap NG
  Baldwin Branch NG built by Union Pacific and later owned by Denver, South Park and Pacific, then by Colo. and Southern Ry. Co.
  Crevasse to Green River NG Construction completed.
  Helper to Tucker (near Detour) NG
  Provo to Ogden Construction completed. NG
  Midvale to Wasatch NG. Purchased Midvale to Sandy from Bingham Canyon and Camp Floyd Railroad Company and constructed from Sandy to Wasatch.

1884

CORPORATIONS:
  SALT LAKE AND FORT DOUGLAS RAILWAY COMPANY incorporated in the Territory of Utah December 2, 1884. Salt Lake City to Red Butte and Emigration, Utah.
CONSTRUCTION:
  None during the year.

1885

None.

1886

CORPORATIONS:
  THE DENVER AND RIO GRANDE RAILWAY COMPANY sold under foreclosure on July 12, 1886.
  THE DENVER AND RIO GRANDE RAILROAD COMPANY incorporated July 14, 1886 in the State of Colorado.
  THE TRINIDAD AND DENVER RAILROAD COMPANY incorporated August 10, 1886 in the State of Colorado. El Moro to Trinidad.
CONSTRUCTION:
  None during the year.

1887

CONSTRUCTION:
  3rd Rail Pueblo to Florence
  El Moro to Trinidad NG
  Rock Creek to Aspen NG

1888

CORPORATIONS:
  SALT LAKE AND EASTERN RAILWAY COMPANY incorporated September 21, 1888 in the Territory of Utah, Mill Creek to Park City, Utah
  THE DENVER CLEAR CREEK AND WESTERN RAILWAY COMPANY incorporated December 18, 1888 in the State of Colorado. Ft. Logan Branch.
CONSTRUCTION:
  Second Track Denver to Littleton, Pikeview to Kelker and Eden to Pueblo
  3rd Rail Florence to Cañon City
  3rd Rail Minnequa to Walsenburg
  Loma Branch to Pictou SG
  3rd Rail Eilers to Leadville
  Chama Lumber Branch Chama to Law's Mill NG 3.16 miles
  Rouse Jct. to old Rouse Mine NG
  Conchita Jct. to Rouse (Santa Clara Mine)
  3rd Rail Cuchara Jct. to Engleville and Trinidad
  3rd Rail Colorado Springs to Manitou

1889

CORPORATIONS:

THE SANTA FE SOUTHERN RAILWAY COMPANY incorporated January 24, 1889 in the Territory of New Mexico. Espanola to Santa Fe.

UTAH WESTERN RAILWAY COMPANY incorporated June 24, 1889 in the Territory of Utah. Merged with Utah Central Railway Company on April 8, 1890.

THE RIO GRANDE WESTERN RAILWAY COMPANY incorporated June 24, 1889 in the State of Colorado and in the Territory of Utah

CONSTRUCTION:

Fort Logan Branch 3-rail
Second Track Pueblo to Minnequa 3-rail
Glenwood to Rifle NG
Aberdeen Jct. to Aberdeen Quarry west of Gunnison NG. Stone for the building of the State Capitol Building at Denver.
Lake City Branch NG
Sugar House or Mill Creek to Park City NG By Salt Lake and Eastern Railway Company

REMOVALS:

Middle Rail removed between El Moro and Engleville and Trinidad.

1890

CORPORATIONS:

UTAH CENTRAL RAILWAY COMPANY incorporated April 8, 1890 in Territory of Utah. Sugar House to Park City, Utah.

CONSTRUCTION:

3rd Rail Fort Logan Branch
Second Track Cleora to Salida 3-rail
3rd Rail Salida to Malta
NG to SG Malta to Aspen
3rd Rail Malta to Eilers
3rd Rail California Gulch Branch
NG to SG Glenwood to Rifle
Rifle to Grand Junction by Rio Grande Junction Railway Company incorporated in the State of Colorado June 26, 1889. Owned jointly by The Denver and Rio Grande Railroad Company and The Colorado Midland Railway Company and operated jointly by those companies. Colorado Midland Railway Company operates under lease over track of The Denver and Rio Grande Railroad Company between Newcastle and Rifle to reach the tracks of the Rio Grande Junction Railway Company.
NG to SG Grand Junction to Helper. Constructed on new location between Crevasse and Cisco SG
Mears Junction to Alamosa Junction NG
Helper to Ogden NG to SG
NG to SG Colton to Scofield
Thistle to Manti NG
NG to SG Bingham Branch
NG to SG Midvale to Sandy
Scofield to Winter Quarters SG
Walsenburg to La Veta NG to SG

REMOVALS:

Middle Rail between Minnequa and Walsenburg removed.
Middle Rail between Cuchara Jct. and El Moro removed.
Lehigh Branch removed.
Grape Creek Branch between Cañon City and Westcliffe flooded out and track removed.

1891

CORPORATIONS:

THE RIO GRANDE GUNNISON RAILWAY COMPANY incorporated September 14, 1891 in the State of Colorado. Wagon Wheel Gap to Creede.

THE TINTIC RANGE RAILWAY COMPANY incorporated May 11, 1891 in the Territory of Utah. Springville to Silver City.

SEVIER RAILWAY COMPANY incorporated May 6, 1891 in the Territory of Utah. Manti to Marysvale, Utah.

CONSTRUCTION:

Wagon Wheel Gap to Creede NG
NG to SG Thistle to Manti

1892

CONSTRUCTION:

Springville to Eureka by Tintic Range Railway Co. Leased to Rio Grande Western Railway Company.

1893

CONSTRUCTION:

Eureka to Silver City by Tintic Range Railway Co. Leased to Rio Grande Western Railway Company.
Crested Butte to Floresta NG (Ruby - Anthracite Branch)

1894

No construction during the year.

1895

CORPORATIONS:

THE RIO GRANDE AND SANTA FE RAILROAD COMPANY incorporated July 1, 1895. Espanola to Santa Fe. In Territory of New Mexico.
No construction during the year.

1896

CONSTRUCTION:

Loma Branch Pictou to Maitland SG
Salina to near Sevier SG
Chama Lumber Spur. Law's Mill to Tierra Amarilla NG 11.56 miles
UTAH admitted to the United States as a state January 4, 1896

1897

CORPORATIONS:

UTAH CENTRAL RAILROAD COMPANY incorporated December 29, 1897 in the State of Utah. Mill Creek to Wilford, Utah.

UTAH EASTERN RAILWAY COMPANY incorporated December 29, 1897 in the State of Utah. Provo Canyon Branch between Mile Post 11 and Heber, Utah.

CONSTRUCTION:

Second Track Soldier Summit to Tucker (Near Detour). Original location on 4% grade.

1898

No construction during the year.

Sugar House (Mill Creek) to Park City leased from Salt Lake and Eastern Railway Company NG

1899

CORPORATIONS:

RIO GRANDE PAGOSA AND NORTHERN RAILROAD COMPANY incorporated April 28, 1899 in State of Colorado. Pagosa Springs Branch.

CARBON COUNTY RAILWAY COMPANY incorporated November 20, 1899 in the State of Utah. Mounds to Sunnyside and Scofield to Clear Creek, Utah.

CONSTRUCTION:

Sunnyside Branch SG

NG to SG La Veta to Alamosa via relocated line over La Veta Pass. New location between La Veta and Wagon Creek Junction (Russell) Grade and curve reductions.

Pleasant Valley Branch Scofield to Clear Creek SG

Provo Canyon Branch Provo to Mile Post 11 constructed by Utah Eastern Railway Company. SG

REMOVALS:

Old NG line between La Veta and Russell via Veta Pass abandoned.

1900

CORPORATIONS:

THE RIO GRANDE RAILROAD COMPANY incorporated July 17, 1900 in the State of Colorado. Construction company for Westcliffe Branch from Texas Creek to Westcliffe, North Fork Branch from Delta to Somerset, and Loma Branch.

CONSTRUCTION:

Second Track Pueblo West to Mile Post 121.58 3-Rail

3rd Rail Alamosa to Monte Vista

Near Sevier to Marysvale SG

Upper 15 miles of Provo Canyon Branch purchased from Utah Eastern Railway Company.

Roper to Mill Creek (Sugar House) SG

NG to SG Mill Creek to Park City. Purchased by Rio Grande Western Railway Company

Pagosa Springs Branch NG

Texas Creek to Westcliffe Westcliffe Branch SG

1901

CORPORATIONS:

THE RIO GRANDE SANGRE DE CRISTO RAILROAD COMPANY incorporated January 8, 1901 in the State of Colorado. Moffat to Cottonwood, Colorado.

CASTLE VALLEY RAILWAY COMPANY incorporated January 15, 1901 in the State of Utah. Salina to Nioche.

COPPER BELT RAILROAD COMPANY incorporated May 18, 1901 in the State of Utah. Tracks to Yampa Smelter, Utah.

CONSTRUCTION:

3rd Rail Monte Vista to Del Norte

3rd Rail Alamosa to Antonito

Dalton to Lark, constructed by others.

Moffat to Cottonwood NG

1902

CORPORATIONS:

THE RIO GRANDE, PUEBLO AND SOUTHERN RAILROAD COMPANY incorporated April 21, 1902 in the State of Colorado. Zinc Junction to Blende, Colorado.

CONSTRUCTION:

Second track MP 121.85 to Goodnight 3-Rail

Delta to Somerset NG

NG to SG Del Norte to Creede SG

Copper Belt Branch SG

Zinc Jct. to Blende SG

NG to SG Castle Rock to Hathaway

REMOVALS:

Middle Rail removed Denver to Pueblo

Middle Rail removed Ft. Logan Branch

Middle Rail removed Arkansas Valley Sampler to Zinc Mines

La Veta to Russell Old NG line over Veta Pass removed.

Middle Rail removed, Alamosa to Del Norte

Douglas Quarry Spur NG removed

1903

CONSTRUCTION:

Denver to Orestod via Corona Pass. (Completed in 1907 by DNW&P RR) (Colorado Construction Co.)

Second Track Rex to Minturn

Second Track Midvale to Salt Lake

Dalton to Lark Purchased.

Copper Belt-Carr Fork Branch to Yampa Mine

Lumberton to El Vado NG By Rio Grande and Southwestern Railroad Co.

Howard Quarry Spur Howard to Calcite SG

Salina to Nioche SG

1904

CONSTRUCTION:

Loma Branch Maitland to Strong or Spanish Fork SG

REMOVALS:

Aberdeen Junction to Aberdeen Quarry NG

1905

CONSTRUCTION:

Orestod to Steamboat Springs begun. (Completed in 1909 by DNW&P RR) Colorado Construction Co.

Carbon Junction to Farmington SG

3rd Rail Carbon Junction to Durango account of standard gauge on the Farmington Branch.

Welby to Garfield SG Garfield Beach Extension

REMOVALS:

Oak Creek Branch

Castle Rock to O'Brien's Quarry abandoned

1906

CONSTRUCTION:

Jansen to Cokedale

NG to SG Montrose to Grand Junction

NG to SG Delta to Somerset

At Montrose and vicinity NG to 3-Rail for interchange of equipment.

Second Track Colton to Soldier Summit

Bingham Branch Extension Loline Jct. to Cuprum SG

1907

CONSTRUCTION:

Loma Branch Spanish Peaks to Kebler No. 2 SG

Denver to Orestod via Corona Pass completed by DNW&P RR

Second Track Red Cliff to Rex

Morrison Branch purchased from San Pete Valley Railway Company

REMOVALS:

Jennings and Potter's Quarry Spur near Kyune. Abandoned

Lake Park Branch near Famington, Utah. Abandoned

Crystal to Nioche. Abandoned

1908

CORPORATIONS:

THE DENVER AND RIO GRANDE RAILROAD COMPANY (CONSOLIDATED) incorporated in the State of Colorado July 27, 1908 and in the State of Utah July 31, 1908.

CONSTRUCTION:

Second Track Florence to Cañon City 3-rail

Nephi to Ephraim Purchased from San Pete Valley Railway Company

Springville to Silver City Purchased from Tintic Range Railway Company

Tropic Spur near La Veta SG

REMOVALS:

Sand Pit to Wasatch Abandoned

1909

CONSTRUCTION:

Orestod to Steamboat Springs. Completed by DNW &P RR Co. (Colo. Constn. Co.)

Second Track Pando to Red Cliff

Second Track Helper to Castle Gate

Second Track Kyune to Colton

1910

CONSTRUCTION:

Second Track Deen to Pando

1911

CONSTRUCTION:

Second Track Goodnight to Swallows

New Double Track Line Southern Junction to Walsenburg Junction SG Colorado & Southern Railway Company owns the northbound track and right of way and The Denver and Rio Grande Western Railroad Company owns the southbound track and right of way. Tracks operated jointly as a double track main line.

Baldwin Branch Leased from Colorado and Southern Ry Co. NG

Parlin to Quartz NG Owned by C&S Ry Co. Operation begun by The D&RGW RR Co. for C&S Ry. under contract.

REMOVALS:

Middle Rail removed between Pueblo and Cleora except at Florence.

Middle Rail removed between Pueblo and Minnequa.

Blue River Branch, operation discontinued.

1912

CONSTRUCTION:

Second Track Detour to Thistle

Reliance Junction to Ojo SG. Constructed along the old roadbed of the original NG main line over Veta Pass abandoned in 1899.

NEW MEXICO admitted to the United States as a state in January 1912.

1913

CONSTRUCTION:

Steamboat Springs to Craig. Commenced by DNW&P RR Co. (Denver and Salt Lake Constn. Co.)

Second Track Castle Gate to Kyune.

New Double Main Track on revised 2% location from Soldier Summit to Detour. New line about 4.49 miles longer than the old 4% Double Main Track.

Spring Canyon Branch constructed for Coal Companies and then purchased by the Railroad Company. In three parts.

NG to SG Sandy to Wasatch

REMOVALS:
> Soldier Summit to Tucker old 4% Double Track line abandoned
> Castle Rock Branch Abandoned
> Coal Creek Branch Abandoned
> Moffat to Cottonwood Abandoned
> Engleville Branch Abandoned

1914
CONSTRUCTION:
> Steamboat Springs to Craig Completed by DNW&P RR Co. (Denver and Salt Lake Constn. Co.)
> Second Track Thistle to Provo constructed by Utah Railway Company on D&RGW RR Co.'s right of way except between Gomex and Springville where tracks diverge for improvement of grade for eastbound traffic.
> Taos Junction to La Madera La Madera Branch NG To serve the McPhee and McGinnity Lumber Co.

1915
No construction during the year.

1916
REMOVALS:
> Copper Belt-Carr Fork Track abandoned.

1917
CORPORATIONS:
> The entire property of The Denver and Rio Grande Railroad Company was taken over by the United States Government along with all other railroads as a war measure and operation was begun under the Director General of Railroads (Hale Holden, Regional Director). For accounting purposes this change was made effective at midnight December 31, 1917.

CONSTRUCTION:
> Longsdale to Bon Carbo

REMOVALS:
> Jennings and Potter's Quarry Spur removed
> Castle Rock to O'Brien's Quarry removed

1918
CORPORATIONS:
> The entire Property of The Denver and Rio Grande Railroad Company passed into the hands of A. R. Baldwin, Receiver, January 26, 1918, who was appointed by the District Court of the United States for the District of Colorado.

CONSTRUCTION:
> El Vado to Gallinas, N. M. NG

REMOVALS:
> Part of the Morrison Branch in Utah removed.

1919
CONSTRUCTION:
> Second Track Bragdon to Eden
> Connecting Tracks at crossings with the AT&SF track between Denver and Pueblo at South Denver, Sedalia, Spruce, Fountain and Bragdon and Paired Track Operation with The AT&SF Ry was begun between South Denver and Bragdon, Colorado. Right hand track operation.
> Goshen Valley Branch constructed from Pearl Junction on the Tintic Branch to Dividend and Iron King. SG Operated by The Denver and Rio Grande Railroad Co.

1920
CORPORATIONS:
> THE DENVER AND RIO GRANDE WESTERN RAILROAD COMPANY incorporated November 15, 1920 in the State of Delaware.
> FEDERAL CONTROL OF RAILROADS was terminated at 12:01 A.M. March 1, 1920 and property was returned to A. R. Baldwin, Receiver. 2¼ years under Government Control.

No construction during the year.

1921
CORPORATIONS:
> THE DENVER AND RIO GRANDE WESTERN RAILROAD COMPANY of Delaware acquired all of the property of The Denver and Rio Grande Railroad Company from its Receiver A. R. Baldwin by Judicial Sale on August 1, 1921 after 3⅝ years in receivership.

No construction during the year.

1922
CORPORATIONS:
> Receivership of The Denver and Rio Grande Western Railroad Company was begun July 21, 1922. Joseph H. Young was appointed by the United States District Court for the District of Colorado, as the Receiver of all of the properties of The D&RGW RR Co. after seven months of operation by the corporation. Name changed to The Denver and Rio Grande Western Railroad System.

No construction during the year.

1923
CORPORATIONS:
> Thomas H. Beacom appointed Receiver of The Denver and Rio Grande Western Railroad System replacing Joseph H. Young, Receiver.

CONSTRUCTION:
> Loma Branch Kebler No. 2 to Alamo No. 1 SG
> SG to NG Durango to Farmington after 18 years of standard operation in a narrow gauge territory.

REMOVALS:

Calumet Branch removed.

Loline Junction to Cuprum. Operation discontinued.

3rd Rail Carbon Jct. to Durango removed account no longer needed after conversion of Farmington Branch to narrow gauge.

1924

CORPORATIONS:

The Denver and Rio Grande Western Railroad System was sold at foreclosure October 29, 1924 and acquired by The Denver and Rio Grande Western Railroad Company (Reorganized) October 29, 1924, from Thomas H. Beacom, Receiver. Sale confirmed by the District Court November 20, 1924. Operation begun 12:01 a.m. December 20, 1924 by the reorganized company, J. S. Pyeatt, President.

CONSTRUCTION:

Second Track Minnequa to Southern Junction SG

Connecting track built between Larimer and Mustang to form the new Capers Branch between Mustang and Capers SG

Track changed around Tunnel No. 3 on the Tintic Branch. Tunnel destroyed by fire and not restored.

REMOVALS:

Castle Rock Quarry Branch removed

Coal Creek Branch removed

Castle Rock Quarry Branch removed

Capers to Graneros Old main line removed

Lascar to Larimer Old main line removed

Blue River Branch removed

Copper Belt Branch removed

Copper Belt-Carr Fork Branch removed

1925

CONSTRUCTION:

Pleasant Valley Branch Line changed Hale to Scofield at Government Expense to allow the construction of Scofield Dam and Reservoir

REMOVALS:

Middle Rail removed Salida to Eiler's near Leadville

Morrison Branch partly removed

Sonora to Graneros removed

Minnequa to Sonora removed

Lake Park Branch removed near Salt Lake City

Bingham Branch Extension removal begun

1926

CONSTRUCTION:

Kenilworth Branch SG replacing the old Kenilworth and Helper Railroad which was impractical to operate account heavy grades.

1927

CONSTRUCTION:

Second Track Walsenburg Jct. to Walsenburg. Joint operation with Colorado and Southern Railway Co.

ABS Gypsum to Palisade

Goshen Valley Branch. Acquired through purchase of the Capital Stock of The Goshen Valley Railway Company.

New Pacific Mine Spur SG near Pictou

1928

CONSTRUCTION:

ABS Cañon City to Salida

Moffat Tunnel completed February 27, 1928. Built and owned by the Moffat Tunnel Commission. 6.21 miles long. Elevation 9239 feet. Line shortened 22.84 miles between Denver and Orestod. Approach tracks at each end also owned by Tunnel Commission.

Second Track Tennessee Pass to West Mitchell.

ABS Salida to Minturn.

CTC Tennessee Pass to Deen

ABS Minturn to Gypsum

ABS Maxwell to Soldier Summit

REMOVALS:

Track of the Denver and Salt Lake Railroad between Newcomb and Vasques over Corona Pass Elevation 11,660 feet, abandoned upon the opening of the Moffat Tunnel for traffic.

Rio Grande and Southwestern Railroad, Lumberton to Gallinas removed.

Bingham Branch Extension removal completed.

1929

CONSTRUCTION:

ABS Pueblo to Goodnight

ABS Swallows to Florence

Cokedale Yard Main track purchased from the American Smelting and Refining Company

ABS Palisade to Green River

ABS Green River to Maxwell

Somerset to Olivers SG

CTC Provo to Midvale

Bingham Branch Extension, portion between Upper Junction and Midas reconstructed on old grade and operation resumed.

REMOVALS:

Right of Way for the old 4% double track main line between Soldier Summit and Tucker Quitclaimed to Utah County and Utah State Road Commission for highway purposes.

Crested Butte to Floresta (Ruby-Anthracite Branch) Abandoned and removed.

Moffat to Cottonwood Removed

1930

CONSTRUCTION:

Baldwin Branch Operation begun for Colorado and Southern Railway under lease. (Operated thus until 1937)

NG to SG Hooper to Alamosa Jct. to avoid transfers. 3-Rail

ABS Soldier Summit to Provo

Kubler Branch. Operated for Colorado and Southern under lease for 7 years (1930 to 1937)

REMOVALS:

Engleville Branch removed

1931

CONSTRUCTION:

ABS Goodnight to Swallows

1932

REMOVALS:

Lascar to Cuchara Jct. removed

Taos Jct. to La Madera Abandoned and removed

Lake City Branch Abandoned

1933

CONSTRUCTION:

Orestod to Dotsero Construction begun by the Denver and Salt Lake Western Railroad Company, for The Denver and Rio Grande Western Railroad Company. (Completed in 1934).

REMOVALS:

Scofield to Winter Quarters removed

Lake City Branch sold to M. B. Burke for $16,000.00

1934

CONSTRUCTION:

Denver to Orestod Operation over Denver and Salt Lake Railway and Denver and Salt Lake Western Railroad through the Moffat Tunnel begun June 15, 1934.

Orestod to Dotsero construction completed by D&SLW RR Co. and placed in operation June 14, 1934. Leased to The D&RGW RR Co. from June 14, 1934 to April 10, 1947, a period of 13 years.

REMOVALS:

Parlin to Quartz NG Colo. and Southern Ry. Operation by D&RGW RR Co. discontinued and track removed by C&S Ry.

1935

CORPORATIONS:

The Books of The Denver and Rio Grande Western Railroad Company were closed October 31, 1935 and new Books opened November 1, 1935 with Trustees Wilson McCarthy and Henry Swan appointed November 18, 1935 by the District Court to administer the properties. Appointments ratified by the I.C.C. December 12, 1935 and they took oath of office December 16, 1935. The Trustees replaced J. S. Pyeatt, President, who had been in office 11 years.

REMOVALS:

Tropic Spur Abandoned and removed

Pagosa Springs Branch Abandoned

1936

CONSTRUCTION:

Walsenburg to Trinidad Operation begun over Colorado & Southern Railway tracks August 3, 1936 under Contract No. 15317 due to the abandonment and removal of The D&RGW RR Co. tracks between those points.

REMOVALS:

Second Track South Denver to Littleton

Second Track Pikeview to Kelker

Cuchara Jct. to Trinidad removed

Cuchara Jct. to Walsenburg Jct. Abandoned

Rouse Jct. to Mayne removed

Howard Quarry Spur to Calcite abandoned and removed

Lake City Branch NG removed

Sand Pit to Wasatch removed

Crystal to Nioche removed

Pagosa Springs Branch removed

1937

CONSTRUCTION:

ABS Florence to Cañon City

Second Track Endo to Lowell

CTC Midwest to Grand Junction

Baldwin Branch Acquired from Colo. and Southern Ry Co. by donation.

ABS Roper to Salt Lake

CTC Midvale to Roper

Kubler Branch Acquired from Colo. and Southern Ry Co. by donation.

REMOVALS:

Cuchara Jct. to Walsenburg Jct. removed

New Pacific Mine Spur near Pictou removed

Zinc Junction to Blende Abandoned

1938

REMOVALS:

Texas Creek to Westcliffe removed

1939

REMOVALS:

Zinc Junction to Blende removed

Reliance Jct. to Ojo removed

1940

CONSTRUCTION:

Second Track Lowell to Ralston

Provo Canyon Branch Line changed between Vivian Park and Heber to new location at Government Expense to allow the construction of the Deer Creek Dam and Reservoir.

Tintic Branch Loop near Mile Post 33 eliminated and line shortened 0.8 mile.

REMOVALS:

Middle rail removed between Eiler's and Leadville

Orient Branch abandoned

1941

CONSTRUCTION:

ABS Denver to Winter Park

CTC Dotsero to Chacra

ABS Orestod to Dotsero

CTC Tunnel to Midwest

REMOVALS:

California Gulch Branch partly removed and partly relocated ending at Rowe Mill.

Mayne to Monson removed

1942

CONSTRUCTION:

ABS Mile Post 78.3 to Mile Post 80 for increased traffic in the vicinity of Camp Carson near Colorado Springs.

CTC Chacra to Tunnel

REMOVALS:

Second Track Cleora to Salida retired

Loma Branch Alamo No. 2 to Alamo

Salina to Crystal Abandoned and removed

Orient Branch removed

1943

CORPORATIONS:

Effective date of reorganization was made January 1, 1943 but the reorganization was not completed until April 1947, or over 4 years later.

CONSTRUCTION:

ABS Kremmling to Orestod

CTC Agate to Maxwell

Sunnyside Branch. Track relocated near Columbia Junction to facilitate handling of very heavy operations from Geneva Mine on the Carbon County Railroad. Grade improvements made near Mounds for same reason.

REMOVALS:

Eureka to Silver City removed

Sandy to Sand Pit removed

Kubler Branch removed

Mammoth Mill Spur All D&RGW RR Co. Operation discontinued account of removal of the connection with Tintic Branch. Jointly owned with OSL RR.

1944

CONSTRUCTION:

CTC Grand Junction to Agate

CTC Maxwell to Helper

Second Track Provo to Bern

REMOVALS:

Half interest of D&RGW RR Co. in Mammoth Mill Spur sold to U. P. R. R.

Leadville to Ibex removed

Chandler Jct. to Chandler Mine removed

1945

CONSTRUCTION:

CTC Denver to Orestod

Second Track Cut-off line past Tabernash to avoid yard.

Second Track Endot to Midvale

REMOVALS:

Part of Morrison Branch in Ephraim removed

1946

CONSTRUCTION:

CTC Gypsum to Dotsero

CTC Nioche to Dotsero

CTC On West Bound Track ONLY Nolan to Kyune

Provo to Orem Purchased from Salt Lake and Utah Railroad. Salt Lake and Utah stopped operation and abandoned line.

REMOVALS:

Baldwin Branch Castleton to Baldwin removed

Park City Branch Cement Quarry to Park City abandoned and removed

Park City Branch tracks in Park City, and the half interest of the D&RGW RR Co. in mine spurs above and east of Park City sold to Union Pacific RR Co.

1947

CORPORATIONS:

Reorganization of The Denver and Rio Grande Western Railroad Company was completed April 11, 1947 with Wilson McCarthy, President. Trusteeship ended after a period of 11½ years.

CONSTRUCTION:

ABS South Denver to Bragdon on paired track operation with AT&SF Ry.

REMOVALS:

Crested Butte to Anthracite removed

MERGERS:

The reorganization included the merger of the following lines as of April 11, 1947:

Denver and Salt Lake Railway Company Denver to Craig

Denver and Salt Lake Western Railroad Company Orestod to Dotsero

Rio Grande Junction Railway Company Rifle to Grand Jct.

Goshen Valley Railway Company Pearl Junction to Dividend and Iron King

1948

CONSTRUCTION:

CTC Bragdon to Pueblo

REMOVALS:

Second Track Tapp to Fuego

San Pete Valley Branch Nephi to Gypsum Mill Sold to the Union Pacific Railroad Company.

Gypsum Mill to Moroni removed

1949

CONSTRUCTION:

Belt Line Junction to Zuni Double Track main line changed to new location around north side of old Utah Junction Yard.

ABS Salt Lake to Ogden

REMOVALS:

Monson to Rouse removed

Sapinero to Cedar Creek removed

1950

REMOVALS:

Reilly Cañon Branch Longsdale to Bon Carbo removed

Ballard and Thompson Railroad Thompson to Sego removed

1951

REMOVALS:

Mears Junction to Hooper removed

Part of Moroni Spur at Ephraim removed and new connection with Marysvale Branch constructed north of Ephraim.

Little Cottonwood Branch State Street to Sandy removed beyond MP 1.94.

Middle Rail removed Hooper to Alamosa Junction

1952

REMOVALS:

Second Track Florence to Cañon City removed

Part of Capers Spur removed

1953

CONSTRUCTION:

NG to SG Montrose to Ridgway eliminating all NG lines in vicinity

REMOVALS:

Loma Branch at and near Alamo No. 2 removed

Ouray Branch Ridgway to Ouray Abandoned

Cedar Creek Branch Abandoned Part of old main line between Gunnison and Montrose

1954

REMOVALS:

Poncha Junction to Sapinero Abandoned

Gunnison to Crested Butte Abandoned

Gunnison to Baldwin Abandoned

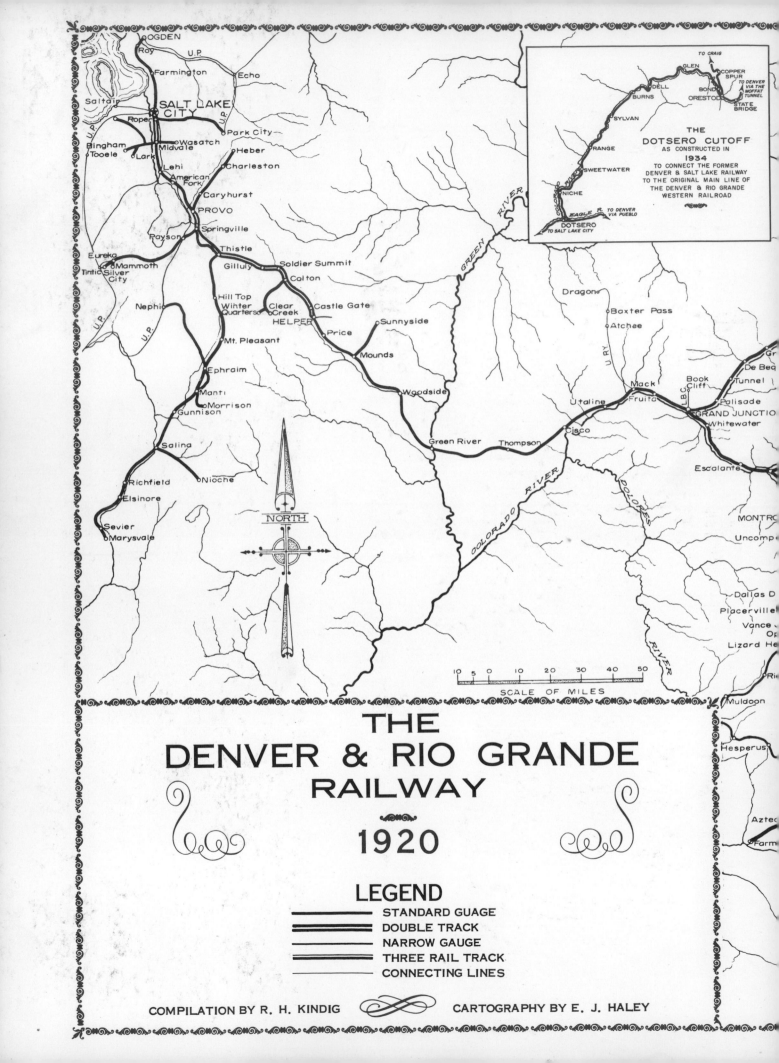

THE
DENVER & RIO GRANDE
RAILWAY

1920

LEGEND

═══════	STANDARD GUAGE
═══════	DOUBLE TRACK
───────	NARROW GAUGE
═══════	THREE RAIL TRACK
───────	CONNECTING LINES

COMPILATION BY R. H. KINDIG   CARTOGRAPHY BY E. J. HALEY

THE
DOTSERO CUTOFF
AS CONSTRUCTED IN
1934
TO CONNECT THE FORMER
DENVER & SALT LAKE RAILWAY
TO THE ORIGINAL MAIN LINE OF
THE DENVER & RIO GRANDE
WESTERN RAILROAD

SCALE OF MILES
10 5 0 10 20 30 40 50